A Quite Interesting Book

THE DISCREETLY PLUMPER SECOND BOOK OF GENERAL IGNORANCE

John Lloyd and John Mitchinson

faber and faber

First published in 2010
by Faber and Faber Ltd
Bloomsbury House
74–77 Great Russell Street
London WC1B 3DA
This paperback edition first published in 2012

Typeset by Palindrome
Printed and bound by CPI Group (UK) Ltd, Croydon, CR0 4YY

ISBN 978–0–571–29072–7

2 4 6 8 10 9 7 5 3 1

THE DISCREETLY PLUMPER
SECOND BOOK OF GENERAL IGNORANCE

CONTENTS

FORETHOUGHT | Stephen Fry

Now, what I want is facts. Teach these boys and girls nothing but Facts. Facts alone are wanted in life. Plant nothing else, and root out everything else. You can only form the minds of reasoning animals upon Facts: nothing else will ever be of any service to them. This is the principle on which I bring up my own children, and this is the principle on which I bring up these children. Stick to Facts, sir!

Nothing but a shudder runs up the spine of the sensible man, woman or child as they read these well-known words of Thomas Gradgrind in Dickens's novel *Hard Times*.

'But surely, Stephen,' you say, in that *way* of yours, 'QI and General Ignorance and all that they are or hope to be represent nothing more than the triumphant distillation of Gradgrindery, fact-dweebiness, trivia-hoarding and information-hugging. The world of noble ideas falls before your world of grinding facts. Facts are the abrasive touchstones on which we test the validity of concepts! Surely, Stephen. Surely, surely, surely! I'm right, aren't I? Aren't I? Oh *do* say I am!'

Well now, bless you and shush and oh you dear things. Calm yourselves and sit down in a semicircle on the play mat while we think about this.

I know it must seem sometimes that QI is a nerd's charter

that encourages boring dorks to vomit undigested boluses of fibrous factoid. QI and its volumes of General Ignorance might appear to some to be nothing more than provisioners of ammunition for tiresome gainsaying did-you-knowers and tedious trotters out of turgid trivia. But look beneath the surface and I hope you will agree that the volume that you hold in your delicate hands is in truth a *celebration*, a celebration of the greatest human quality there is. Curiosity. Curiosity has wrongly, by those with a vested interest in ignorance and their own revealed truths, been traduced and eternally characterised as a dangerous felicide, but you, dearest of dear, dear readers, know that Curiosity lights the way to glory.

Let us put it another way: the *lack* of curiosity is the Dementor that sucks all hope, joy, possibility and beauty out of the world. The dull torpid acedia that does not care to find out, that has no hunger and thirst for input, understanding and connection will desertify the human landscape and land our descendants squarely in the soup.

Do we want our species to make its way, foreheads thrust out, knuckles grazing the ground, into a barren of tedium and brutish unquestioning blindness, or do we want to skip through the world filled with wonder, curiosity and an appetite for discovery?

This screamingly overwrought preface that is even now embarrassing you to the encrimsoning roots of your scalp, is called *Forethought* in honour of Prometheus, the greatest of the Titans of Greek mythology. Prometheus, whose brother Atlas was busy holding up the world, looked at us poor newly made humans and loved us and felt sorry that we were animals so close to gods yet still lacking . . . *something* . . .

Prometheus climbed up Olympus and stole that something from the gods, bringing it down carefully preserved in a fennel stalk. It was fire. Fire that gave us technology, but more than that, it was *iskra,* the spark, the divine fire, the quality that drove us to *know.* The fire that allowed us to rise up on a level with the gods.

The Greeks rightly understood that if there *were* such creatures as gods, they were (it is self-evident) capricious, inconsistent, unjust, jealous and mean. And indeed Zeus, their king, was outraged that Prometheus, one of their own, had given humans great creating fire. He punished the Titan by chaining him to the Caucasus mountains. Every day an eagle (or vultures depending on your source) came to peck out his liver, which (Prometheus being an immortal) grew back each night. This eternal torture he underwent for humans, that we might, each one of us, have the divine spark, the immortal fire that drives us to ask Why? Who? When? What? Where? and How?

The name Prometheus means Forethought. We can repay him his daily agony by being, every day, curious, wondering and entirely on fire.

I adore you widely.

SECOND THOUGHTS |
John Lloyd and John Mitchinson

When we compiled the original Book of General Ignorance in 2006 – aided by the doughty and indefatigable QI Elves – we laboured under the misconception that we might have mined the Mountain of Ignorance to exhaustion, depleting its resources forever.

Nothing could be further from the truth.

Six years on, six series later, there is so much more ignorance available that we've had to deliberately cull it in order to make this *Second Book of General Ignorance* tolerably portable.

We hope you'll have as much fun reading it as we've had putting it together.

It is a wonderful thing that we, 'The Two Johnnies' (aged 61 and 49 respectively) can honestly say that we genuinely do 'learn something new every day'.

Thank you for allowing us to do that.

THE DISCREETLY PLUMPER SECOND BOOK OF GENERAL IGNORANCE

Everybody is ignorant, only on different subjects.
Will Rogers (1879–1935)

Who made the first flight in an aeroplane?

We don't know his name but he beat the Wright Brothers to it by fifty years.

He worked for Sir George Cayley (1773–1857), an aristocratic Yorkshireman and pioneer of aeronautics, who carried out the first truly scientific study of how birds fly. Cayley correctly described the principles of 'lift, drag and thrust' that govern flight and this led him to build a series of prototype flying machines. His early attempts with flapping wings (powered by steam and gunpowder engines) failed, so he turned his attention to gliders instead.

In 1804 he demonstrated the world's first model glider and, five years later, tested a full-sized version – but without a pilot. More than three decades passed before he finally felt ready to trust his 'governable parachute' with a human passenger. In 1853, at Brompton Dale near Scarborough, the intrepid baronet persuaded his reluctant coachman to steer the contraption across the valley. It was this anonymous employee who became the first human ever to fly in a heavier-than-air machine.

The coachman, so the story goes, was not impressed. He handed in his notice as soon as he landed, saying, 'I was hired to drive, not to fly.' A modern replica of Cayley's glider, now on show at the Yorkshire Air Museum, successfully repeated the flight across Brompton Dale in 1974.

But wings weren't Sir George's only legacy. With his work on the glider's landing gear, he literally reinvented the wheel. Needing something light but strong to absorb the aircraft's impact on landing, he came up with the idea of using wheels whose spokes were held at tension, rather than being carved from solid wood. These went on to transform the development of the bicycle and the car and are still widely used today.

And that wasn't all. Cayley was a remarkably prolific inventor, developing self-righting lifeboats, caterpillar tracks for bulldozers, automatic signals for railway crossings and seat belts. Even more remarkably, he offered all these inventions for the public good, without expecting any financial reward.

The Wright Brothers made their famous flights half a century later, in 1903. They were inspired by Cayley and by another unsung hero of aviation, Otto Lilienthal (1848–96), a Prussian known as the 'Glider King'. He was the first person to fly consistently: in the decade before the Wright Brothers, he made over 2,000 glider flights before falling to his death in 1896. His last words were humble and poignant: 'Small sacrifices must be made.'

STEPHEN *Who invented the aeroplane?*
RICH HALL *It's Orville and Wilbur Wright.*
KLAXON *'The Wright Brothers'*
PETER SERAFINOWICZ *Is it the Wrong Brothers?*

How many legs does an octopus have?

Two.

Octopuses have eight limbs protruding from their bodies, but recent research into how they use them has redefined what they should be called. Octopuses (from the Greek for 'eight feet') are *cephalopods* (Greek for 'head foot'). They use their back two tentacles to propel themselves along the seabed, leaving the remaining six to be used for feeding. As result, marine biologists now tend to refer to them as animals with two legs and six arms.

An octopus's tentacles are miraculous organs. They can stiffen to create a temporary elbow joint, or fold up to disguise their owner as a coconut rolling along the sea floor. They also contain two-thirds of the octopus's brain – about 50 million neurons – the remaining third of which is shaped like a doughnut and located inside its head, or mantle.

Because so much of an octopus's nervous system is in its extremities, each limb has a high degree of independence. A severed tentacle can continue to crawl around and, in some species, will live for several months. An octopus's arm (or leg) quite genuinely has a mind of its own.

Each arm on an octopus has two rows of suckers, equipped with taste-buds for identifying food. An octopus tastes everything that it touches. Male octopuses also have a specialised arm in which they keep their sperm. It's called the hectocotylus and is used for mating. To transfer the sperm, the male puts his arm into a hole in the female's head. During copulation the hectocotylus usually breaks off, but the male grows a new one the following year.

The way octopuses mate was first described by Aristotle (384–322 BC) but for over 2,000 years no one believed him. The French zoologist Georges Cuvier (1769–1832) redis-covered the process in the nineteenth century and gave the hectocotylus its name. It means 'a hundred tiny cups' in Greek.

Genetic variations sometimes cause octopuses to grow more than eight limbs. In 1998 the Shima Marineland Aquarium in Japan had a common octopus on display that had 96 tentacles. It was captured in nearby Matoya Bay in December 1998 but died five months later. The multi-armed cephalopod managed to lay a batch of eggs before its death. All the offspring hatched with the normal number of arms and legs, but none survived longer than a month.

Octopuses occasionally eat their own arms. This used to be blamed on stress, but is now thought to be caused by a virus that attacks their nervous system.

MEERA SYAL *Do you know how octopuses mate?*
STEPHEN *Tell, tell.*
ALAN *With difficulty.*
MEERA *They mate with their third right arm.*
ALAN *Do they?*
MEERA *Yes!*
CLIVE ANDERSON *We all do that.*

What colour are oranges?

That depends.

In many countries, oranges are green – even when ripe – and are sold that way in the shops. The same goes for lemons, mangoes, tangerines and grapefruit.

Oranges are unknown in the wild. They are a cross between tangerines and the pomelo or 'Chinese grapefruit' (which is pale green or yellow), and were first grown in South-East Asia. They were green there then, and today they still are. Vietnamese oranges and Thai tangerines are bright green on the outside, and only orange on the inside.

Oranges are subtropical fruit, not tropical ones. The colour of an orange depends on where it grows. In more temperate climes, its green skin turns orange when the weather cools; but in countries where it's always hot the chlorophyll is not destroyed and the fruits stay green. Oranges in Honduras, for example, are eaten green at home but artificially 'oranged' for export.

To achieve this, they are blasted with ethylene gas, a by-product of the oil industry, whose main use is in the manufacture of plastic. Ethylene is the most widely produced organic compound in the world: 100 million tons of it are made every year. It removes the natural outer green layer of an orange allowing the more familiar colour to show through.

Far and away the world's largest producer of oranges is Brazil (18 million tons a year), followed by the USA, which grows fewer than half as many. American oranges come from California, Texas and Florida. They were often synthetically dyed until the Food and Drug Administration banned the practice in 1955.

You can't tell the ripeness of an orange by its colour, no matter where it's from. If an orange goes unpicked, it can stay on the tree till the next season, during which time fluctuations in temperature can make it turn from green to orange and back to green again without the quality or flavour being affected.

The oranges you see on display in your supermarket certainly *appear* to be completely orange, but you may now start to worry they've been gassed. Don't.

Ethylene is odourless, tasteless and harmless, and many fruits and vegetables give it off naturally after they're picked. Ethylene producers include apples, melons, tomatoes, avocados and bananas. The gas isn't bad for you, but it can affect other kinds of fruit and veg – which is why you should keep apples and bananas separate from, say, lemons or carrots (and, of course, oranges).

Ethylene has other uses apart from making plastics (and

detergents and antifreeze) and altering the colour of an orange. If you want to speed up the ripening process of an unripe mango, keep it in a bag with a banana.

What's the name of the most southerly point of Africa?

It's not the Cape of Good Hope.

The residents of nearby Cape Town often have to explain this to visitors. The southernmost point of the continent is the altogether less famous Cape Agulhas, 150 kilometres (93 miles) south-east of the Cape of Good Hope.

The usual reason given for the Cape of Good Hope's fame (and its name) is that it was the psychologically important point where sailors, on the long haul down the west coast of Africa on their way to the Far East, at last began to sail in an easterly, rather than a southerly, direction.

On the other hand, it might have been an early example of marketing spin.

Bartolomeu Dias (1451–1500), the Portuguese navigator who discovered the Cape of Good Hope and became the first European to make the hair-raising trip around the foot of Africa, named it Cabo das Tormentas ('Cape of Storms'). His employer, King John II of Portugal (1455–95), keen to encourage others to adopt the new trade route, overruled him and tactfully rechristened it Cabo da Boa Esperança ('Cape of Good Hope').

The King died childless, aged only forty. Five years later Bartolomeu Dias also died. He was wrecked in a terrible storm – along with four ships and the loss of all hands – off the very cape he had so presciently named.

Cape Agulhas is equally treacherous. It is Portuguese for 'Cape of Needles', after the sharp rocks and reefs that infest its roaring waters. The local town is home to a shipwreck museum that commemorates 'a graveyard of ships'.

Because of its isolation and rocky, inaccessible beach, the area is rich in wildlife. On land, it is home to the critically endangered micro-frog (*Microbatrachella capensis*) and the Agulhas clapper (*Mirafra (apiata) majoriae*), a lark whose mating display involves much noisy wing-flapping.

In the waters offshore, between May and August, the sea boils with billions of migrating South African pilchards (*Sardinops sagax*). These shoals form one of the largest congregations of wildlife on the planet, equivalent to the great wildebeest migrations on land, and can stretch to be 6 kilometres (3.7 miles) long and 2 kilometres (1.2 miles) wide. Hundreds of thousands of sharks, dolphins, seals and seabirds travel in the fishes' wake, snacking on them at will but making little impact on the overall numbers.

Cape Agulhas is at 34° 49' 58" south and 20° 00' 12" east and it is the official dividing point between the Atlantic and Indian oceans. If you sailed past it, along the relatively unimpressive, gradually curving coastline, you probably wouldn't even notice it but for the cairn that marks the tip's exact location.

What's the hardest known substance?

It's not diamonds any more.

In 2005 scientists at Bayreuth University in Germany created a new material by compressing pure carbon under extreme heat. It's called hyperdiamond or aggregated diamond nanorods (ADNR) and, although it's incredibly hard, it looks rather like asphalt or a glittery black pudding.

It's long been known that one form of pure carbon (graphite) can be turned into another (diamond) by heat and pressure. But the Bayreuth team used neither. They used a third form of pure carbon, fullerite, also known as buckminsterfullerene or 'buckyballs'. Its sixty carbon atoms form a molecule shaped like a soccer ball, or like one of the geodesic domes invented by the American architect Richard Buckminster Fuller (1895–1983).

The carbon atoms in diamond are arranged in cubes stacked in pyramids; the new substance is made of tiny, interlocking rods. These are called 'nanorods' because they are so small – *nanos* is Greek for 'dwarf'. Each is 1 micron (one millionth of a metre) long and 20 nanometres (20 billionths of a metre) wide – about 1/50,000th of the width of a human hair.

Subjecting fullerite to extremes of heat (2,220 °C) and compression (200,000 times normal atmospheric pressure) created not only the *hardest*, but also the *stiffest* and *densest* substance known to science.

Density is how tightly packed a material's molecules are and is measured using X-rays. ADNR is 0.3 per cent denser than diamond.

Stiffness is a measure of compressibility: the amount of force that must be applied equally on all sides to make the material shrink in volume. Its basic unit is the pascal, after Blaise Pascal (1623–62), the French mathematician who helped develop the barometer, which measures air pressure. ADNR's stiffness rating is 491 gigapascals (GPa): diamond's is 442 GPa and iron's is 180 GPa. This means that ADNR is almost three times harder to compress than iron.

Hardness is simpler to determine: if one material can make a scratch mark on another, it's harder. The German mineralogist Friedrich Mohs (1773–1839) devised the Mohs Hardness scale in 1812. It starts at the softest end with talc (MH1). Lead is fairly soft at MH1½; fingernails are graded MH2½ (as hard as gold); in the middle are glass and knife blades at MH5½. Ordinary sandpaper (which is made of corundum) is MH9, and right at the top end is diamond at MH10. Since ADNR can scratch diamond, it is literally off the scale.

And there's more disappointing news for diamond fans: they aren't 'forever'. Graphite (which, oddly enough, is one of the *softest* known substances, as soft as talc) is much more chemically stable than diamond. In fact all diamonds are very slowly turning *into* graphite. But the process is imperceptible. There's no danger of anybody suddenly finding their earrings have become pencils.

What's the strangest substance known to science?

H_2O.

Water, or hydrogen oxide, is the strangest substance known to science. With the possible exception of air, it's also the most familiar. It covers 70 per cent of the earth and accounts for 70 per cent of our own brains.

Water is oxygen linked to hydrogen (the simplest and most common element in the universe) in the simplest way possible. Any other gas combined with hydrogen just produces another gas: only oxygen and hydrogen make a liquid.

And it's a liquid that behaves so differently from any other that theoretically it shouldn't exist. There are sixty-six known ways in which water is abnormal, the most peculiar being that nothing else in nature is found simultaneously as liquid, solid and gas. A sea full of icebergs under a cloudy sky may appear natural, but in chemical terms it is anything but. Most substances shrink as they cool, but when water falls below 4 °C it starts to expand and become lighter. That's why ice floats, and why wine bottles burst if left in the freezer.

Each water molecule can attach itself to four other water molecules. Because water is so strongly bonded, a lot of energy is needed to change it from one state to another. It takes ten times more energy to heat water than iron.

Because water can absorb a lot of heat without getting hot, it helps keep the planet's climate steady. Temperatures in the oceans are three times more stable than on land and water's transparency allows light to penetrate its depths, enabling life in the sea. Without water there would be no life at all. And, though you can put your hand right through it, it's remarkably difficult to compress and water hit at speed is as hard as concrete.

Although the bonds between water molecules are strong, they aren't stable. They are constantly being broken and remade: each molecule of water collides with other water molecules 10,000,000,000,000,000 times a second.

So many things can be dissolved in water that it's known as the 'universal solvent'. If you dissolve metal in acid, it's gone forever. If you dissolve plaster in water, when all the water has evaporated, the plaster is still there. This ability to dissolve stuff without eradicating it also paradoxically makes water the most destructive substance on the planet. Sooner or later, it eats away everything – from an iron drainpipe to the Grand Canyon.

And it gets everywhere. There are substantial deposits of ice on the moon and on Mars: traces of water vapour have even been detected on the cooler patches of the sun's surface. On Earth only a tiny fraction of all the water is in the atmosphere. If it fell evenly throughout the world, it would produce no more than 25 millimetres or an inch of rain. Most of Earth's water is inaccessible, locked deep inside the planet, carried down when tectonic plates overlap, or held inside the mineral structure of the rocks themselves.

If this hidden water were released it would refill the oceans thirty times over.

At what temperature does water freeze?

Pure water doesn't freeze at 0 °C, nor does seawater.

For water to freeze, it needs something for its molecules to latch on to. Ice crystals form around 'nuclei', such as small particles of dust. If there are none of these, you can get the temperature of water down to −42 °C before it freezes.

Cooling water without freezing it is known as 'supercooling'. It has to be done slowly. You can put a bottle of very pure water in your freezer and supercool it. When you take the bottle out and tap it, the water will instantly turn to ice.

Cooling water extremely fast has a completely different effect. It bypasses the ice stage (which has a regular crystalline lattice structure) and transforms into a chaotic amorphous solid known as 'glassy water' (so called because the random arrangement of molecules is similar to that found in glass). To form 'glassy water' you need to get the water temperature down to −137 °C in a few milliseconds. You won't find glassy water outside the lab on Earth, but it's the most common form of water in the universe − it's what comets are made of.

Because of its high salt content, seawater regularly falls below 0 °C without freezing. The blood of fishes normally freezes at about −0.5 °C, so marine biologists used to be puzzled by how fish survived in polar oceans. It turns out that species like Antarctic icefish and herring produce proteins in the pancreas that are absorbed into their blood. These prevent the formation of ice nuclei (much like antifreeze in a car radiator).

Given the peculiarities of water at low temperatures, it won't surprise you to learn that the boiling point of water, even at normal pressure, isn't necessarily 100 °C either. It can be much more. Again, the liquid needs to be warmed slowly and in a container that has no scratches. It is these that contain the small pockets of air around which the first bubbles form.

Boiling happens when bubbles of water vapour expand and break the surface. For this to happen, the temperature must be high enough for the pressure created by the vapour bubble to exceed the atmospheric pressure. Under normal conditions this is 100 °C, but if the water is free of places where bubbles could form, more heat is needed to overcome the surface tension of the bubbles as they struggle into life. (It's the same reason that blowing up a balloon is always harder at the beginning.)

This explains why a boiling hot cup of coffee in the microwave can explode all over you once removed or stirred. The movement sets off a chain reaction, so that all the water in the coffee vaporises at high speed.

One last watery oddity: hot water freezes faster than cold water. Aristotle first noted this in the fourth century BC, but it was only accepted by modern science in 1963. This resulted from the persistence of a Tanzanian schoolboy called Erasto Mpemba, who proved it by repeatedly demonstrating that a hot ice cream mixture set more quickly than cold. We still don't know why it does.

Where is the largest known lake?

It's 842 million miles away, halfway across the solar system.

In 2007 the Cassini–Huygens space probe sent back pictures of Titan, the largest of Saturn's moons. Near the moon's northern pole, radar imaging revealed a giant lake estimated to cover 388,500 square kilometres (150,000 square miles), significantly bigger than the Caspian Sea, the largest lake on Earth at 370,400 square kilometres (143,244 square miles).

The lake is called Kraken Mare – *mare* is Latin for 'sea' and the kraken is a sea monster from Norse mythology.

Titan has many lakes and they are the only bodies of stable liquid known to exist anywhere other than on Earth. But the liquid isn't water: Titan's average temperature is −181°C, so any water would be frozen solid. They are lakes of liquid gas – methane and ethane, the main ingredients of natural gas on earth – and they are so cold that they may even contain frozen methane-bergs.

Titan's chemical composition is thought to be very similar to that of Earth during the period when life first appeared here, and it is the only moon in the solar system with an atmosphere.

In 2004 Ladbrokes the bookmaker, in a joint publicity stunt with *New Scientist* magazine, offered odds of 10,000 to 1 against life being discovered on Titan. Would this be worth risking a titan on? (A 'titan' is the £100 million note used by the Bank of England for inter-bank accounting purposes.)

On balance, probably not. The development of DNA on Titan is unlikely because of the extreme cold and the lack of liquid water. However, some astrobiologists have suggested that Titan's hydrocarbon lakes might sustain forms of life that would inhale hydrogen in place of oxygen. Another theory is that life could have reached Titan from Earth, through microbes clinging to rocks smashed out of Earth's orbit by asteroid impacts. This theory is called panspermia (from *pan* 'all' and *sperma* 'seed' in Greek) and was used to explain the presence of life on Earth as long ago as the fifth century BC, when the Greek cosmologist Anaxagoras first proposed it.

What is certain is that, as the sun gets hotter, the temperature on Titan will also rise, making the conditions for life more likely. Whether, in six billion years or so, Ladbrokes will still exist to pay out any winnings is much less probable.

The Cassini–Huygens probe is named after the Italian astronomer Giovanni Domenico Cassini (1625–1712), who discovered four of Saturn's smaller moons between 1671 and 1684, and the Dutch polymath Christiaan Huygens (1629–95), who discovered Titan in 1654. Among Huygens's other achievements were working out the theory of centrifugal force, publishing a book on the use of probability in dice games, building the first pendulum clock and writing the first ever physics equation.

Where is the world's saltiest water?

Not in the Dead Sea.

The saltiest water in the world is found in Don Juan Pond in the Dry Valleys of north-eastern Antarctica. Also known as Lake Don Juan, it's really more of a puddle, with an average depth of less than 15 centimetres (6 inches). Its water is so salty that it doesn't freeze, despite the surrounding air temperature of −50°C. The water is 40 per cent salt − eighteen times saltier than seawater and more than twice as salty as the Dead Sea (which is only eight times saltier than the oceans).

Don Juan Pond was discovered by accident in 1961 and

named after two US Navy helicopter pilots, Lieutenants Donald Roe and John Hickey (hence Don John or 'Don Juan' in Spanish), who carried in the first field party to study it.

It's probably the most interesting puddle on Earth. Given that Antarctica's Dry Valleys are the driest, coldest places on the planet, it's astonishing that there's water there at all. It didn't come from the sky – it's too cold and windy there for rain or snow – it seeped up from the ground, slowly becoming saltier as the top layer of water evaporated. In spite of these unpromising conditions, the first researchers were amazed to discover it contained life: slender mats of blue-green algae that harboured a flourishing community of bacteria, yeast and fungi.

Since that first expedition, for reasons that are unclear, the water level in the pond has more than halved and no life remains. But even this is significant, because its waters still contain nitrous oxide (better known as laughing gas), a chemical previously believed to require organic life to produce it. This has now been shown to be a by-product of the reaction between the salts in the pond and the volcanic basalt rock that surrounds it.

If liquid water is found on Mars, it is likely to be in the form of cold, briny pools, just like Don Juan Pond. And we now know that at least some of the nitrogen-rich chemicals needed to produce life can occur in even the harshest environment.

Unlike Don Juan Pond, there is still plenty of life in the Dead Sea. There are no fish, but it is teeming with algae. This supports microbes that feed on it called *Halobacteria*. They belong to the Archaea domain, the oldest life forms on the planet. Archaea are so ancient that, on the evolutionary timescale, human beings are closer to bacteria than bacteria are to Archaea. Like the former inhabitants of Don Juan Pond, *Halobacteria* are 'extremophiles', surviving in conditions once believed impossible for life.

The *Halobacterium* is also known as the 'Renaissance Bug' because it can mend its own DNA (which is damaged by high salt concentrations). If this can be harnessed, it could be of great benefit to cancer sufferers. It might even enable manned space flight to Mars, by helping astronauts protect their DNA from exposure to the fierce radiation of interplanetary space.

Where did most minerals in the world come from?

Life on Earth.

There are about 4,300 minerals in the world today, but in the primordial dust that was to become the solar system there were fewer than a dozen. All the chemical elements were already there, but minerals were very rare before the sun and the planets formed.

Unlike all the other planets, Earth's crust is a patchwork of constantly moving tectonic plates ('tectonic' is from the Greek for 'construction'). No one knows why, but one theory is that all the water on the earth's surface caused cracks in it, like damp from a flooded bathroom seeping through a plaster ceiling. As the plates of the young Earth jostled together, they created immense heat and pressure, pushing the number of minerals up to perhaps a thousand.

Then, 4 billion years ago, life appeared. Microscopic algae began using sunlight to convert the carbon dioxide that made up most of the atmosphere into carbohydrates for food. This released oxygen as a by-product. Oxygen is both the most abundant and the most reactive element in the planet's crust. It forms compounds with almost anything. As it bonded with silicon, copper and iron, hundreds of new minerals were created. Although we think of oxygen as a gas, almost half the rocks on Earth are made from it.

While oxygen was being released into the atmosphere, carbon was also being sucked into the sea. Carbon, the basis of life, is as stable as oxygen is reactive. Its stability has made it the core of millions of organic compounds, including all the proteins, fats, acids and carbohydrates that go to make up living things. As the complexity of life on Earth increased, new minerals were created. Marine creatures died and drifted to the seabed, the thick layers of their shells and skeletons destined to become limestone, chalk and marble. Meanwhile, over millions of years, the sludge of rotting plants provided the ingredients for coal and oil. More life, and more diversity of life, meant more minerals. Two-thirds of all the minerals on earth were once alive.

This 'parallel evolution' of life and rocks gives clues to what we should look for on other planets. If certain minerals are detected, it's a good bet that they came into being alongside particular types of organism.

Are we depleting the world's mineral reserves? Oil aside, none of the evidence suggests so. Although vegetables grown in the UK and the USA over the past fifty years have shown significant drops in the levels of the trace minerals they contain, this is the result of artificial fertilisers, which promote faster growth at the expense of the plants' ability to absorb nutrientsfrom the air and soil.

This may explain why people say that food 'tasted better during the War'. They're probably right.

What are trees made from?

Air.

Most of the material that turns a tiny seed into a mighty tree comes from the sky, not the ground.

Small amounts of essential minerals come from the soil, but by far the majority of a tree's bulk is processed air. The tree's leaves convert light energy from the sun into chemical energy. This is used to recombine the carbon from carbon dioxide in the air and the hydrogen from rainwater into carbohydrates. The main one is cellulose, better known as wood.

When the chemical reaction is complete, the tree releases the oxygen it doesn't need back into the air. A medium-sized tree generates about the same amount of oxygen that each one of us needs to breathe.

This is the miracle of photosynthesis. Since all life depends on plants to eat, it is probably the most important biological process on earth.

Giant sequoia trees are the heaviest living things ever to have existed. They can weigh up to 6,000 tons, and reach over 95 metres (300 feet) in height and 12 metres (40 feet) in diameter. Their bark is up to 1.5 metres (5 feet) thick, but the seeds are minuscule, weighing 0.009 gram (1/3,000th of an ounce) each, approximately one billionth the weight of the fully grown tree.

Giant sequoias are also the fastest-growing trees in the world: for this they need not just air, but fire. The trees rely on the heat of forest fires to open their tough seed cones and to expose the bare soil. So the US Forest Service deliberately sets fire to the sequoia groves on a regular basis.

At the other end of the scale, the smallest trees in the world are the dwarf willows that grow on the tundra of Greenland. Fully grown, they struggle to reach 2 inches tall.

In 2008 a Norway spruce (*Picea abies*) found growing in

Sweden was carbon-dated to an astonishing 9,555 years old, taking the prize for both the oldest living plant and the oldest living organism. (Definitions of a 'single' organism are tricky, though: there are groves of quaking aspens in Utah that have root systems thought to date back 80,000 years.)

If it weren't for recycling, the paper the world gets through in one day would use up 12 million trees — about 250 square kilometres of forest.

How can you tell the age of a tree in a rainforest?

It almost certainly won't have any rings, so don't bother trying to count them. Your best bet is probably radiocarbon dating.

The living fibre of a tree's trunk is known as vascular tissue (from the Latin *vasculum* meaning 'little vessel') because, like the blood vessels in a body, it carries the water and nutrients to the leaves and flowers. Trees in temperate climes grow in a stop-start fashion, depending on the season, and this creates the annual growth ring. Plenty of water and a long, warm season of growth will create a wide ring; drought or frost will produce a narrow one.

There is only one recorded case of British oak trees failing to create an annual ring. This was in 1816, the 'year of no summer', when the world's climate was plunged into crisis by the eruption of Mount Tambora in Indonesia. Counting a tree's rings and relating the number to the date (technically known as dendrochronology) is remarkably accurate for temperate species of tree, but it isn't much use in the tropics, where there is little difference between seasons and most trees have no discernible rings.

In 2005 a team of Brazilian and American scientists conducted a large-scale research project to calculate the age of trees in the Amazon rain forest. They used radiocarbon dating methods similar to those employed by archaeologists when calculating the date of organic artefacts. (All organic material contains traces of carbon-14, the radioactive form of carbon. This decays at a fixed rate, enabling the material's age to be calculated accurately.) The results were surprising – more than half of those trees recorded with trunk diameters of as little as 10 centimetres (4 inches) were already 300 years old, and many of the large canopy trees were 750 to 1,000 years old. This slow growth rate seems to be the result of nutrient-poor soil and the lack of light underneath the canopy.

Why do trees live for so long? One of the secrets of their longevity is that, unlike most animals, they can close off diseased or damaged portions of themselves without killing the whole organism. Even cleverer, some trees defy the ageing process by generating 'clones', or genetically identical shoots, so that, even when one trunk dies, the network of roots can send out a new one. Perhaps the most famous of these is the quaking aspen (*Populus tremuloides*), which can form groves of several hundred trees, each of which is a 'limb' of one vast, living thing. Some of these colonies have been traced back 80,000 years. Recent evidence, however, suggests the number of male reproductive cells declines as they age, so, although they are very old, they aren't immortal.

Of the trees that *don't* use this trick, the oldest surviving example was until recently believed to be Methuselah, a bristlecone pine in California, which is, at 4,765 years old, older than Stonehenge or the pyramids. The Norway spruce (*Picea abies*) in the Dalarna province of Sweden that was carbon-dated as 9,555 years old grew as it did because cold weather had stopped the roots from growing for thousands of years, so it stayed a shrub until a century ago, when warmer weather encouraged it to sprout a new trunk. Called 'Old Tjikko' (after the dog owned by the geologist who discovered it), it claims the prize for both the oldest living plant and the planet's oldest living organism of any kind.

STEPHEN *Where's the best place in the world to discover an entirely new species?*

ALAN *What about the Amazon rainforest, where they're discovering new things all the time?*

KLAXON

STEPHEN *You'd have to travel thousands of miles, you'd have to park there, you'd have to look, you know . . .*

ALAN *Park?*

DAVID MITCHELL *Everyone knows it's a nightmare, parking.*

STEPHEN *I'm suddenly worried that my brain let me say that.*

Which came first, the chicken or the egg?

The egg. Final answer.

As the geneticist J. B. S. Haldane (1892–1964) remarked, 'The most frequently asked question is: "Which came first, the chicken or the egg?" The fact that it is still asked proves either that many people have never been  taught the theory of evolution or that they don't believe it.'

With that in mind, the answer becomes obvious. Birds evolved from reptiles, so the first bird must have come out of an egg – laid by a reptile.

Like everything else, an egg is not as simple as it looks. For a start, the word 'egg' is used in two different ways. To a biologist, an egg is an ovum (Latin for egg), the tiny female reproductive cell which, when fertilised by a male sperm (Greek for seed), develops into an embryo. Both the ovum and the sperm are called gametes (from the Greek *gamete*, 'wife', and *gametes*, 'husband').

In a hen's egg these two tiny cells merge in the 'germinal spot' or blastodisc (from *blastos*, Greek for 'sprout'). Around this is the yolk, which provides most of the nutrition for the growing chick. The word 'yolk' comes from Old English, *geolca*, 'yellow' (until the late nineteenth century it was often spelt 'yelk'). Around the yolk is the egg white or albumen (from the Latin *albus*, 'white') which is also nutritious but whose main purpose is to protect the yolk, which is held in place in the centre of the egg by two twisted threads called chalazae. (*chalaza* is Greek for 'hailstone': the knotted white cord looks like a string of minute pearls or balls of ice.) Around the albumen is the shell, which is made from calcium carbonate – the same stuff that skeletons and indigestion pills are made from. It's porous so that the chick can breathe, and the air is kept in a pocket between the albumen and the shell. Membranes separate each part and together it's known as a cleidoic egg – from the Greek *kleidoun*, meaning 'to lock up'. A chicken makes the whole thing from scratch in a single day.

Because its shell is porous, if you keep an egg for a long time, the yolk and albumen dry out, sucking air inside. That's why rotten eggs float. To find out what colour egg a hen will lay, examine her earlobes. Hens with white earlobes lay white eggs; hens with red earlobes lay brown ones. The colour of a hen's egg depends on the breed of the chicken: it has nothing to do with diet.

In 1826 the Estonian biologist Karl Ernst von Baer (1792–1876) proved that women produce eggs like other animals. Since the time of Aristotle, everyone had thought that a male seed was 'planted' in the woman and nurtured in the womb. (The first observation of semen under a microscope by Anton van Leeuwenhoek (1632–1723) in 1677 seemed to confirm this: he thought he had seen a miniature *homunculus*, or 'little man', in each sperm.) It wasn't until the 1870s that the embryo was proven to develop from the union of egg and sperm and it took another twenty years before German biologist August Weismann (1834–1914) discovered that sperm and ovum carried only half the parent's genes. The sperm is one of the smallest cells in the human body – it's only a twentieth the size of an ovum – whereas the ovum is one of the largest. It's twelve times bigger than the average cell, but still only the size of a full stop on this page.

Can you name a fish?

Don't even try: there's no such thing.

After a lifetime's study of the creatures formerly known as 'fish', the great palaeontologist Stephen Jay Gould (1941–2002) concluded they didn't exist.

The point he was making is that the word 'fish' is applied indiscriminately to entirely separate classes of animal – cartilaginous ones (like sharks and rays); bony ones (including most 'fish', from piranhas and eels to seahorses and cod); and ones with skulls but no backbones or jaws (such as hagfish and lampreys). These three classes split off from one another far longer ago than the different orders, families and genuses did from each other, so that a salmon, for example, has more in common with (and is more closely related to) a human than a hagfish. To an evolutionary biologist, 'fish' is not a useful word unless it's on a menu.

And this isn't just a quirk particular to Gould. The *Oxford Encyclopedia of Underwater Life* comments: 'Incredible as it may sound, there is no such thing as a "fish". The concept is merely a convenient umbrella term to describe an aquatic vertebrate that is not a mammal, a turtle, or anything else.' It's equivalent to calling bats and flying lizards 'birds' just because they happen to fly. 'The relationship between a lamprey and a shark', the *Encyclopedia* insists, 'is no closer than that between a salamander and a camel.'

Still, it's better than it was. In the sixteenth century seals, whales, crocodiles and even hippos were called 'fish'. And, today, cuttlefish, starfish, crayfish, jellyfish and shellfish (which, by any scientific definition, aren't fish at all) still are.

Stephen Jay Gould made the same point about trees. The 'tree' form has evolved many times in the course of history: its ancestors were unrelated plants such as grasses, roses, mosses and clovers – so, for Gould, there's no such thing as a tree either.

One fish that absolutely doesn't exist is the 'sardine'. It's a generic term used for around twenty different small, soft-boned, oily fish. And only once they're in a can. In the UK, they're usually pilchards, often called – optimistically – 'true sardines', although the Latin name (*Sardina pilchardus*) points up the confusion. Sometimes what you get in a sardine can is a herring, sometimes it's a sprat (which glories in the scientific name *Sprattus sprattus sprattus*).

What it isn't, is a 'sardine'. Nor even, as we now know, a fish.

ALAN *At night all the ugly fish come out. And it's really interesting.*

STEPHEN *You don't need to be pretty out there.*

ALAN *That's right. You go to the Red Sea and, in the day, the fish are beautiful, colourful fish. And then at night, they're all bug-eyed. They limp around and you're not allowed to touch them.*

And they all kind of look at you. And you shine a light at them
and they go 'No! No! Don't look at me, don't look at me!'

How does a shark know you're there?

You don't have to be bleeding for one to track you down.

Sharks have an astonishingly powerful sense of smell. They can detect blood at a concentration of one part in 25 million, the equivalent of a single drop of blood in a 9,000-litre (2,000-gallon) tank of water.

It's the currents that determine the speed and direction of a smell's dispersal in water, so sharks swim into the current. If you are bleeding, even slightly, a shark will know. If the current is running at a moderate 3½ kilometres per hour (about 2¼ miles per hour), a shark 400 metres (a quarter of a mile) downstream will smell your blood in seven minutes. Sharks swim at nearly 40 kilometres per hour (25 miles per hour), so one could reach you in sixty seconds. Faster currents make things worse – even allowing for the fact that the shark has more to swim against. In a riptide of 26 kilometres per hour (16 miles per hour), a shark less than half a kilometre (a quarter of a mile) downstream would detect you in a minute and take less than two to reach you – giving you three minutes in total to escape.

Sharks also see very well, but even a short-sighted shark with a bad head cold (not that it happens) would still be able to find you. Sharks have excellent hearing in the lower frequencies and can hear something thrashing about at a distance of half a kilometre (a third of a mile). So you could try being very quiet indeed.

A blind, stone-deaf shark with no nose would still find you

without breaking stride. Sharks' heads are riddled with jelly-filled canals by the name of the 'ampullae of Lorenzini' after Stefano Lorenzini, the Italian doctor who first described them in 1678. We've only recently discovered what their purpose is: to register the faint electrical fields generated by all living bodies.

So, as long as you're not bleeding, not moving and your brain and heart aren't working, you should be fine.

And there's some more good news – sort of. Californian oceanography professor Dr Jamie MacMahan has found that the standard view of a riptide is wrong – it doesn't run out to sea but is circular, like a whirlpool. If you swim parallel to the shore, he says, there's a 50 per cent chance you'll be swept out into the ocean deeps. But, if you just tread water, there's a 90 per cent chance of being returned to shore within three minutes – perhaps just in time to escape the shark.

If a shark does find you, try turning it upside down and tickling its tummy. It will enter a reflex state known as 'tonic immobility' and float motionless as if hypnotised. Killer whales exploit this by flipping sharks over on to their backs and holding them immobile in the water until they suffocate. You have about fifteen minutes before the shark gets wise to your ruse. Careful, though: not all species of shark react the same way. Tiger sharks, for example, respond best to a gentle massage around the eyes. According to shark expert Michael Rutzen, it's just like tickling trout: 'All you have to do is defend your own personal space and stay calm.'

Having said all this, relax. Sharks almost never attack people. Figures from all twenty-two US coastal states, averaged over the last fifty years, show that you are seventy-six times more likely to be killed by a bolt of lightning than by a shark.

Does the Mediterranean have tides?

Yes it does, despite what every tour guide tells you.

Most of them are very small: just a few centimetres back and forth on average. This is because the Mediterranean is cut off from the Atlantic (and the huge effect of the pull of the moon on it) by the narrow Straits of Gibraltar.

Right next door to the entrance to the Med, sea levels can change by around 80 centimetres (3 feet) but in the Gulf of Gabes off the coast of eastern Tunisia, the tidal elevation can be as much as 2.5 metres (8 feet) twice a day.

This is because tides are caused not only by the gravitational effect of the moon but also by atmospheric pressure, depth, salinity, temperature and the shape of the coastline.

The relatively big tides in the Gulf of Gabes result from its shape. It is a wide, shallow basin, about 100 kilometres (60 miles) wide by 100 kilometres long. The gulf acts as a funnel, the tidal energy forcing water into a progressively smaller space, thereby increasing the rise in sea level – and, correspondingly, lowering it on the way out. The same thing happens on a much greater scale in the Bristol Channel, which has a tidal range of over 9 metres (30 feet).

Tidal effects are at their strongest when the sun and moon are on the same side of the earth (new moon), or on the opposite side (full moon), and their gravitational pulls combine to create the strong 'spring' tides ('spring' in the sense of 'powerful forward movement', not the season).

The Phoenicians founded Gabes in about 800 BC. Pliny the Elder first noted its unusually large tides in AD 77 in his *Natural History*. He also recorded that Gabes was second only to Tyre in the production of the expensive purple dye made from murex shells, which the Phoenicians discovered (hence the Greek for purple, *phoinikeos*), and which was highly prized by the Romans: the *toga purpurea* was worn only by kings, generals in triumph and emperors.

The Mediterranean is bigger than you might think. At 2,500 square kilometres (965,000 square miles) it covers the same area as Sudan, the largest country in Africa, and would comfortably swallow Western Europe (France, Spain, Germany, Italy, Greece, Britain, the Netherlands, Belgium, Switzerland and Austria combined). Its coastline stretches for 46,000 kilometres (28,000 miles) or about twice the length of the coastline of Africa. Nor is it particularly shallow: its average depth is over 1½ kilometres (about a mile) while the North Sea's is a mere 94 metres (310 feet) and, at its deepest point, in the Ionian Sea, it reaches down nearly 5 kilometres (over 3 miles), substantially deeper than the average depth of the Atlantic.

Six million years ago, the Mediterranean dried out completely in the so-called Messinian Salinity Crisis. This created the largest salt basin that ever existed and raised the sea level of the rest of the world by 10 metres (33 feet). Three hundred thousand years later, the rock barrier at the Straits of Gibraltar gave way – in a cataclysm called the Zanclean Flood – producing the world's largest-ever waterfall and refilling the whole of the Mediterranean in as little as two years. The tide would have risen 10 metres every day. But it wouldn't have gone out again.

STEPHEN *The Mediterranean was once the biggest dry lake in the world. In the late Miocene era.*

ALAN *The water came rushing in over the Strait of Gibraltar.*

STEPHEN *You're quite right. Six million years ago.*

ALAN *I know this because I saw it in the Plymouth Aquarium.*

JIMMY CARR *That must have been fabulous for all the towns around Spain and Portugal that rely on tourism. When that came in, they went: 'This is fantastic. Finally these jet-skis are going to get an outing.'*

Which birds inspired Darwin's theory of evolution?

Many smart people would answer 'finches', but actually it was mockingbirds.

The great passion of the young Charles Darwin (1809–82) was killing wildlife. As a student at Cambridge, when the shooting season started, his hands shook so much with excitement he could hardly load his gun. Though studying medicine and divinity to please his father, he dismissed lectures as 'cold, breakfastless hours, listening to discourses on the properties of rhubarb'.

But he was also an enthusiastic amateur biologist and fossil-hunter and was keen to see the tropics, so he signed on as a 'gentleman naturalist' for HMS *Beagle*'s second survey expedition (1831–6). He almost didn't get the job: the captain was keen on physiognomy and thought that Darwin's nose indicated laziness. Charles later noted that 'I think he was afterwards well satisfied that my nose had spoken falsely'.

The story goes that, during the voyage, Darwin noticed that finches on different islands in the Galapagos had distinctive beaks, which led him to guess that each type had adapted for a specific habitat and evolved from a common ancestor. It's true that Darwin's theory of evolution by natural selection originated aboard the *Beagle*, but it had nothing to do with finches. Though Darwin did collect finch specimens from the Galapagos, he showed very little interest in them until years later. He was no ornithologist in those days and wasn't even aware that the finches were of different species. It wouldn't have helped much if he had been, because he didn't label them to show where they'd been caught. He mentioned them only in passing in his journals and they are not mentioned once in *On the Origin of Species* (1859).

The mockingbirds were a different matter. Intrigued by the

variations between the populations on two nearby islands, Darwin took careful note of every mockingbird he encountered. Gradually, as his journals show, he began to realise that species were not immutable: they could change over time. Out of that insight all his subsequent theories on evolution grew.

Because the finches are a perfect example of Darwin's theories in action, later scientists assumed that they must have been the birds that inspired him. One of these was the evolutionary biologist David Lack (1910–73) whose 1947 book, *Darwin's Finches,* fixed the idea (and the term) in the popular consciousness.

Darwin's book on the voyage of the *Beagle* was an immediate best-seller, and the trip made the captain's name too. Robert Fitzroy (1805–65) went on to become a vice-admiral, Governor General of New Zealand and the inventor of weather forecasting – one of the sea areas in the Shipping Forecast is named after him.

The finches got famous, too, as we know. The fifteen species of *Geospizinae* are still popularly known today as Darwin's Finches – although it turns out they're not finches at all, but a different kind of bird called a tanager.

Where's the most convenient place to discover a new species?

In your own back garden.

You can cancel that expensive (and possibly dangerous) trip up the Amazon.

In 1972 an ecologist called Jennifer Owen started to note down all the wildlife in her garden in Humberstone, a suburb of Leicester. After fifteen years she wrote a book about it. She had counted 422 species of plant and 1,757 species of animal, including 533 species of parasitic Ichneumon wasp. Fifteen of these had never been recorded in Britain, and four were completely new to science.

Suburban gardens cover 433,000 hectares (well over a million acres) of England and Wales. If so many new species can be found in just one of them, this must be true of others. Between 2000 and 2007, the Biodiversity in Urban Gardens in Sheffield project (BUGS) repeated Dr Owen's work on a bigger scale. Domestic gardens account for some 23 per cent of urban Sheffield, including 25,000 ponds, 45,000 nest boxes, 50,000 compost heaps and 360,000 trees. These present, as Professor Kevin Gaston, BUGS' chief investigator, put it '175,000 separate conservation opportunities'. One of BUGS' discoveries was what may be a new, minuscule species of lichen, found in the moss on an ordinary tarmac path.

To more or less guarantee discovering a new species, all you need is a garden, a lot of time and patience, and a lot of expertise. In the words of the eighteenth-century naturalist Gilbert White (1720–93), 'In zoology as it is in botany: all nature is so full, that that district produces the greatest variety which is the most examined.' In 2010 London's Natural History Museum found a new species of insect in its own garden. They are baffled by what it is, as it doesn't match any of the more than 28 million specimens inside the museum itself.

Part of the fun of discovering a new species is that you get the chance to choose what it's called. A recently discovered beetle with legs resembling overdeveloped human biceps was named *Agra schwarzeneggeri*; a fossilised trilobite with an hourglass-shaped shell was called *Norasaphus monroeae* after Marilyn Monroe; and *Orectochilus orbisonorum* is a whirligig beetle dedicated to singer Ray Orbison because it looks like it's wearing a tuxedo. In 1982 Ferdinando Boero, now a professor at Lecce University in Italy, but then a researcher at Genoa, had a more underhand motive in naming the jellyfish he discovered *Phialella zappai* – it was a cunning plan to persuade his hero Frank Zappa to meet him. It worked: they remained friends for the rest of the musician's life.

British-born astrobiologist Paul Davies of Arizona State University urges us all to search for new unknown forms of life. 'It could be right in front of our noses – or even in our noses,' he says.

The one thing you don't want to find in your nose is an Ichneumon wasp. These unpleasant insects caused Darwin to lose his religious faith. 'I cannot persuade myself', he wrote, 'that a beneficent and omnipotent God would have designedly created the Ichneumonidae with the express intention of their feeding within the living bodies of caterpillars.'

What kind of bird is *Puffinus puffinus*?

Before you answer, bear in mind that *Rattus rattus* is a rat, *Gerbillus gerbillus* is a gerbil, *Oriolus oriolus* is an oriole, *Iguana iguana* is an iguana, *Conger conger* is a conger eel and *Gorilla gorilla gorilla* is emphatically a gorilla.

And *Puffinus puffinus*?

Bad luck, that's the Manx shearwater. It's unrelated to the puffin.

Scientific names for animals are usually composed of two words: the genus comes first, followed by the species. The species of a living thing is defined as that group with which it can reproduce. Its genus is analogous to its tribe: a group of species that are clearly related to each other. When the names of an animal's genus and its species are the same that's called a tautonym (from the Greek *tautos* 'same' and *onoma* 'name'). For example, the bogue fish is *Boops boops* and *Mops mops* is the Malayan Free-tailed bat.

Where there is a third part to the name of a species, it is used to indicate a subspecies. So the triple tautonym *Gorilla gorilla gorilla* (the Western Lowland gorilla) is a subspecies of *Gorilla gorilla* (the Western gorilla). The Tiger beetle subspecies *Megacephala (Megacephala) megacephala* has a name that translates as 'bighead (bighead) bighead'. Sometimes a subgenus is also given in brackets such as *Bison (Bison) bison bison*, which (for the avoidance of doubt) is a kind of bison.

Tautonyms for animals are not uncommon, but are strictly forbidden for plants under the International Code of Botanical Nomenclature.

There are three species of puffin and they belong to the genus *Fratercula*, Latin for 'little brother', because their plumage resembles monastic robes.

There are about thirty species of shearwater, all of which share the genus name *Puffinus*, which comes from an Anglo-Norman word meaning 'fatling'. This refers to the chubbiness of the young birds, and hints at their culinary uses. They were eaten both fresh and pickled and, because they swim so well under water, were for a long time thought to be half fish, which allowed Catholics to eat them on Fridays and during Lent. Shearwater chicks are easily mistaken for puffins: which probably explains the confusion over the name. Puffins (and particularly their hearts) are a national delicacy in Iceland.

The oldest living bird ever recorded in Britain was a Manx Shearwater. It was found by chance in 2002 by the staff of the bird observatory on Bardsey Island in North Wales. They were delighted to discover that ornithologists had ringed it in 1957, when it must already have been at least five years old. It's reckoned to have covered around 8 million kilometres (5 million miles) over more than half a century, flying to South

America in the winter and back again to Britain for the *Puffinus puffinus* breeding season.

JEREMY CLARKSON *You don't want to listen to this, but I once had some whale. And they said to me: 'Would you like me to grate some puffin on that?'*

Can you name three species of British mouse?

Two points each for Harvest mouse, House mouse, Field mouse and Wood mouse – and four points for Yellow-necked mouse – but minus ten for dormouse.

The dormouse is more of a squirrel than a mouse.

Admittedly, it does look rather mouse-like – except for its tail, which is furry. (Mice have scaly tales.) It also has fur inside its ears – which mice don't. In fact, the dormouse is generally furrier all round. This to keep it warm in winter: it's the only British rodent that hibernates.

The 'dorm-' part of its name means 'sleepy' and sleeping is what it's best at. The golden-coloured Common (or Hazel) dormouse can spend three-quarters of its life asleep. It's also known as the 'seven-sleeper' because it regularly spends seven months of the year dormant, though warmer winters now mean its hibernation lasts five and a half weeks less than it did twenty years ago.

If you want to get involved with dormice, you'll need to go on a Dormouse Handling Course and apply for a government dormouse licence. The British dormouse population has fallen by 70 per cent in the last quarter century and it is now strictly illegal to disturb, let alone kill, this rarely seen nocturnal creature.

The much larger Edible (or Fat) dormouse (*Glis glis*) is even less common in Britain than the Common dormouse (*Muscardinus avellanarius*). It's grey and white and could easily be mistaken for a small squirrel with big ears. It was introduced to Britain in 1902 by Lord Rothschild, as part of his wildlife collection in Tring Park, Hertfordshire – since when escapees have spread across the Chilterns. They can be a serious pest in lofts and outbuildings and can cause fatal damage to young trees. It's legal to shoot them.

The Romans were very keen on eating Edible dormice, though there's no evidence that they brought them to Britain. They kept them in earthenware pots called *dolia*, fattening them up on a diet of walnuts and currants, and storing the pots in special dormouse gardens or *glisaria*. Recipes included roast stuffed dormouse and honey-glazed dormouse with poppy seeds.

It's a taste that survives in many parts of Europe, where dormouse hunting is illegal but often done. In Calabria in southern Italy, where tens of thousands are eaten annually, the Mafia allegedly controls the lucrative dormouse trade.

In 2007 fifteen Calabrian restaurateurs were charged with serving *Glis* stewed in wine and red pepper. They all denied the allegations. Their defence was that the meat in the casseroles wasn't dormouse – it was only rat.

How far are you from a rat?

It's much further than you think.

The idea that you are 'never more than 6 feet away from a rat' is wrong by a factor of ten. Of course, it depends where you live: some of us live close to hundred of rats, others live near

none. But rats, although they happily live off our rubbish, don't like to get too close. Rentokil, the pest control company, estimates that the average city dweller is at least 21 metres (70 feet) from the nearest one.

The bad news is that rats in the UK now outnumber people. According to the National Rodent Survey, there are around 70 million rats in the country: 10 per cent more than the current human population.

Rats carry seventy or so infectious diseases including salmonella, tuberculosis and Weil's disease. They are also responsible for consuming a fifth of the world's food supply each year. Their sharp teeth (which never stop growing) enable them to gnaw through almost anything, causing a quarter of all electric cable breaks and disconnected phone lines in the process.

Plus, they brought the fleas that gave us bubonic plague. And they have those nasty, scaly tails.

It was the Black or Ship rat (*Rattus rattus*) that brought the plague. It sought out human company because our living conditions were so squalid. Slovenly disposal of food waste causes 35 per cent of rat infestations: broken sewers only 2 per cent.

Today, *Rattus rattus* is one of the UK's rarest mammals. Only small clusters remain, around big ports like London and Liverpool and on remote islands like Lundy, where they still are regularly (and legally) culled. The Black rat doesn't appear on any endangered lists – presumably because it's a rat.

Any rat you see today is almost certain to be the larger, stronger Brown or Norway rat (*Rattus norvegicus*), which arrived in the UK less than 300 years ago. They have nothing to do with Norway (they originated in northern China) and they don't carry plague. In fact, their use in laboratory experiments saves many human lives.

The dreaded rat's tail is actually a device for regulating body temperature. It acts as a long, thin radiator (rather like an elephant's ears), which is why it isn't covered in hair.

ALAN *You know, all the rats in England all face the same direction at any given time . . .*

BILL BAILEY *'Cause they're magnetic, aren't they, rats?*

ROB BRYDON *It's very hard for rat couples who have that, kind of, reversed polarity going on. You know, when you can't put two magnets together? There are rats who fall in love, and they are destined to be together, and they can't kiss.*

What kind of animal is 'Ratty' from *The Wind in the Willows*?

You won't be surprised to hear that he's not a rat.

The Wind in the Willows by Kenneth Grahame (1859–1932) began as a series of letters to his young son, Alistair (nicknamed 'Mouse'). After being rejected by several publishers, it came out in book form in 1908 – the same year that Grahame retired after thirty years working at the Bank of England.

Ratty, one of the main characters, is a water vole (*Arvicola amphibius*), colloquially known as a 'water rat'. As a child, Kenneth Grahame would have seen plenty of water voles, nesting in the riverbanks near his grandmother's home at Cookham Dean on the Thames – but today they are one of

Britain's most endangered species. Water voles underwent a catastrophe after the fur trade started farming imported American mink in the 1920s. Unlike native predators, mink can follow voles right into their tunnels. Escaped mink (and their descendants) have been eating vast numbers of voles ever since, wiping them out entirely in many places.

This is bad news for future archaeologists. Voles are the world's fastest-evolving mammals, dividing into new species up to a hundred times faster than the average vertebrate. This allows archaeologists to use the so-called 'vole clock'. Carbon dating only works up to about 50,000 years ago. For older digs, the investigators use fossilised vole teeth – tiny things about the size of a fingernail clipping. The ways they have altered at different stages in voles' evolution are so specific that items found alongside them can be dated with great accuracy.

Water voles are vegetarian but, in 2010, researchers in Berkshire were amazed to discover they had been eating the legs of toads. It's thought that pregnant voles needing extra protein were responsible, but it seems like poetic justice given all the trouble that Toad caused Ratty in the book.

Early reviews of *The Wind in the Willows* were damning. Arthur Ransome (1884–1967), author of *Swallows and Amazons*, wrote that it was 'like a speech to Hottentots made in Chinese'. It only started to sell after Grahame sent a copy to US President Theodore Roosevelt (1858–1919), who adored it.

Grahame's own life was much less delightful than the riverside idyll he wrote about. His mother died when he was five, causing his father to drink himself to death. As Secretary to the Bank of England, he spent his time collecting fluffy toys and writing hundreds of letters in baby language to his equally strange fiancée, Elspeth. In 1903 he survived an assassination attempt when a 'Socialist Lunatic' shot him at work (the Governor wasn't available). Luckily, the fire brigade managed to subdue the terrorist by turning a hose on him.

The life of his troubled son, Alistair ('Mouse'), was even worse. Blind in one eye from birth, his childhood hobbies included lying down in front of passing cars to make them stop. He had a nervous breakdown at school and then took to calling himself 'Robinson' – the name of his father's would-be assassin. In 1920, while an undergraduate at Oxford, Alistair lay face down across a railway track in Port Meadow and was decapitated by a train.

What kind of animal did Beatrix Potter first write about?

It wasn't a rabbit – or a hedgehog, or a frog – or anything remotely cute. The first living things that Beatrix Potter wrote about were fungi.

Fungus is Latin for mushroom. You might think it's pushing it a bit to call a mushroom an animal, but fungi are biologically closer to animals than they are to plants. Since 1969 they've had their own kingdom (along with yeasts and moulds) and they're neither plant nor animal.

The English author and illustrator Beatrix Potter (1866–1943) was educated by governesses and grew up isolated from other children. From the age of fifteen she recorded her life in journals, using a secret code that wasn't unravelled until twenty years after her death. She had lots of pets: a bat, newts, ferrets, frogs and two rabbits (Benjamin and Peter), whom she took out for walks on leads. She spent her summers in Scotland and the Lake District where her close observation of nature led her to become an expert on fungi or 'mycologist'.

Although an amateur, Potter kept up with all the latest advances in mycology.

Her first published work, presented at the Linnaean Society in 1897, was *On the Germination of Spores of Agaricineae*. It had to be read out for her by her uncle, because women were not allowed to address meetings. She applied to study at the Royal Botanic Gardens at Kew, but was turned down for the same reason – and the Royal Society refused to publish at least one of her papers. A hundred years later, the Linnaean Society, at least, had the grace to issue a belated posthumous apology.

Potter was an early pioneer of the theory that lichens were a partnership between fungi and algae – two separate organisms rather than one – and she produced a series of detailed drawings to support her hypothesis. This idea, later confirmed as correct, was considered heretical by the British scientific establishment at the time, but her scientific illustrations were greatly admired. This proved useful when she came to write her children's books.

The first of Beatrix Potter's twenty stories for children began life in 1893, as a letter to a young boy named Noel Moore, whose mother had been one of her governesses. The ex-governess loved the story and persuaded her to publish it. Frederick Warne brought it out in 1902, and by Christmas *The Tale of Peter Rabbit* had sold 28,000 copies. Within a year, Peter Rabbit was so popular he had become a soft toy, making him the world's first licensed character.

Peter Rabbit was inspired by a pet rabbit named Peter Piper, bought for the young Beatrix in Shepherd's Bush for 4s 6d. He was trained to 'jump through a hoop, and ring a bell, and play the tambourine'. Although he brought her fame and financial security, Potter was baffled by the success of her creation: 'The public must be fond of rabbits! What an appalling quantity of Peter.'

Beatrix Potter borrowed the names for many of her characters from tombstones in Brompton Cemetery in London, which was near the family home in South Kensington. Peter Rabbett, Jeremiah Fisher, Mr Nutkins, Mr Brock and Mr McGregor are all buried there.

Which animal dreams most?

You might think it's the ones that sleep most, like the dormouse or the sloth, or perhaps humans, who have the most complex brains. But it's none of these. The greatest dreamer of all is the duck-billed platypus.

All mammals (but only some birds) dream. What happens to them when they do, or why they do it at all, is much less well understood.

The dream state is known as Rapid Eye Movement (REM) sleep and it was discovered in 1952. Eugene Aserinsky, a graduate physiology student at the University of Chicago, used a device called an electroculogram to record the eye-movements of his eight-year-old son. He noticed a distinct pattern as he slept during the night and pointed it out to his supervisor, Dr Nathaniel Kleitman. An electro-encephalograph (EEG) was then used to measure the brain activity of twenty sleeping people. To the researchers' amazement, this showed that, when the subjects' eyes were moving rapidly, their brain activity was so vigorous that they should really have been awake. Waking them from REM sleep led to vivid recall of their dreams – which didn't happen when their eyes were still.

Zoologists soon found that many animals also undergo the same process. Cats, bats, opossums and armadillos all have extended periods of REM sleep but, surprisingly, giraffes and elephants get very little and dolphins have none at all. The animal with by far the longest REM sleep is the duck-billed platypus (*Ornithorhynchus anatinus*), one of the oldest of all mammals. They spend eight hours a day in the dream state, four times as much as an adult human.

REM sleep is different from either normal sleep or waking: it is a third state of existence in which the brain is racing, but the body is virtually paralysed. It seems that the animals most at risk from predators dream least. Ruminants like elephants and sheep have few dreams; a platypus, with few enemies, can afford plenty. Dolphins, who need to rest while afloat but still keep breathing, don't sleep at all in the traditional sense. One half of their brain and body goes to sleep at a time, while the other half is fully awake – including one of their eyes. This may explain why they don't have REM: the conscious eye would be jiggling about all over the place.

Platypuses sleep so deeply that you can dig open their burrows without waking them. Though much of this is REM sleep, unlike almost all other animals, the brains of sleeping platypuses aren't as active as when they were awake. So we can't say for certain that they are dreaming.

But then, we can't be absolutely sure that any animal dreams – because we can't ask them – we can only say it of ourselves. No one knows why we dream. Assuming an average life of sixty-five years, with two hours' REM a night, we would spend 8 per cent of our lives dreaming (about five years).

Eugene Aserinsky got his doctorate but, angry at having to share the credit for REM with Dr Kleitman, gave up sleep research for ten years. He died aged seventy-seven when his car ran into a tree. Kleitman kept at it, earning himself the title the 'Father of Sleep Research', and outlived Aserinsky by a year. He died aged 104.

Which animal drinks most?

The biggest boozer after man is the Pen-tailed tree shrew of Malaysia.

Ptilocercus lowii, a rat-sized animal with a tail shaped like a quill pen, gets through nine units of alcohol a night (the equivalent of nine single whiskies, five pints of beer or five 175-millilitre glasses of wine).

Its staple diet is nectar from the flowers of the Bertram palm, which ferments as a result of natural yeasts in the plant's spiky buds. This brew weighs in at 3.8 per cent ABV (alcohol by volume) – about the strength of a decent pale ale – and the Pen-tailed tree shrew spends an average of two hours a night sipping it.

The nectar of the Bertram palm is among the most alcoholic of any naturally occurring food. German researchers from the University of Bayreuth were first alerted to the presence of alcohol in the plant by its wafting, yeasty aroma, and what looked very much like a foamy 'head' on the nectar.

Analysis of the tree shrew's hair revealed blood-alcohol levels that would be dangerous in most mammals, but it never gets drunk. If it did, it wouldn't have lasted long as a species. Being small and edible makes for a tough enough life, but being small, edible and permanently confused would be fatal.

The Pen-tailed tree shrew has somehow evolved to break down the alcohol without becoming intoxicated, and it may also have benefited from the so-called 'aperitif effect'. First noted in humans, this is the fact that alcohol stimulates the appetite, so we eat more. The higher an animal's calorie intake, the more energy it has and the more likely it is to survive. As the Pen-tailed tree shrew appears to have discovered, the smell of fermentation in a fruit indicates that it has reached its peak calorific level.

The first record of humans drinking alcohol dates from 9,000 years ago, when brewing was invented in Mesopotamia. But the Bayreuth research suggests we may have inherited the taste for it from our pre-human past. The common ancestor of shrews and man was a small mammal that lived between 55 and 80 million years ago. The closest living match to this nameless creature is thought to be the Pen-tailed tree shrew. If we can work out why it likes alcohol so much (and why it never gets drunk), we may reach a better understanding of why humans like to drink, how we can do it without becoming legless, and maybe discover a hangover cure along the way.

In the oldest surviving work of literature on earth – the 4,000-year-old *Epic of Gilgamesh* – Shamhat, a temple prostitute, tames Enkidu, a hairy wild man raised by animals, by taking him to bed for a week and plying him with seven jars of beer. The result that is he starts to wash, puts on clothes for the first time and abandons his former animal friends, 'having acquired wisdom'.

STEPHEN *Name a green mammal*
BILL BAILEY *A really, really jealous shrew.*

How do elephants get drunk?

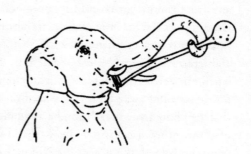

African tourist brochures often tell of elephants blundering around drunk after eating the fermented fruit of the marula tree, but it's a complete myth.

The marula tree (*Scelerocarya birrea caffera*) is a member of the mango family and elephants do indeed love its plum-sized yellow fruit. And it's not just the elephants' favourite – warthogs, monkeys, antelopes, giraffes and zebras all enjoy eating both the fruit and the bark of the tree.

In fact they like the fruit so much that none of them leave it lying on the ground long enough to allow it to rot and start to ferment. Elephants like their fruit fresh and visit the trees often to check whether their lunch is ripe. They are so eager that they will sometimes push the tree over to get what they want. Even if elephants liked rotten fruit, there's none on the ground because it's all been eaten by other species.

A study by Steve Morris of the University of Bristol calculated that, even if there *were* rotten fruit on the ground and the elephants *did* eat it, they would have to consume about 1,500 marula fruit, all at the same time, to get tipsy.

The myth can be traced back to a wildlife movie called *Animals Are Beautiful People* (1974) by the South African film director Jamie Uys (1921–96). His scenes of elephants, warthogs and baboons getting drunk on marula fruit were almost certainly staged. All Uys's other films were comedies, and one, *Funny People* (1978), was a spoof show similar to *Candid Camera* or *Beadle's About*.

The Bristol University study suggested that any odd behaviour by elephants around marula trees might be due to another form of 'intoxication' altogether. The bark is host to the grubs of the Lebistina beetle, traditionally used by the San Bushmen to poison their arrows.

Elephants can get drunk – but only by drinking alcohol. They can detect the pleasant smell of ethanol (pure alcohol) up to 10 miles away. In 1999 a herd of elephants broke into thatched huts in a village in India and polished off several vats of fermenting rice wine. They then went on a drunken rampage through the other huts, killing four unlucky villagers.

People have been eating marula fruit, which is rich in vitamin C, for 10,000 years. The tree has many other uses. The wood is used for carvings, the inner bark is made into rope and the skin of the fruit into substitute coffee. The bark also contains antihistamines (used to cure dysentery, diarrhoea and malaria), and caterpillars (which are collected and eaten roasted).

Marula beer is the favourite drink of the people of Swaziland. Drinkers claim it doesn't give you a hangover but, in 2002, the Swazi authorities banned it, citing a huge increase in drink driving, street brawls and absenteeism at work.

Amarula Cream, a sweet liqueur distilled from the fruit, is a speciality of South Africa, where it is served as an after-dinner *digestif*. It has a picture of an elephant on the label.

What's the world's most aggressive mammal?

It's not tigers or hippos.

According to *Scientific American* in 2009, the world's most fearsome land mammal is the Honey badger (*Mellivora capensis*). The *Guinness Book of Records* also lists it as 'the most *fearless* animal in the world'.

Honey badgers live in Africa and Asia in vacant burrows abandoned by other creatures such as aardvarks, and they aren't badgers. They're called that because they bear a superficial resemblance to regular badgers (*Meles meles*) and because they love honey. Badgers and Honey badgers are unrelated members of the weasel family, *Mustelidae*, the largest group of carnivores. It includes ferrets, polecats, minks and wolverines, but the Honey badger is a one-off: the only species in the genus *Mellivora*, which means 'honey-eaters'.

Honey badgers use their large and powerful claws to ravage termite mounds, rip through the wire round chicken coops and, especially, tear beehives apart. They are led to the hives by honeyguide birds, which call out when they find one, and take their share when the Honey badger has eaten its fill.

One of the things that makes the Honey badger such an indomitable adversary is its very loose-fitting skin: if it's caught from behind it is able to twist around inside its own skin and fight back. As a result, they have few predators and will attack most animals when provoked, even humans. They have fought or killed hyenas, lions, tigers, tortoises, porcupines, crocodiles and bears. They eat venomous snakes, which they grab in their jaws and devour in fifteen minutes. They also eat young Honey badgers: only half the cubs survive to adulthood.

Legend has it that a Honey badger's attack methods are below the belt. The first published record of this was in 1947 when a Honey badger was allegedly observed to castrate an adult buffalo. They are also said to have emasculated wildebeest, waterbuck, kudu, zebra and man. In *Top Gear*'s 2009 Botswana special, Jeremy Clarkson reported: 'The honey badger does not kill you to eat you. It tears off your testicles.'

In Pakistan, they are called 'Bijj' and are said to take away dead bodies from graves. Such is the animal's terrifying reputation that, during the Iraq war, British troops in Basra were accused of having unleashed a plague of man-eating bear-like beasts to terrify the locals. They turned out to be Honey badgers, which had been driven into the city by the flooding of marshland.

ROSS NOBLE *You know what annoys me, right, is the term to 'badger' somebody. Because badgers don't actually badger. If you were going to badger somebody you'd move into their garden and you'd just sleep a lot . . .*

What is Australia's deadliest creature?

Spider? Snake? Shark? Not at all: the most dangerous Aussie animal of all is the horse.

According to the National Coroners Information System, between 2000 and 2006 there were 128 animal-related deaths in Australia, and horses were responsible for thirty-six of them. Many resulted from someone colliding with a horse while driving, or falling off one while riding. A quarter of all animal-related deaths in Australia take place on the road.

The second most deadly Australian animal in the period was the cow – with twenty deaths – followed by the dog with twelve. Sharks killed eleven people; snakes killed eight; crocodiles or alligators, four; spiders, only three. One person met their doom at the hands of a cat.

There is no such thing as a 'deadly' spider (in the sense of being fatal to humans, that is). People *can* die of spider bites – as a result of allergies or lack of medical attention – but the same can be said of scratches from cats, stings from bees or hypersensitivity to peanuts. More people die from wasp- and bee-stings every year than from spider bites.

According to spider expert Rod Crawford, curator of arachnids at the Burke Museum in Washington, 'There is no spider species anywhere that can properly be called "deadly". I know of no species on earth capable of causing death in humans. In nine out of ten cases, even if its bite is left untreated.'

Spiders may be less dangerous to us than we think, but they are deadly to insects and to one another: they are predatory, territorial carnivores. Put 10,000 spiders in a sealed room and you will eventually end up with a single, enormously fat spider.

Some Australian spider species have turned this cannibalistic urge to their advantage. Male Australian Redbacks (*Lactrodectus hasselti*) actually compete to be eaten. Offering themselves as lunch to the females while they mate ensures their sperm gets taken on board ahead of the competition.

STEPHEN *What makes Australian spiders so dangerous?*
ROB BRYDON *It's their cunning and their organisation, Stephen. And the fact they're willing to put the man-hours in. They will stalk you for weeks. They'll look for patterns in your behaviour and they'll strike when you least expect it.*

Which animal has saved the most human lives?

It's not the faithful dog, the loyal horse or the brave carrier pigeon, but the oldest surviving species on the planet: the horseshoe crab.

If you've ever had an injection you quite possibly owe your life to the North American horseshoe crab (*Limulus polyphemus*). An extract of its blood, Limulus amebocyte lysate, or LAL, is used by the pharmaceutical industry to test drugs, vaccines and medical devices like artificial kidneys to ensure they are free of dangerous microbes. No other test works as easily or reliably.

Horseshoe crabs live in shallow coastal seas, which are often polluted. A litre of such seawater can contain over a thousand billion toxic bacteria. Horseshoe crabs have no immune system and can't develop antibodies to fight infection. Instead, their blood contains a miraculous ingredient that disables invasive bacteria and viruses by clotting around them, and it is this that is used to make LAL. To find out if anything intended for medical use is contaminated or not, all you have to do is expose it to some LAL: if it doesn't clot, it's fine.

Unlike humans, the blood of horseshoe crabs has no haemoglobin – which uses iron to carry oxygen – instead it has haemocyanin, which uses copper. As a result, their blood is blue. It sells for about $15,000 a litre.

To obtain the blood, horseshoe crabs are 'harvested' rather than killed. Up to a thousand of them a week are collected by hand from small boats with a clam rake, and brought to the lab alive. Although 30 per cent of their blood is taken, they recover quickly when put back in the water. The crabs are bled once a year and their blood is freeze-dried and shipped around the world.

Horseshoe crabs aren't, in fact, crabs. They're not even crustaceans. More closely related to ticks, scorpions and spiders, they are the last surviving members of the once thriving *Xiphosura* ('sword-tail') order, and they've been scuttling around the Atlantic coast of America and the seas of South-East Asia unchanged since the Ordovician era, 445 million years ago. That's 75 per cent of the entire time that animal life has existed on the planet and 200 million years before the dinosaurs arrived. Not bad for something that looks like a fancy computer mouse or a small tin hat.

It's their smooth, curved shells that helped them survive for so long. They're hard for predators to overturn and expose the soft underside, though Native Americans once used them as bailers to scoop water out of their canoes.

As well as their extraordinary blood – now known to be able to detect meningitis and cancer as well – horseshoe crabs can endure extremes of heat and cold and go for a year without eating.

They also have ten eyes. Which is odd, because Polyphemus, the giant of Greek mythology they're named after, only had one.

STEPHEN *It's the blood of the horseshoe crab.*
JACK DEE *When you get given it, do you walk out sideways?*

What's the best way to treat a jellyfish sting?

Don't urinate on it!

There's a well-established urban myth that urinating on a jellyfish sting relieves the pain.

In fact, it doesn't – and could make it worse.

The sting of a jellyfish comes from specialised cells in the skin of its tentacles called cnidocytes (literally 'nettle-jars', from Greek *cnide*, 'stinging nettle', and *cytos*, a 'vase' or 'vessel').

Each small, bulb-shaped capsule holds a coiled, barbed, thread-like tube, filled with poison and sealed in under high pressure. On the outside of each cell is a tiny hair called a cnidocil (Latin *cilia* for 'eyelashes'). Touching this 'hair-trigger' explodes the cell's minuscule toxic harpoon into your skin in 700 billionths of a second.

It is the fastest known mechanism in nature.

Feeling or scratching a jellyfish sting is not a good idea. It sets off any other unfired sting cells clinging to the skin, and you get stung on your hand as well.

Brush off any loose tentacles with a towel and splash the sting with salt water to wash away any unfired cells. Fresh water is no good: the change in the salt content of the water also activates the cells and injects more venom.

There's a lot of fresh water in urine – you can survive by drinking it if you have to – and, depending on who's doing the urinating, a lot of other stuff as well. It may contain harmful bacteria that can infect the wound. (Don't be fooled by the 'fact' that human urine is sterile. It is when it leaves the bladder, but it has to pass through the urethra which contains plenty of germs, all of them waiting to multiply in a warm, hitherto unoccupied medium like urine.)

Many Australian beaches have supplies of vinegar (5 per cent acetic acid) available in case of jellyfish stings. This can work – if you know the species you've been stung by. But some jellyfish have acid stings and some have alkaline ones. Vinegar is a good temporary remedy for the deadly Australian box jellyfish, but only exacerbates the sting of the Portuguese man of war.

Pain is not necessarily the worst thing about jellyfish

stings. They can cause anaphylactic shock. Watch out for swelling, itching, rashes or shortness of breath. If you spot any of these symptoms, don't waste valuable time urinating on the patient – call a doctor.

What causes pins and needles?

Ordinary pins and needles have nothing to do with poor circulation.

They happen when pressure on a part of the body compresses the nerve cells and impedes the blood flow. When the pressure is released and the blood flow returns to normal, numbness gives way to tingling as oxygen and glucose are restored to the nerves. This can affect anywhere on the body – though it's usually found in arms, legs, hands or feet – and passes within a few minutes. The technical term for it is 'transient paraesthesia', Greek for 'altered feeling'.

If you suffer from *chronic* pins and needles, however, you might want to get a professional opinion. It can be symptomatic of a stroke, brain tumour, brain abscess, multiple sclerosis, rheumatoid arthritis, HIV, Lyme disease, cancer, alcoholism, malnutrition, exposure to radiation or whiplash injury.

Disturbing though that list is, it won't lead to the onset of belonephobia, the 'fear of pins and needles'. That only applies to fear of sharp points (*belone* is Greek for 'needle'). There is no such word as paraesthesiaphobia – at least, there wasn't until just now.

The indescribably peculiar feeling you get when you bang your 'funny bone' is a close relative of transient paraesthesia. The 'funny bone' isn't a bone – it's the ulnar nerve, which is unusually near the surface. The twinge comes from it getting jammed up against an actual bone, the humerus, which starts at the shoulder and ends at the elbow. Banging it produces dysaesthesia, meaning an unpleasant sensation, as opposed to paraesthesia, which is merely an unusual one.

A good way to get pins and needles is to sit on one of your feet, a pose that was very popular in nineteenth-century Turkey. In the travel book *Constantinople in 1828* by Charles Macfarlane, the author noted that the polite sitting position for ladies in Smyrna was 'with one leg on the sofa bent under them, and the other hanging over the edge'. This led a visiting Frenchman to ask whether 'this unipedal exhibition' meant that 'all the women in the city had but the one leg'.

In the USA 27 November is official Pins and Needles Day, though few people know why. It commemorates the opening night, in 1937, of a unique Broadway musical. *Pins and Needles* was produced by the International Ladies' Garment Workers' Union, and the cast was made up of union members. Despite being ignored by mainstream theatre critics, the show ran for 1,108 performances, a record only overtaken by *Oklahoma!* in 1945.

Finally, in case you're wondering, acupuncturists *do* claim to be able to treat pins and needles. They may not ask you how you got them: paraesthesia is one of the side effects associated with acupuncture.

What causes a hernia?

It's not the strain of lifting something heavy.

Hernia is Latin for 'rupture' and is the condition in which a bodily organ (or part of one) breaks through into a part of the body it shouldn't be in. This could be the brain pro-truding through a defect in the skull, or a loop of intestine escaping from the abdominal cavity and ending up in the chest.

The most common use of the word hernia refers to tissue that has protruded through the abdomen. Heavy lifting never *causes* this – although straining the abdominal muscles by lifting something heavy might make an existing, unnoticed hernia more prominent.

A hernia is caused by a lack of collagen (the protein in skin and muscle tissue that makes it flexible) in the affected area. This can be the result of genetic abnormalities, of smoking (which breaks down the collagen in your body) or just the general wear-and-tear of advancing age. Only one in ten people who are diagnosed with a hernia will have discovered it by straining themselves.

The most common type of hernia in the UK is the inguinal hernia (from Latin *inguen*, 'groin'), in which a segment of bowel slips down into the scrotum, using the same route as the descending testes during puberty. If it gets caught, and cannot return easily, it can 'strangulate' – causing vio-lent vomiting and abdominal pain and requiring immediate surgery.

But this misfortune is a weakness that you are born with: it's not caused by strenuous exercise.

Why should you avoid the free peanuts in bars?

You'll have heard about the scientists who tested a bowl of peanuts in a bar and found traces of urine belonging to twenty-seven different people. Johnny Depp certainly has; he mentioned it during an appearance on *The Tonight Show* with Jay Leno in July 2005.

This alarming tale is trotted out again and again, and it's in the back of many people's minds every time they reach for the bar snacks.

As far as we know, there has never been any such scientific study but, in 2003, the London *Evening Standard* conducted an informal tour of six London bars and took away samples of the free snacks. Tests showed that four of the six contained enterobacteria, which are also found in faeces.

There is certainly cause for concern about many people's attitudes to toilet hygiene. In 2000 the American Society for Microbiology asked a thousand people whether or not they washed their hands when visiting a public lavatory and 95 per cent said they always did. The Society's researchers weren't convinced and so they set up hidden cameras to see how people actually behaved. The percentage of those who really *did* wash their hands turned out to be 58 per cent. Another US survey produced the even odder statistic that 8 per cent of Americans are so frightened of catching germs from lavatories that they flush with their feet.

The French, at least, are more honest – or perhaps less paranoid: 56 per cent of men and 66 per cent of women admitted to researchers that they *never* wash their hands after visiting *les toilettes*. This prompted a French engineer to develop a device that locked users inside restaurant lavatories until they'd done so.

The peanut factoid is sometimes told about bowls of complimentary mints in restaurants, with exactly the same wording. When the news of this reached Canada and was reported in the *Ottawa Sentinel* in 1994, the regional health authorities sent out their inspectors to ensure that all such mints were either ready-wrapped, or were offered in such a way that they could 'only be handled by one person at a time'.

Which is riskier: nuts or mints? The answer turns out to be ice cubes.

Recent official studies of both hotels and pubs in Cardiff and fast-food joints and bars in Chicago found that at least 20 per cent of all ice cubes were contaminated with 'faecal matter' caused by staff failing to wash their hands.

In January 2010 a study at Hollins University in Roanoke, Virginia reported that almost half the drinks from ninety local soda fountains tested positive for coliform bacteria, indicating possible faecal contamination.

On a more optimistic note, they also noted that there were no reported outbreaks of food-related illness in Roanoke at the time of the study.

But please, now wash your hands. And don't shake anyone else's.

Which item in the bathroom has the most germs?

It's not the lavatory.

The most likely candidate is your toothbrush. According to a 2010 research study by the University of Manchester, the average toothbrush hosts up to 100 million bacteria, including various strains of staphylococcus which cause skin rashes, *E. coli* which can cause diarrhoea and the viruses that cause all three types of hepatitis. A damp toothbrush not only picks up germs from our mouth (which contains more than 600 different species of bacteria), it is also vulnerable to the spray from a flushed toilet, which coats all objects within 1.8 metres (6 feet) in a fine bacteria-rich mist.

But before we start panicking and dipping our toothbrush

in Domestos each morning, it's worth bearing in mind that most of these bacteria are harmless unless they enter the bloodstream and, even then, pose very little threat to a healthy adult or child. It's only certain mutant strains of *E. coli*, for example, that cause disease in humans. Most bacteria in our mouths and gut perform a useful function in helping us to digest our food. By rinsing and drying our toothbrushes after we use them (and closing the toilet lid before we flush) we significantly reduce the risk of bacterial infection.

Used properly, household bleach is also a very effective disinfectant – particularly on hard surfaces – but we've only recently discovered how it works. In 2008 a team at the University of Michigan, led by molecular biologist Dr Ursula Jakob, demonstrated that bleach 'cooks' the protein inside bacteria, rather as heat cooks the protein in egg white. Once the molecular structure has been transformed, the change is irreversible and the bacteria die.

Even so, no bleach can claim to kill *all* known germs. Tests have shown that the active ingredient in bleach, sodium hypochlorite, is ineffective in killing the waterborne intestinal parasites that cause giardiasis (2 million cases in the US each year) and cryptosporidiosis (10,000 cases a year).

But germs don't just live in bathrooms. Our desks harbour far more microbes than the average toilet seat. That's because we tend to clean our toilets regularly, but we rarely clean our workstations. According to research carried out by the University of Arizona in 2004, an average office desk is home to 10 million microbes. That's 3,250 microbes per square centimetre (20,961 per square inch). The most germ-laden item is the telephone, with 3,895 microbes per square centimetre (25,127 per square inch), followed by keyboards (511 per square centimetre or 3,295 per square inch) and the computer mouse (260 per square centimetre or 1,676 per square inch). Toilet seats, by contrast, average only 15 microbes per square centimetre or 95 per square inch. The most germ-intensive item in the bathroom after the toothbrush was the toilet *handle* – not surprising now we know that one in two people lie about washing their hands.

For that very reason 8 per cent of Americans claim they now flush the loo with their feet.

DAVID MITCHELL *It's like one of those adverts that sort of says, 'There are more germs on your chopping board than on your loo seat.'*

STEPHEN *That's right.*

DAVID *To which the answer is, 'Well, clearly, that's fine, then! We're not all dying, or constantly having diarrhoea, so they're saying in the advert, "The very thing we are selling you is unnecessary." '*

What is household dust made from?

The composition of house dust has been extensively studied because of its role in allergies. Not much of it is dead skin.

It's quite difficult to get meaningful data because dust varies so widely from country to country, house to house, and even room to room. It also depends on the season and on the lifestyle of the householder – whether you have a pet, how often you clean, whether you open the windows etc.

What is clear is that the allegation that house dust is 70 per cent human skin is wildly exaggerated. More common sources of dust include flakes of animal skin, sand, insect waste, flour (in the kitchen) and lots and lots of ordinary dirt.

The dead skin we shed each year would be enough to fill a

small flour bag, but most of it is drained away in bathwater or eaten by dust mites.

Dust mites are tiny, fat, eight-legged members of the spider family. They live in beehives and in birds' nests as well as in human homes. Half a teaspoon of dust may contain as many as 1,000 mites and 250,000 droppings.

They also live in beds, but the idea that dead dust mites and their waste products make up half the weight of your mattress or pillow is nonsense.

Bedding manufacturers (particularly in the USA) are in no hurry to discourage these rumours.

Most people who react badly to dust are actually allergic to dust mite faeces. Enzymes excreted from the mite's gut attack the respiratory passages, causing hay-fever-like symptoms or asthma.

Such allergies aside, there's no reason to worry about mites: you're already supporting a thriving community of them on your face.

Follicle mites (*Demodex follicularum*) live exclusively on human beings. They are long (about a hundredth of an inch) and slim (to fit snugly into the follicles). They have microscopic claws and needle-shaped mouthparts, which they use to pierce skin cells. They can't walk backwards, so once they've burrowed head first into somewhere comfortable like the base of your eyelashes, they're stuck for life. They eventually dissolve away harmlessly *in situ*, rear end last.

This rear end is an interesting sight: unlike dust mites, follicle mites create so little waste that they don't even need an anus.

STEPHEN *Now, what is house dust mostly composed of?*
VIC REEVES *Rust.*
STEPHEN *'Rust'! I don't think mostly of rust, no.*
VIC *If you live in an iron house like me . . .*

What might land on your head if you live under a flight path?

A huge block of frozen urine? It has never happened and it never will.

Aeroplanes do not dump the contents of their lavatories overboard. The waste is contained in a holding tank, which is emptied when the aircraft lands. Great care is taken to ensure that this tank is secure. Even if a mad pilot wanted to jettison it, access to the tank is located on the outside of the plane.

On very rare occasions, ice can fall from aeroplanes. Some 3 million flights pass through British airspace every year; in the same period, the Civil Aviation Authority gets just twenty to thirty reports of possible icefalls. The CAA investigates all such complaints by checking the relevant flight paths. Over the past twenty years, they estimate that five people have been hit by small amounts of falling ice.

In July 2009 a lump of ice the size of a football crushed the roof of a car in Loughborough, Leicestershire, but no flights were in the area at the time and the incident has been put down to a freak conglomeration of hailstones.

If ice does fall from a plane, it is either water that has frozen on the wings owing to the high altitude (which melts off as the plane comes into land) or water from the air-conditioning system that has leaked through a faulty seal on to the fuselage. Aircraft toilets often add a blue chemical to the water to deodorise the waste and break down any solids, but any blue ice that falls to the ground is a result of a fault in the input pipe. It cannot come out of the toilet itself or from the holding tank, which is a fully integrated, sealed unit.

In the USA the Federal Aviation Authority is equally adamant. No American has ever been hit by anything falling from an aircraft lavatory. Phone calls to the FAA complaining about brown droplets coming from the sky always increase during the bird migration season. The FAA also blames so-called 'blue ice' on incontinent birds that have been eating blueberries.

Like planes, modern trains in the UK carry chemical retention tanks, but some older rolling stock still offloads its toilet waste straight on to the tracks.

Around Britain's coastline, there are 20,000 pipes pumping untreated sewage into the sea. These 'combined sewer overflows', or CSOs, are intended as a last resort when there is a danger of an urban sewage system flooding. But heavy rainfall in recent summers means that some have been in almost constant use. As a result, in 2009, almost half of Britain's beaches were 'not recommended' for swimming by the Marine Conservation Society's *Good Beach Guide*.

Resorts that failed to come up to scratch included fashionable destinations such as Rock in Cornwall, Sandgate in Kent and West Sands in St Andrews. It was the worst result for Britain's beaches for eight years and bad enough for the European Commission to decide to take the UK to court to try to get CSO discharges banned.

ALAN *Urine. Frozen urine. It kills you and you just look like you've pissed yourself. To death.*

What are your chances of surviving a plane crash?

They're very good indeed: especially if you're in the cheap seats.

In the USA, between 1983 and 2000, there were 568 plane crashes. In 90 per cent of them there were survivors and, out of a total of 53,487 people onboard, 51,207 survived. According to *Popular Mechanics* magazine the safest place to be in the event of a crash is at the back, well behind the wings, where there is a 69 per cent survival rate. Sitting over (or just in front of) the wing reduces your chances of getting out alive to 56 per cent. The worst place to be is right up at the front in first class, where the survival rate falls to 49 per cent. Which is an outrage, considering how much you have to pay to sit there.

According to the world's leading 'fire safety engineer', Professor Ed Galea of the University of Greenwich, the biggest danger is seatbelts. In an emergency, passengers panic and revert to what they are familiar with: they struggle to open them like a seatbelt in a car, resulting in (sometimes fatal) delay. Fire is, of course, a major problem, largely because of smoke inhalation. Your safest bet is to sit on the aisle close to an exit. Before take-off, make a note of how many rows there are between you and the nearest door. That way, even if the cabin is filled with smoke, you'll still be able to crawl your way out by feel.

Until recently, it was thought impossible for a passenger airliner to make a successful emergency landing on water. The margin for error is so small. To prevent the plane breaking up on impact, the pilot must slow down as much as possible – but without losing lift – and raise the nose of the plane to 12 degrees so that the tail hits the water first. The wings must be perfectly level: if one wing-tip hits the water before the other the plane will cartwheel and break up. The fuel must be used up or dumped: its weight would cause the plane to sink even if it did land successfully. Then there's the weather, and sea conditions, either of which could wreck the plane, no matter how calmly the pilot behaves.

Despite such unnerving obstacles, there have been at least half a dozen successful emergency landings by airliners on water, including one off the coast of Sicily in 2005. The most recent and spectacular example occurred in January 2009 when an Airbus A320, US Airways Flight 1549, ditched in the Hudson River in New York. Shortly after take off, the plane hit a flock of geese and Captain Chesley 'Sully' Sullenberger III had to make a forced landing on the water. He did this perfectly, saving the lives of all 155 people on board.

Airline statisticians like to say that you are ten times more likely to be hit by a comet than to die in a plane crash. This is because, once every million years or so, an extraterrestrial body collides with Earth. The next time this happens it will probably wipe out half the world's population but, as far as we know, the last time anyone was hit by a comet was 12,900 years ago.

It is the case, however, that you are many times more likely to die in the taxi on the way to and from the airport than you are on the flight itself.

DAVID MITCHELL *I imagine your survival swings on the whistle that you get on the life jacket.*

JIMMY CARR *It does rather rely on someone having quite selective hearing, and going, 'I didn't hear that plane go down,' but . . .*

What's the word for the fear of heights?

It's not vertigo.

The fear of heights is called acrophobia (from the Greek *akros,* 'highest').

Reactions include clinging, crouching, or crawling on all fours as well as the usual symptoms associated with other phobias such as sweating, shaking and palpitations. Acrophobia is unusual among phobias in that it can actually cause what the person is frightened of. A panic attack at height may lead them to lose control and fall.

Vertigo (Latin for 'whirling') is a recognised medical condition. It's a type of dizziness where sufferers feel they are moving when they are in fact stationary. Women are two to three times more likely to suffer from it than men and it gets more common with age. Up to 10 per cent of people experience some form of vertigo in their lives. Vertigo doesn't necessarily take place high above the ground and it's not the same thing as acrophobia.

The confusion wasn't helped by Alfred Hitchcock's film *Vertigo* (1958). In the movie, an ex-police detective (Jimmy Stewart) suffers from acrophobia as a result of witnessing a fellow officer fall to his death in a rooftop chase. His condition haunts him and the film comes to a climax when he apparently fails to prevent the woman he loves falling from a bell tower. He is unable to climb the stairs due to his crippling fear of heights and an attack of vertigo.

In real life, people with acrophobia may never suffer from vertigo – and vice versa.

A sensible caution towards high places seems to be built into all of us. In 1960, psychologists E. J. Gibson and R. D. Walk created the 'visual cliff experiment' in which infants from different species (including human babies) had to cross a transparent glass panel with an apparently sharp drop-off point beneath it. They found that all the species in the experiment saw and avoided the cliff as soon as they were old enough to manage independent movement – six months for a human or one day in chicks.

While not everyone is frightened of heights, acrophobia appears to be the second most common human phobia of all.

The first is fear of public speaking.

What's the world's second-highest peak?

Actually, it's also Everest.

Mount Everest's main summit is the highest point on the Earth's surface measured from sea level. It rises 8,850 metres (29,035.4 feet) into the sky. The second-highest separate mountain is K2, but the unremarkable bump of Everest's south summit is in fact higher, at 8,750 metres (28,707 feet). This beats K2 – 8,611 metres (28,250 feet)– by almost 140 metres (460 feet).

K2 is not in the Himalayas. It's in a range called the Karakorum – the initial K of which gives K2 its rather functional name.

K2 was a temporary label given to it by Lieutenant Thomas Montgomerie (1830–78) a young officer in the Great Trigonometric Survey of India, which lasted through most of the nineteenth century. He named the biggest peaks he saw in the Karakorum range K1, K2, K3, etc., in the order that he came across them.

K1, which he first saw in 1856, is only the twenty-second highest mountain in the world, but it already had (and has) a local name: Masherbrum. And so, as it eventually turned out, did all the others in Montgomerie's list – except K2.

K2 hadn't been given a local name (and still hasn't) by either the Pakistanis in the south or the Chinese in the north. The reason for this is the mountain's remoteness. Despite its majestic height, it cannot be seen from any of the villages in the area – and it's possible that no one even knew of its existence until the Great Trigonometric Survey. An early attempt to name it Mount Godwin-Austen – after another surveyor, Henry Godwin-Austen (1834–1926) – was rejected by the Royal Geographical Society. But K2 is informally known as 'The Savage Mountain' – one in four people who attempt to get to the summit die, and it has never been conquered in winter.

The south summit of Everest may be a long way up, but it is only a cone of snow and ice about the size of an ordinary dinner table. For most climbers it is just another stop on the way to the highest point on Earth, a time to change oxygen bottles and admire the view of the final slopes of the main summit.

The south summit is inside what mountaineers call the 'Dead Zone' (above 8,000 metres or 26,246 feet). Although Everest kills fewer people proportionally than K2, many more people climb it. As a result, the Dead Zone is full of rubbish and frozen corpses. In 2010 a team of twenty Sherpas began a concerted effort to tidy it all up. As well as removing several bodies, they expect to clear 3,000 kilograms (about 3 tons) of old tents, ropes, oxygen cylinders, food packaging and camping stoves from the mountain.

Pedants should be aware that the English name for the world's highest mountain should be spoken aloud as *EEV-uh-rest*, not *EV-uh-rest*.

This is how Sir George Everest (1799–1866), the Welsh-born Surveyor General of India, after whom it is named, pronounced his surname.

How can you tell how high up a mountain you are?

Make some tea.

The traditional method of estimating the height of a mountain while you're on one is by taking the temperature of a pot of boiling water.

Water boils when the pressure of the steam trying to escape from it exceeds the pressure of the air above it.

Air pressure decreases with altitude in a rather neat (if non-metric) way. For every 300 metres (1,000 feet) gained in height, the boiling point of water reduces by 1 °C.

So, at 4,500 metres (15,000 feet, the summit of Mont Blanc) water boils at 84.4 °C. At the top of Everest it boils at 70 °C and at nearly 23,000 metres (75,000 feet) it would boil at room temperature (not that any room would be at room temperature at that altitude).

This form of measurement is called hypsometry (from the Greek *hypsos*, 'height' and *metria,* 'measure').

In his travelogue *A Tramp Abroad* (1880), Mark Twain (1835–1910) tells how, on an expedition to the Swiss Alps, he tried to calculate the altitude by boiling his barometer in bean soup. This gave 'a strong barometer taste to the soup' which was so unexpectedly popular he had the expedition cook make it every day. The cook used two barometers, one in working order, the other not – the soup from the former went to the Officers' Mess, the latter to the Other Ranks.

The Challenger Deep in the Marianas Trench in the Pacific is the deepest known part of the world's oceans.

The pressure there is 1,100 times that at sea level, so if you wanted to make a cup of tea you'd have to wait awhile.

The kettle would start to boil at 530 °C.

How can you tell which way is north in a forest?

It's old woodsman's lore that moss always grows on the north side of the trees, but it doesn't.

Mosses prefer shady places but they can grow on the south, west and east of trees (as well as the north), if there's enough moisture to sustain them. The presence of moisture depends as much on the direction of the prevailing wind as on being out of the sun. And, although a tree in isolation tends to have more shade on its northern side, trees in wooded areas throw shade on one another, making it perfectly possible for the south side to be the mossy one.

Can you tell which way is north from the sun? If you face the sunrise in the east, north is 90° to your left, isn't it?

This isn't foolproof either. The sun only rises *exactly* in the east on two days a year, at the spring and autumn equinoxes, when night and day are of equal length. (*Equinox* is Latin for 'equal night'.) In Britain, as a general rule, the sun rises in the south-east and sets in the south-west in winter; and rises in the north-east and sets in the north-west in the summer.

A more reliable method is to wait for nightfall and use the stars. Find the constellation of Ursa Major (Latin for 'Great Bear'), better known as the Plough or Big Dipper. It looks a like a pan with a handle. Make a line between the two stars on the side of the pan opposite the handle and follow it upwards.

Polaris – the North Star – is the next bright star you find along that line. It's not *exactly* north; but it's good enough for someone hopelessly lost in a forest.

Unfortunately, this doesn't work so well in the southern hemisphere. The nearest star to the celestial South Pole, sometimes called *Polaris Australis*, or the 'Southern Pole star', is Sigma Octantis in the constellation Octans, but it's barely visible without a telescope.

The North Star isn't always due north, either. This is because Earth wobbles as it spins. Think of the Earth as a ball, spinning round an imaginary stick that passes through each pole. Because of the gravitational pull of the Sun and Moon, the stick moves slightly over time, slowly tracing a circle in the sky. This means that the end of the stick isn't always pointing directly at Polaris: it's either moving slowly towards or away from it.

You don't need to worry about that for a while yet, though. The movement is *very* slow: each rotation of that circle takes 25,765 years to complete. For our Bronze Age ancestors in 3000 BC, the star Thuban in the constellation of Draco was closer to north. In 12,000 years time it will be Vega in the constellation Lyra. Polaris will be back in pole position again by AD 27800.

Meanwhile, a neat trick is to use your watch. Point the hour hand at the sun. Taking the middle of the angle formed between that and the number twelve gives a fairly good approximation to south.

STEPHEN *You can float a razor blade on water and, if it's magnetised, it would act as a compass.*

ROB BRYDON *But if you were lost in the forest and you were getting pretty despondent, and you thought, 'I'll float a razor blade on the water', you would be tempted, wouldn't you, as you looked at that razor blade, to end it all?*

Do people really go round and round in circles when they're lost?

Yes, they do. In situations where there are no navigational clues – such as in a snowstorm or thick fog – human beings who are convinced they're walking in a straight line always end up going round in circles.

Until very recently this peculiar effect was explained away by the not very convincing theory that one of our legs is stronger than the other, so that over a period of time we tend to veer in the direction of the weaker leg. But research carried out in 2009 by the Max Planck Institute for Biological Cybernetics in Tübingen has shown that it's not our legs, but our brains, that are at fault.

Volunteers were set down in a particularly empty bit of the Sahara in southern Tunisia or the dense, flat Bienwald Forest in south-west Germany and tracked as they walked, using GPS (the Global Positioning Satellite). When the sun or moon was out, they were perfectly capable of walking in a straight line. As soon as these were absent, the volunteers started to walk in circles, crossing their own path several times without noticing it. When another group of volunteers was blindfolded, the effect was even more obvious and immediate: the average diameter of the circle they walked was only 20 metres (66 feet).

This is far too rapid a change of course for the 'stronger leg' theory to explain. What the research proved is that, deprived of any visual points of reference, people have no instinctive sense of direction.

Vision is by far the most important of all human senses. Processing visual information uses 30 per cent of the brain's activity, whereas smell, the directional aid used by most mammals, accounts for just 1 per cent. Only birds are as visually dependent as we are, but they navigate using 'magnetoception', the ability to plug into the Earth's magnetic field. Embedded in their brains are crystals of an iron-based mineral called magnetite.

The bones of human noses also contain traces of magnetite, which suggests we may once also have had 'magnetoception' but have forgotten how to use it.

In 2004 Peter König, a cognitive scientist at the University of Osnabrück in Germany, made a belt that he wore round his waist constantly, even in bed. It had thirteen pads linked to a sensor that detected Earth's magnetic field: whichever pad was pointing north vibrated gently like a cellphone. Over time, König's spatial awareness radically improved. Wherever he was in the city, he found he knew intuitively the direction of his home or office. Once, on a trip to Hamburg, over 160 kilometres (100 miles) away, he correctly pointed towards Osnabrück.

When he finally removed the belt, he had a powerful sensation that the world had shrunk and that he had become 'smaller and more chaotic'. The belt had reactivated − or perhaps re-educated − a sense he didn't realise he had. It may be that our bodies have been faithfully sending out magnetoception signals all the time, but that our brains have lost the ability to interpret them.

STEPHEN *Why do we walk in circles if we're lost?*
ALAN *Homing pigeons: we're descended from homing pigeons.*

What's the best way to weigh your own head?

Self-decapitation?
Are you sure?

A severed head has less than five seconds of consciousness left, so you wouldn't have much time to enjoy the results of your experiment.

Resting your head on the bathroom scales is another idea but it's very inaccurate: your neck would still be supporting some of the weight.

The simplest way is to stick your head in a bucket.

The density of most people's heads is very close to that of water. Put a bucket in a large tray, fill it to the brim with water and then dunk your head in it. Weighing the water that spills over into the tray will give you a fairly good approximation of the weight of your head.

For an encore, you can repeat the experiment with your whole body, using larger containers. You can then compare the amount of water displaced by your head to the amount displaced by your whole body, and work out what fraction of your total body weight your head is.

To ensure 100 per cent accuracy, though, what you really need is a CT scan.

Computed Tomography (CT) scanners use X-rays to produce an extensive series of images of objects in cross-section. (Tomography is Greek for 'writing in slices'.) The information can be used to analyse any part of the human body and determine the exact density at each point within it. From this, a SAM – or Specific Anthropomorphic Mannequin

– can be generated: a 3-D computer model that, among other things, will tell you the exact weight of your head.

If you're not particularly bothered about accuracy and only want to know *roughly* what your head weighs, according to the anatomy department at Sydney University the weight of an adult human head (with hair removed), cut off at the third vertebra down, is between 4.5 and 5 kilograms (9.9 and 11 pounds).

If you like to be accurate to the point of extreme pedantry, you might be able to use this. It was the Greek mathematician Archimedes (about 287–212 BC) who discovered you could measure the volume of irregular objects by seeing how much water they displaced. He supposedly found this out while he was sitting in his bath and was so excited that he jumped out and ran naked through the streets of Syracuse yelling 'Eureka!' (Greek for 'I've found it!')

How do snakes swallow things bigger than their heads?

They don't, as you may have heard, 'dislocate their jaws': they stretch them.

Most of the bones in a snake's head – including the two halves of the jaw – are not locked in position, as in mammals, but are attached by a flexible ligament.

One of these bones links the snake's lower jaw to its upper jaw in a double-jointed hinge. It's called the quadrate bone because it is connected at four points.

We have this quadrate bone too, but it's no longer attached to our jaw. Instead, it has migrated up into the ear and shrunk down in size to become the incus, or 'anvil', bone. This combines with two other bones called the malleus (or 'hammer') and the stapes ('stirrup'), to produce the miracle of efficiency that is the human middle ear.

The three-bone arrangement amplifies sound and is capable of much more acute hearing than the reptile system, where the eardrum is connected directly to the inner ear by just the single 'stirrup' bone. So, while we can't swallow a goat whole, we can at least hear much better than snakes can.

Despite their big mouths, snakes sometimes bite off more than they can chew.

In 2005 the remains of a 1.8-metre (6-foot) alligator were found in the Florida Everglades National Park, protruding from the stomach of a 4-metre (13-foot) Burmese python. The python had tried to swallow the alligator whole and had then exploded. The alligator is thought to have clawed at the python's stomach from the inside, leading it to burst.

Burmese pythons come from South-East Asia and are one of the six largest snakes in the world. In their natural habitat, they can grow to more than 6 metres (20 feet) long. They now infest the Everglades: all of them are pets that have been abandoned by, or escaped from, their owners.

In 1999 a study at Cornell University estimated that the control of invasive species cost the US a staggering $137 billion a year. In the following five years 144,000 more Burmese pythons were blithely imported into the United States.

In 2010 Florida finally passed a law banning the importation of Burmese pythons, but too late. They thrive in the hot, wet climate of the local swamps (along with dozens of other non-native species like monitor lizards and vervet monkeys). Fights between alligators and Burmese pythons are a not uncommon sight and are a popular tourist attraction. The result is quite often a draw.

Where does a snake's tail begin?

You might think a snake is just one long tail with a head at one end, but in fact only about 20 per cent of a snake is tail.

The word *vertebra* is Latin for 'joint'. Human beings have thirty-three vertebrae, which form the spinal column and the bones in the neck. Depending on the species, snakes can have over ten times as many. The great majority of these sprout a pair of ribs. Just as with people, snakes don't have ribs in their head. And, at the other end (also as with people), where the ribs stop, the tail begins. The human 'tail' is called the coccyx; in a snake, its tail starts after its cloaca.

All reptiles, birds and amphibians have a cloaca. It's named after the Cloaca Maxima, an early sewage system that ran through the Forum in ancient Rome. In snakes the cloaca is a small, flexible vent on its underside: the reptilian equivalent of a bottom. So a snake's tail starts, just like a lizard's or a pheasant's, behind its behind.

Although controlled by a sphincter muscle, as in mammals, it differs from a mammal's anus by providing a common passage for the removal of both urine and faeces. It's also used for mating and egg laying. Stored inside a male snake's tail are his two penises (known as hemipenes or 'half-penises'). To mate, he turns each one inside out, so that they poke out of his cloaca. They look rather like exotic varieties of mollusc, adorned with various knobs, spines and protuberances. Each is inserted, in turn, into the female's cloaca, which is of a matching design to deter interlopers from other snake species.

Recent studies have shown that, while a snake can't be referred to as 'right-handed', they are definitely 'right-penised': the hemipenis on the right side tends to be larger and is the one inserted first. Another use for the cloaca in some snake species is 'popping'. This is where air is expelled from it in a series of sharp bursts, indistinguishable in timbre and volume from high-pitched human farts. The foul smell (and surprise value) helps keep predators at bay.

If a snake is kept in too small a space, it may attack and eat its own tail, thinking it's a rival. Some snakes have been known to choke on their own tails.

The Ouroboros (Greek for 'tail-eater') is an ancient symbol of a snake swallowing its own tail. It appears in Egyptian, Greek, Norse, Hindu and Aztec mythology and represents the cyclical nature of things. In the *Timaeus* (360 BC), Plato credited the origin of life in the universe to such a circular, self-consuming creature and the Swiss psychologist Carl Jung (1875–1961) believed it was an archetype, a concept hard-wired into our unconscious.

The Ouroboros unlocked one of the great scientific puzzles of the nineteenth century: the chemical structure of benzene. Found in crude oil, benzene is a powerful solvent used in the manufacture of dyes and plastics. First isolated in 1825, it was used as paint stripper, aftershave and to decaffeinate coffee before it was discovered to be dangerously toxic. Though its chemical formula, C_6H_6, was known, its atomic structure baffled everyone until the German chemist August

Kekulé (1829–96), after years of work, had the sudden insight that it was a ring of six carbon atoms. These were attached to each hydrogen atom with a single bond, but to each other with alternating single and double bonds.

Kekulé's solution transformed organic chemistry. The breakthrough came to him in a daydream, when the image of a snake with its tail in its mouth suddenly came to mind.

ALAN *When I was a kid, there was a rattlesnake on TV, every week. It was, like, a big thing in the '70s. Every week, in something, there was always a rattlesnake. And nowadays, there's never a rattlesnake on TV.*

What are the chances of a coin landing on heads?

It isn't fifty–fifty.

If the coin is heads up to begin with, it's more likely to land on heads. Students at Stanford University recorded thousands of coin tosses with high-speed cameras and discovered the chances are approximately fifty-one–forty-nine.

The researchers showed that coin tossing is not a strictly random procedure, but a measurable event that obeys the laws of physics. If each coin is subject to exactly the same initial conditions and exactly the same initial force, then its spin will produce an even chance of landing on heads or tails.

However, the slightest difference in the conditions – speed and angle of spin, height of the coin from the ground, which side is facing up to start with – will affect the result. The Stanford research showed that, averaged over many tosses, these changes were significant enough to prevent a fifty–fifty probability.

The toss of a coin can be a serious matter. In the third European Football Championships in 1968, Italy and Russia drew 0–0 in the semi-final. There were no penalty shoot-outs in those days (and there was no time in the schedule to fit in a replay), so the result was decided by the toss of a coin. Russia lost and Italy went through to the final and won the Championship.

In cricket, although winning the toss doesn't seem to affect the results of daytime cricket matches, statistical analysis from University College London suggests that, in day–night games, winning the toss and batting first (during daylight) increases the chances of victory by almost 10 per cent.

Under British electoral law, if a vote finishes in a dead heat, the result is determined by lot.

In the 2010 UK council elections, there were tied votes in Great Yarmouth and Bristol. In one, the victory went to the candidate who drew the highest card from a pack; in the other, the returning officer drew the name from a hat.

Perhaps they'd seen the Stanford research and decided to give the coin-toss a miss . . .

SEAN LOCK *I still can't get my head round the notion that it's just as likely to be 1, 2, 3, 4, 5, 6 on the lottery – and I still go 'it just wouldn't happen'. You know why? You know why? Because it's a lottery. I mean, the clue's in the title.*

What does biting a coin prove?

If you can leave teeth marks in a gold coin, it's almost certainly a fake.

People who've watched too many old pirate movies think that, because gold is a soft metal, the way to prove a gold coin is genuine is by biting into it. While this theoretically works with a pure gold coin, it ignores the fact that all 'gold' coins minted for circulation in the UK and America since Tudor times have contained copper. This made them more durable (and hard to the bite).

In 1538 Henry VIII set the levels of purity and weight for the gold sovereign. By law, the coin had to contain 91.6 per cent gold – the rest being copper – and weigh half a troy ounce. ('Troy weight' was a French system of measurement named after the famous Troyes fair, the medieval version of an international trade convention.) Each coin was minted to a standard diameter and thickness.

Gold is very difficult to counterfeit, but its high value made it worth trying. The simplest method was to mix lead with gold, or to gild lead coins.

But, though gold is relatively soft, it's also denser than almost all other metals – almost twice as dense as lead. To test a coin, all a merchant or banker had to do was weigh and measure it and compare it to the royal standard. Because gold is so heavy, a fake coin would either be too light or too big. A lead coin of the same *thickness* and diameter as a sovereign would be only a third as heavy. A lead coin of the right *weight* and diameter would be twice as thick.

A much more successful ploy for forgers was adulteration. The trick was to remove small amounts of metal from legal coinage, melt down the scraps and recast new coins. There were three ways of doing this: 'clipping' (filing tiny fragments from the coin's edges); 'drilling' (taking the coin and punching small holes in it, which were then hammered shut); and 'sweating' (shaking a bag of coins for long enough to create a dust of gold and copper).

Sir Isaac Newton (1643–1727) became obsessed with the underworld of counterfeiting gangs after he was made Warden of the Royal Mint in 1696. His secret career as an alchemist had made him something on an expert at assessing the purity of metals. By his reckoning, one in five coins in circulation in England were false. He took on the criminal networks, collecting evidence by frequenting taverns and brothels in disguise. In 1699 he ensnared the master forger William Chaloner, who once boasted he had 'coined' 30,000 guineas of false gold (the equivalent of £50 million today). Chaloner was convicted of treason and publicly hanged, drawn and quartered.

About 40,000 gold sovereigns are still minted in the UK every year, to the same purity standard laid down under Henry VIII. Sovereigns are no longer legal tender but are kept as gold bullion, which is a tradable commodity. The average world market price of gold in 2009 was about £20,500 per kilogram.

Who invented the catflap?

It wasn't Sir Isaac Newton.

It's an appealing idea that the father of gravitation, the leading theoretical scientist of his day and arguably the most famous celebrity in Europe at the start of the eighteenth century, invented something as mundane as the cat flap. Sadly, the evidence doesn't stack up.

To this day, students at Cambridge are told that, while an undergraduate at Trinity College, Isaac Newton cut two holes in the door of his lodgings – a large one for his pet cat and a smaller one for its kittens. The story plays on a classic stereotype, the genius with no common sense – because there's no need for the smaller door. But we know it never happened. Newton's secretary and distant relative, Humphrey Newton, was explicit: his master 'kept neither dog nor cat in his chamber'. Also, the doorways of most Cambridge lodgings of the period had a system of double doors. The outer doors were thick and heavy, and usually carved from a large piece of oak. The inner door acted as a draught excluder. Sawing holes through both would have been a major DIY project. And a self-defeating one – turning Newton's rooms into a wind tunnel.

Nobody knows where the catflap myth started, but we do have a source for the legend of the apple tree: Newton himself. Never one for self-deprecation, he likened his discovery of gravity to Adam being expelled from the Garden of Eden, as both featured the sudden acquisition of knowledge through an apple.

Newton often told the story during his lifetime, but, over a century later, the German mathematician Karl Friedrich Gauss (1777–1855) offered his own version of events. 'Undoubtedly,' he said, 'the occurrence was something of this sort: There comes to Newton a stupid importunate man, who asks him how he made his great discovery. Newton wanted to get rid of the man, told him that an apple fell on his nose; and this made the matter quite clear to the man, and he went away satisfied.'

Newton certainly had a reputation for grumpiness. He didn't suffer fools (or anyone else) gladly, and preferred solitary study to human company. At times his eccentricities seem to have shaded into genuine mental illness, particularly in 1692, when he complained of 'great disturbance of mind'. Historians have variously ascribed the other symptoms he exhibited – insomnia, obsessive behaviour, lack of appetite and the delusion that his friends were turning on him – to depression, Asperger's syndrome and even mercury poisoning. Recent tests on a lock of his hair showed abnormally high levels of mercury, perhaps caused by decades of secret alchemical experimentation.

Whatever afflicted him, it didn't prevent Newton from producing *Principia Mathematica* (1687), the most influential scientific book of all time, or from building a successful second career as a civil servant and administrator. He lived until he was eighty-four and died a very wealthy man, leaving assets worth £31,821 (equivalent to £49 million in today's money).

STEPHEN *There are people in history who were said to be agelastic, including Isaac Newton, who was supposed to have laughed only once in his life.*

CLIVE ANDERSON *When an apple fell on his head.*

STEPHEN *No, when someone asked him what was the point of studying Euclid, and he burst out laughing.*

JIMMY CARR *Yeah, that is a good one, though.*

What did Molotov invent?

Molotov didn't invent his 'cocktails'. They were named after him as an insult.

Vyacheslav Mikhailovich

Skriabin (1890–1986) took the pen name 'Molotov' (*molot* means 'hammer' in Russian) as a young Bolshevik party organiser and underground journalist in pre-Revolutionary Russia. He became Stalin's most loyal deputy, and was one of only four members of the 1917 revolutionary government to survive Stalin's purges of the 1930s.

The story of the Molotov cocktail begins in 1939 when, as Soviet foreign minister, Molotov secretly authorised the illegal invasion of Finland, weeks after the Second World War had started. In the early phases of the invasion, he claimed in radio broadcasts that the cluster bombs Soviet planes were dropping were actually food parcels for starving Finns.

The Finnish resistance was stronger than the Soviets had anticipated and the invasion lasted through the bitter winter of 1940. The Finns' secret weapon was a handmade incendiary device made from a bottle filled with flammable liquid and stoppered with a wick. They had borrowed the idea from General Franco's Fascist troops, who had recently emerged as victors in the Spanish Civil War. The Fascists had produced these hand-held bombs to disable the Soviet-built tanks used by the left-wing Republican government forces. The Finns christened them 'Molotov's cocktails', the joke being that they were 'a drink to go with his food parcels'. They used a government vodka distillery to produce more than 450,000 of them. Their fame spread and, by the end of the War, combatants on all sides knew them as 'Molotov cocktails'.

The disinformation about food parcels was typical of Molotov. He wasn't a soldier; he was a bureaucrat, skilled in the use of propaganda. The Finnish war resulted from the Molotov–Ribbentrop pact that he had signed with the Nazis in August 1939. (Von Ribbentrop was Molotov's opposite number, the German foreign minister.) This was a secret agreement for the USSR and Germany to carve up Poland and the Baltic states between them. It wasn't made public until after war had ended – Molotov went to his grave denying it had ever existed – but it made possible the German invasion of Poland (which began the Second World War) as well as the Soviet invasion of Finland. It also allowed Molotov to destroy Polish resistance by authorising the murder of all 22,000 members of the Polish officer corps at Katyn forest in March 1940.

The short-lived pact with Germany wasn't Molotov's only legacy. During the Soviet purges of the 1930s, it had been his idea to use lists to sentence people to death, greatly speeding up the process. In 1937–8, he personally signed 372 orders for mass executions – more than Stalin himself – leading to the murder of more than 43,000 people.

Vegetarian, teetotal and a studious collector of first editions (many were dedicated to him by authors he later sent to the Gulag), Molotov was the last surviving Bolshevik. He died, an unrepentant Stalinist, in 1986, just after Mikhail Gorbachev announced the *perestroika* (restructuring) reforms that would lead, five years later, to the dissolution of the USSR.

Why was the speed camera invented?

It was designed to speed cars up, not slow them down.

A Dutch engineer called Maurice Gatsonides (1911–98) devised the first speed camera. Far from being a road-safety campaigner, Gatsonides was Europe's first professional rally driver. The pinnacle of his career came in 1953 when he won the Monte Carlo Rally in a Ford Zephyr by just three seconds.

His world-famous invention was driven by a desire to improve his speed round corners. The first 'Gatsometer' consisted of two pressure-sensitive rubber strips stretched across the road. Driving over the first strip started a stop-watch; crossing the second stopped it. This was the world's first reliable speed-measuring device. Gatsonides then added a flash camera which made it even more accurate. It enabled him to see just how much extra speed he could squeeze out of a corner by approaching it along a different line.

Gatso soon realised that his camera could also be used to catch speeding motorists. He founded Gatsometer BV in 1958 and over the next twenty years gradually refined his invention, introducing a radar beam to replace the rubber pressure strips in 1971. The 'Gatso 24' is now installed in more than forty countries. In many languages, speed cameras of any kind are simply known as 'Gatsos'.

The first Gatsos in the UK were installed in Nottingham in 1988, after a triple fatality at a traffic-light-controlled junction. Having been slow to adopt the new technology, the UK now leads Europe in the use of speed cameras. In 2007 the UK had 4,309 of them (compared with 1,571 in 2001), more than France and Italy combined.

Do they work? The evidence suggests that they do. A four-year survey by the UK Department for Transport, published in 2006, reported that the overall speed past camera sites was reduced by an average of 6 per cent, and the number of people killed or seriously injured by 42 per cent. While the motoring lobby points out that driving too fast is the main cause in only 14 per cent of fatal accidents – compared with 'driver distraction' which accounts for 68 per cent – the enforcement of speed limits has had a massive impact on the number of collisions. In the ten years since 32 kilometres per hour (20 miles per hour) limits were introduced in London, the number of accidents has halved.

Dislike of speed cameras is nothing new. The Automobile Association was established in 1905 to help motorists avoid police speed traps which (then as now) many felt were more to do with extorting money than road safety. All drivers speed at some point: 75 per cent admit to doing it regularly. But for all the grumbling, according to the Department for Transport, 82 per cent of us think speed cameras are a good thing.

Gatsonides certainly thought so. 'I am often caught by my own speed cameras and find hefty fines on my doorstep,' he once confessed. 'I love speeding.'

JEREMY CLARKSON *There's a marvellous new club in Holland called the Tuf Tuf Club that goes around destroying speed cameras.*

STEPHEN *Oh, really?*

JEREMY *You get prizes if you can think of the most imaginative way. My favourite one was to put some of that builders' foam in. It just bursts and then sets in a rather ugly, Dr Who-y special effect. Which is quite good.*

What's the word for a staircase that goes round and round?

It's not 'spiral', it's helical.

A spiral is a two-dimensional curve which radiates out from a fixed, central point. The longer it gets, the less curved it becomes, like a snail shell. A helix is a three-dimensional curve, like a spring or a Slinky, which doesn't change its angle of curve no matter how long it gets.

In the Scottish Borders there's a legend that the Kerr family built their castle towers with helical staircases that went round in the opposite direction to everybody else's. Because most of the male Kerrs were left-handed, this gave them an advantage in defending the stairs against a right-handed swordsman.

Sadly, it isn't true: Kerrs are no more left-handed than any other family. A 1972 study in the *British Medical Journal* reported a 30 per cent incidence of left-handedness among Kerrs against a 10 per cent incidence in the British population generally, but the research turned out to be flawed. It had been based on a self-selecting sample, i.e. left-handed people with the surname Kerr were encouraged to come forward, and so the results were badly skewed. A later and more careful study in 1993 found no such tendency.

What's more, the staircase trick wouldn't work: if a defender was left-handed then an anticlockwise staircase would indeed allow him to use his sword more effectively, but it would also give a right-handed attacker the same advantage. So, a staircase that twisted the other way would only be useful when defending against another Kerr (not impossible given their bloodthirsty reputation).

The Chateau de Chambord in the Loire Valley has a double-helix staircase: two staircases which wind around each other so that people going up don't bump into people coming down – and the cliff-top fortifications at Dover have a *triple-*helix staircase (known as the 'Grand Shaft') designed to get three columns of troops down to harbour level simultaneously.

The most famous of all double helixes is the molecule called deoxyribonucleic acid, better known as DNA. Francis Crick and James Watson first described its structure in 1953, although they were inspired by an X-ray photograph of DNA taken by Rosalind Franklin (1920–58), who almost beat them to it.

If you unravelled all the DNA strands in your body they'd stretch for 1,000 billion kilometres (620 billion miles), which is nearly 7,000 times further than the distance to the sun, and further away in the other direction than the edge of the Solar System.

To put that in perspective, to count to 620 billion you would have to have started 20,000 years ago, in the middle of the last ice age.

What's so great about the golden ratio?

Every Dan Brown fan has heard of this mysterious figure that crops up everywhere – in the human body, in ancient architecture, in the natural world – and whose appeal nobody can explain. The truth is that it doesn't appear in most of the places it's supposed to, and many of the claims about it are false.

The golden ratio (also known as 'the golden mean' or the 'divine proportion') is a way of relating any two quantities – such as the height (a) of a building to the length (b) – in the following simple way.

$$\frac{a+b}{a} = \frac{a}{b}$$

If a=1, then b=0.6180339887 . . .

In the nineteenth century, this ratio was given the name phi – φ – after the great Greek sculptor Phidias (490–430 BC), who supposedly used it in the proportions of his human figures. The reason that such a simple formula produces such a complicated, unharmonious looking number is that phi (φ), like pi (π), cannot be written as a neat fraction, or 'ratio', so it is called an irrational number. Irrational numbers can only be expressed as an infinite string of decimal places that never repeat themselves. A prettier way of expressing phi in maths is: ($\sqrt{5}+1$) divided by 2.

A 'golden spiral' is one that gets further from its central point by a factor of φ for every quarter turn it makes. A frequently quoted example of this is the beautiful shell of *Nautilus pompilius*, a member of the octopus family. But in fact this is a 'logarithmic spiral', not a golden one. In 1999 the American mathematician Clement Falbo measured several hundred shells and showed quite clearly that the average ratio was 1 to 1.33: a long way from 1.618. (If you did want to use a shell to demonstrate the golden mean, the abalone would do well, but they're not nearly as photogenic as the nautilus.)

The Greeks knew about the golden ratio, and the Parthenon is the usual example given of its use in architecture. But any diagrams showing how its side or front elevations demonstrate a 'golden rectangle' always either include some empty air at the top or leave out some steps at the bottom.

The golden ratio was forgotten for hundreds of years after the fall of Rome, until Luca Pacioli (1446–1517), a Franciscan monk and Leonardo da Vinci's tutor, wrote about it in *De Divina Proportione* (1509). Leonardo did the illustrations for the book but, despite what it says in *The Da Vinci Code*, he did not use the golden ratio to compose either the Mona Lisa or his famous 1487 drawing of a man in a circle with his limbs extended.

The latter is called Vitruvian Man after the Roman architect Vitruvius, who lived in the first century BC and is sometimes called 'the world's first engineer'. He based his buildings on the proportions of the ideal human body, where the height is equal to the span of the arms and eight times the size of the head. He didn't use φ at all, whether or not Phidias once used it for a similar purpose.

What kind of stripes make you look slimmer?

Vertical ones, surely?

Nope.

According to research carried out in 2008 at the University of York, it is stripes running *across* the body that make the wearer appear more trim.

The experiment asked people to compare over 200 pairs of pictures of women wearing dresses with either horizontal or vertical stripes and say which of them looked fatter.

The results showed conclusively that, with two women of the same size, the one wearing the horizontal stripes appeared to be the thinner of the two. In fact, to make the women *appear* to be the same size, the one in the horizontal stripes had to be 6 per cent wider.

Led by psychologist Dr Peter Thompson, the York team had been puzzled that the conventional view that vertical stripes are 'slimming' went against a famous optical illusion, the Helmholtz square, in which a square filled with horizontal lines appears taller than one filled with vertical ones.

Hermann von Helmholtz (1821–94) was a German polymath. Not only was he a qualified physician and a theoretical physicist, he also helped found the discipline of experimental psychology and transformed the science of optics, writing the standard textbook on the subject and, in 1851, inventing the ophthalmoscope, an instrument which enabled people to see the inside of the eye for the first time.

On the matter of striped dresses, von Helmholtz was absolutely categorical: 'Frocks with cross stripes on them make the figure look taller.'

For some reason, everyone has steadily ignored him for well over a century. When Sheriff Joe Arpaio of Maricopa County,

Arizona, reintroduced striped prison uniforms in 1997, female inmates begged him to make the bars vertical so they wouldn't look fat. He said: 'I told them I am an equal-opportunity incarcerator – the men have horizontal stripes, and so will the women.'

Striped prison uniforms, first introduced in the early nineteenth century, made it easier to spot escapees in a crowd. But they were also intended as a psychological punishment. In the Middle Ages, striped clothes were the pattern of choice for prostitutes, clowns and other social outcasts – whether or not they were overweight.

One piece of received fashion wisdom the York team did confirm was that black really does make you look slimmer. This research was provoked by another famous optical illusion, in which a black circle on a white background appears smaller than a white circle on a black background.

ROB BRYDON *I have a friend who's quite short and he likes to wear vertical stripes because they make him look taller.*

DAVID MITCHELL *Only when he's not standing next to anyone. It's not going to make him look taller than a taller man. It's all relative. You won't just say: 'Oh, there's a normal size man next to an enormous man' and then go: 'Oh thank God, he's taken his striped shirt off, it's actually a tiny man next to a normal man.'*

How many eyes do you need to estimate depth and distance?

One.

You'd think that we need both eyes, but we don't.

It is true that most depth perception is created by the different angles of vision produced by each eye. It's the way that 3-D film works, combining the output of two different cameras. When we look at something we create a single 'field of view', with the visual information split between the right and the left eye. The right-hand field from both eyes is sent to the right side of the brain; the left half of the field is sent to the left side. The brain merges them into a single solid-looking image.

However, our brains can still judge distance with a single eye. If you lose sight in one eye, the brain processes information from the remaining eye and plots it against the motion of your body. It then combines these visual and non-visual clues to create a sense of depth.

In fact, it turns out that you don't need eyes to 'see' at all.

Over thirty years, US neuroscientist Paul Bach-y-Rita (1934–2006) experimented with 'sensory substitution'. He had noticed that, although different parts of the body collect different types of sensory information, the way they're transmitted – electrical nerve impulses – is always the same. In theory, this meant the nervous system could be rewired, swapping one sense for another.

In 2003 he began to test a device called the BrainPort. This uses a camera attached to the head to record visual images, which are translated into electrical signals that are sent to electrodes attached to the tongue. (The tongue has more nerve endings than anywhere on the human body except the lips.) What the tongue feels is a sequence of pulses of different length, frequency and intensity, which corresponds to the visual data. Gradually the brain learns to 'see' the image being sent to the tongue. The results are remarkable: after a while, people wearing the device can recognise shapes, letters – even faces – and catch balls that are thrown to them. Brain scans show that even blind people using it are having their visual cortex stimulated.

Darting movements of the eyes are called saccades (from the French *saquer* 'to twitch', and pronounced 'suck-hards'). They are the fastest movements produced by the human body.

Our eyes are also continually vibrating. These tiny, imperceptible movements, each covering 20 arcseconds (or 1/5,000th of a degree) are called microsaccades. They are an essential component of vision: without them we'd be blind. In order to send nerve impulses to the brain, the rod and cone cells need to be continually stimulated by light. Microsaccades ensure that light keeps striking the retina, but the brain edits them out as unnecessary.

One spooky way of demonstrating how much the brain edits our sight is to stand facing a mirror and look at one eye and then the other. You won't be able to see your eyes moving (although it's quite obvious to anyone else).

What's the natural reaction to a bright light?

Squinting or shading the eyes is instinctive for most people, but at least a quarter of us respond to bright lights by sneezing.

This is called the photic sneeze reflex (from *photos*, Greek for 'light') or, with rather heavy-handed humour, the ACHOO syndrome (Autosomal-dominant Compelling Helio-Ophthalmic Outburst).

It was first medically described in 1978, but people have been known to sneeze after looking at the sun since Aristotle; he blamed the effect of heat on the nose. Francis Bacon (1561–1626) disproved Aristotle's theory in the seventeenth century by going out into the sun with his eyes closed; he suffered from photic sneeze reflex, but with his eyes shut nothing happened. Since the heat was still there, he decided that the sneezing must be caused by light; he guessed that the sun made the eyes water and this water irritated the nose.

In fact, the disorder is caused by confused signalling from the trigeminal nerve, the one responsible for sensation in the face. (Trigeminal means 'triple-origin' because the nerve has three main branches.) Somewhere along its passage to the brain the nerve impulses from around the eye and inside the nose become scrambled, and the brain is tricked into thinking that a visual stimulus is a nasal one. The result is that the body tries to 'expel' the light by sneezing.

Photic sneeze reflex affects between 18 per cent and 35 per cent of people. It most often occurs when someone leaves a dark place such as a tunnel or a forest and emerges into bright sunlight. The usual number of sneezes is two or three, but it can be as many as forty. This surprisingly common trait is inherited. Both men and women can get it, and they have a fifty–fifty chance of passing it on to their children. Because it's genetic, it isn't equally distributed but occurs in geographical clusters.

'Honeymoon rhinitis' is another genetic condition where people are attacked by uncontrollable sneezing during sex. One theory is that the nose is the only part of the body other than the reproductive system (and, strangely, the ears) to contain erectile tissue. It may be that the 'arousal' impulse, in some people, triggers both the nose and the genitals simultaneously.

An interesting side effect of this is that, like Pinocchio, our noses really do get bigger when we lie. Guilt causes blood to flow to the erectile tissue in the nose. This is an automatic reflex, and explains why people who are not very good liars often give themselves away by touching or scratching their noses or ears.

How do you know when the sun has set?

'When it has disappeared below the horizon' is the wrong answer.

The sun has already set when its lower edge touches the horizon.

As the setting sun falls in the sky, its light passes through the atmosphere at an increasingly shallow angle and is bent more and more as the amount of air it has to pass through increases. At the end of the process, the light is bent so much that we can still apparently see the sun even though it's physically below the horizon. By coincidence, the degree of bending is almost equal to the width of the sun – so when we see the lower rim of the sun kiss the horizon, the whole of it has in fact completely disappeared.

What we're looking at is a mirage. The bending of the light also has the effect of reducing the apparent distance between the top and bottom of the sun. This can cause the sun to appear oval.

When sunlight travels through the atmosphere, green light is bent very slightly more than red light – as when passing through a prism. This means that the top of the setting sun has a very thin green rim – too thin to be seen by the naked eye. Very occasionally, when atmospheric conditions are right, this green rim can be artificially magnified and it shines for a second or so just as the sun disappears from view. This phenomenon is known as the 'green flash' and is considered a good omen by sailors.

Another common mirage is the one you see on a road in summer. Hot tarmac heats the air above it, producing a sharp shift in its density, which causes light to bend. You think you see water; what you're actually seeing is a reflection of the sky. The brain tells you it's water, because water also reflects the sky.

Desert mirages are the same: the thirsty adventurer only ever 'sees' water.

Any other images of the type associated with mirages in cartoons and films (palm trees, ice-cream vans, dancing girls, etc.) are just figments of a heat-addled imagination.

STEPHEN *Light from the setting sun passes through our atmosphere at a shallow angle; it is gradually bent as the air density, i.e. the pressure, increases. Not dissimilar to the image of your legs when you sit in a swimming pool. Our brains cannot accept that light is bent. The effect is to artificially raise the sun in the last few minutes of its decline, through the thickness of the atmosphere at that shallow angle there. And by coincidence, the amount of bending is pretty much equal to the diameter of the sun, so it's exactly, exactly as it is there, that it's actually disappeared.*

PHILL JUPITUS *I hate this show.*

What are the highest clouds called?

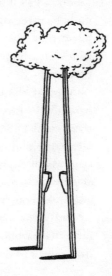

'Everyone knows' that the wispy cirrus clouds are the highest – but they aren't.

Clear midsummer evenings can occasionally reveal one of the loveliest and least understood phenomena of the night sky. Noctilucent ('night-shining') clouds are silvery blue streaks that form so high up in the atmosphere they catch the sun's light, even at night. At over 80 kilometres (50 miles) in altitude, they are seven times higher than the highest cirrus clouds.

The word atmosphere is Greek for 'globe of vapour'. Earth's atmosphere is a succession of layers of gas, stretching about 100 kilometres (62 miles) into space. We live in the troposphere (*tropos* is Greek for 'change'), which is warm and moist and is where all the clouds (except the noctilucent ones) form. At 11 kilometres (7 miles) up, the stratosphere starts (*stratum* is Latin for 'covering'): it contains the protective ozone layer. The outermost layer is the mesosphere, somewhat confusingly called the 'middle sphere' because it's between the other, inner layers and space. It starts nearly 5 kilometres (about 3 miles) up and is 32 kilometres (20 miles) thick. It's too high for most aircraft and too low for space flight, and it's nicknamed the 'ignorosphere' because we know so little about it.

Noctilucent clouds form right on the boundary of the mesosphere and space. Clouds need water vapour and dust particles to form and the mesosphere is so dry and cold (about −123 °C) it was first thought that noctilucent clouds must be made of something other than water vapour. Now we know they are made of tiny ice crystals − a fiftieth of the width of a human hair − but we still don't understand how they form.

Another thing we don't know about them is whether they have always existed or not. No one had ever reported seeing them until 1885 when they were first named by Otto Jesse, a German cloud enthusiast. This was just two years after the eruption of Krakatoa and at a time when the industrial age was at its peak. It seems that this was the first time dust had ever got high enough for clouds to form in the mesosphere.

Today, the mesosphere is getting cooler still, as a result of increased carbon dioxide (CO_2) emissions. At the same time, ironically, carbon dioxide is busy heating up the troposphere.

CO_2 naturally absorbs heat. In the thin air of the mesosphere, it simply sucks it up. But, in the troposphere, nearer the Earth's surface, where the gases are more densely packed, CO_2 collides continually with other substances (such as water vapour). This releases heat and causes global temperatures to rise and is known as the 'greenhouse effect'.

Over the past three decades, the number of noctilucent clouds has more than doubled, which has led some scientists to liken them to miner's canaries: their eerie beauty warning of the dangers of climate change to come.

How much does a cloud weigh?

A *lot*.

A popular unit of measurement for cloud-weight seems to be the elephant. According to the National Center for Atmospheric Research in Boulder, Colorado, an average cumulus cloud weighs about 100 elephants, while a big storm cloud tips the scales at 200,000 elephants.

This is nothing compared to a hurricane. If you extracted the water from a cubic metre of hurricane, weighed it and then multiplied it by the number of cubic metres in the whole hurricane cloud, you would find that a single hurricane weighs *40 million* elephants. That's twenty-six times more elephants than exist on the planet.

Which raises an obvious question: how can something that weighs as much as even *one* elephant float in the sky? The answer is that the weight is distributed across a vast number of tiny water droplets and ice crystals spread over a very large area. The biggest droplets are only 0.2 millimetre (less than 0.008 inch) across: you'd need a million of them to make a teaspoon of water. Clouds form on top of updraughts of warm air. The rising air is stronger than the downward pressure of the water droplets, and so clouds float. When the air cools, and sinks, it begins to rain.

In order to rain, the water in the clouds has to freeze before it falls. If the air temperature is low enough, it will fall as snow or hail; if not, the frozen drops melt on their way down. One puzzle is why there is so much rain in temperate climates like Britain, where clouds rarely get cold enough to freeze pure water. Catalysts like soot and dust help, providing nuclei around which ice can form, but there isn't enough pollution of that kind to create all the rain.

The answer seems to be airborne microbes. Certain kinds of bacteria are first-class 'ice nucleators', to the extent that they have the magical ability to *make* water freeze. Adding *Pseudomonas syringae*, for example, to water, makes it freeze almost instantly, even at relatively warm temperatures of 5–6 °C.

The rain they 'seed' carries the bacteria to earth where they use their ice-making powers to mush up plant cells, including many crops, so they can feed on them. Air currents then sweep them back up into the atmosphere again, causing more rain.

If this theory is right, the implications are enormous: merely growing the kind of crops that these ice-making bacteria like could wipe out droughts forever.

How much of the Moon can you see from the Earth?

It's not half.

Because the Moon takes exactly the same amount of time to

revolve around its own axis as it does to orbit the Earth, we only ever see one face of it.

But the Moon's motion is not quite regular. As it goes round, it shifts backwards and forwards and side to side, revealing rather more of itself than half. This is known as 'libration', from the Latin *librare*, 'to swing', after the balancing movements of a pair of scales, or *libra*.

Galileo Galilei (1564–1642) discovered it in 1637, and it comes in three forms.

Latitudinal libration is caused by the fact that the Moon is slightly tilted on its axis. This means that from a fixed point on the Earth's surface the Moon appears to rock first towards and then away from us as it passes by, allowing us to glimpse a little more of its top and bottom in turn.

Longitudinal libration, or side-to-side motion, results from the fact that Moon travels round the Earth at a slightly uneven speed. It always *rotates* at the same rate but, because it's travelling round the Earth in an ellipse rather than a circle, it's going faster when it's closer to the Earth and slower when it's further away. We can see more of its trailing edge when it's going away from us, and more of its leading edge when it's coming towards us.

Finally, there's *diurnal* ('daily') *libration*. Because the Earth is also rotating on its axis, at different times of day we're looking at the moon from a different angle. This allows us to see a bit round the back of the Moon's western edge as it rises, and a bit more round the back of its eastern edge as it sets.

The net result is that in any one month (each twenty-eight-day orbit of the Moon) we see 59 per cent of the Moon's surface. The Soviet spacecraft Luna 3 took the first pictures of the 'dark' side of the Moon in 1959.

The fact that the Moon always shows the same face to the Earth is known as 'tidal locking'. Many of the 169 known moons in the solar system are synchronised in this way: including both the moons of Mars, the five inner moons of Saturn and the four largest of Jupiter's moons, known as the 'Galilean satellites' after Galileo who also discovered them in 1610.

Earth has a similar relationship with Venus. Despite spinning in the opposite direction to Earth, when Venus is closest to us (every 583 days) it always presents the same face. No one knows why. Astronomical bodies become tidally locked when they are relatively close to each other: Venus never gets nearer to us than 38 million kilometres (24 million miles). So it might just be chance.

STEPHEN *There is this strange thing called libration, which is like vibration beginning with an 'l'. It was a thing that was noted by quite a few of the early astronomers . . .*

ROB BRYDON *Can I say, sorry Stephen, but that's not an acceptable way of defining a word: 'Libration, it's like vibration but beginning with an l.'*

What's the best planet in the solar system to take your annual holiday?

It has to be Venus. The weather's appalling but the value for money is unbeatable.

Venus rotates so slowly around its axis that its day is longer than its year. A fortnight's break on Venus would last over fifteen years.

Because Venus spins in the opposite direction to all the other planets except Uranus, the sun rises in the West and sets in the East. You won't see it, though: the sky is clogged with thick clouds of sulphuric acid.

Take sensible clothing. The surface of Venus is hot enough to melt aluminium and the atmospheric pressure is equivalent to being half a mile under the sea on Earth. The 'air' can hardly be described as 'fresh' either: it's mostly unbreathable carbon dioxide.

The speedy rotation of long-haul destination Neptune means that a day there is eight hours shorter than on Earth, but its huge orbit means a year is the equivalent of 165 earth years, and each of the four seasons lasts about four decades. Forty years of summer sounds good – until you learn that Neptune's average temperature at that time of year is −200 °C.

Jupiter is almost big and hot enough to be a star, but not an ideal holiday destination unless you enjoy gas, of which it mainly consists. A layer of black liquid hydrogen, 43,500 kilometres (27,000 miles) thick, crushes carbon into diamonds that are literally as big as the Ritz and precipitates neon (rather than water) from the atmosphere, to create brilliant, bright red rain.

Saturn's spectacular rings are over 112,600 kilometres (70,000 miles) wide, but may disappoint tourists on closer inspection. They are only 9 metres (30 feet) thick and mostly made from ice particles, some as small as 1¼ centimetres (½ inch) in diameter. There's also nowhere to stand or sit down. Saturn is so lacking in density that if you could find a lake big enough, it would float.

Those who like a bit of historical information on holiday might as well stay home. Despite their variety, the planets (and the Sun) are all the same age, formed simultaneously about 4.5 billion years ago.

RICH HALL *You know, uh, Venus is made entirely out of felt . . . I would like three points, please.*

What can you hear in space?

In space, no one can hear you scream, but that's not to say that there's no noise there.

There are gases in space, which allow sound waves to travel, but interstellar gas is much less dense than Earth's atmosphere. Whereas air has 30 billion, billion atoms per cubic centimetre, deep space averages fewer than two.

If you were standing at the edge of an interstellar gas cloud and a sound came through it towards you, only a few atoms a second would hit your eardrums – too little for you to hear anything. An extremely sensitive microphone might do better, but humans are effectively deaf in space. Our ears aren't up to it.

Even if you were standing next to an exploding supernova, the gases from the explosion would expand so rapidly that their density would decrease very fast and you'd hear very little.

Sound doesn't travel well on Mars, either: its atmosphere is only 1 per cent as dense as ours. On Earth, a scream can travel a kilometre (⅗ of a mile) before being absorbed by the air; on Mars, it would be inaudible at a distance of 15 metres (50 feet).

Black holes generate sound. There's one in the Perseus cluster of galaxies, 250 million light years away. The signal was detected in 2003 in the form of X-rays (which will happily travel anywhere) by NASA's Chandra X-ray Observatory satellite.

No one will ever hear it, though. It's 57 octaves lower than middle C: over a million billion times deeper than the limits of human hearing.

It's the deepest note ever detected from any object anywhere in the universe and it makes a noise in the pitch of B flat – the same as a vuvuzela.

How do you open a parachute?

Not with a ripcord any more.

The traditional way of opening a parachute was to pull a handle attached to a stainless steel cable known as a ripcord. Since the 1980s, pilot chutes, packed into a pocket in the parachute harness, have replaced ripcords. The pilot chute is much smaller than the main parachute – about a metre or 3 feet in diameter – and is usually released by the jumper pulling it out of its pocket and throwing it into the air. The sudden jerk as the pilot chute inflates removes the release pin for the main chute, which then opens. This is much safer than ripcords, as there is less chance of jamming.

Modern parachute canopies aren't shaped like jellyfish any more, either. They are rectangular and made of a double layer of parallel tubular cells, a bit like an airbed. The back and sides of each cell are closed, but open at the front. As the tubes fill with air, the canopy forms a wedge, similar to the shape of a hang-glider. And, just as with hang-gliders, parachutes can be steered. The control cords also allow the jumper to slow down or speed up the rate of descent.

If the main parachute fails, there is a second or 'reserve' parachute to open and, even if the jump causes a loss of consciousness, there is an AAD, or Automatic Activation Device, which automatically releases the reserve parachute at about 230 metres (750 feet). The fatality rate for parachute jumps is one in 100,000, but almost none of these are caused by faulty equipment. Most result from reckless manoeuvres or from landing too fast; changes in wind conditions; or 'canopy collisions', where two parachutes get entangled.

Modern parachutists descend at about 40 kilometres per hour (25 miles per hour). In freefall, a body's terminal velocity – where air resistance prevents it from falling any faster – is about 200 kilometres per hour (125 miles per hour). In normal atmospheric pressure, and with an un-controlled posture, it takes about 573 metres (1,880 feet) or 14 seconds to reach this speed.

At higher altitudes, where the air is much less dense, a faster fall is possible. In 1960 US air force pilot Joseph Kittenger leapt from a balloon at 31,333 metres (102,800 feet) and reached a speed of 988 kilometres per hour (613 miles per hour), close to the speed of sound. Despite continuing to dive head first, he began to spin rapidly and blacked out, coming round when his chute opened automatically around 1.6 kilometres (a mile) above the ground. He is now helping skydiver Felix Baumgartner prepare to break his fifty-year-old record. Baumgartner plans to dive from a balloon at 36,500 metres (120,000 feet or 23 miles). He aims to reach a speed of 1,110 kilometres per hour (690 miles per hour). This will make him the first person to break the sound barrier outside an aircraft. No one knows what the physical effects of supersonic speed will be on a human body.

Leonardo da Vinci is often credited with inventing the idea of a parachute, but the concept predates his famous 1485 drawing. An anonymous manuscript from a decade earlier shows a man wearing rather comical Italian dress and a nonchalant expression, holding on to a cone-shaped canopy. One can only hope it was never tested: it was much too small to slow his descent at all.

STEPHEN *I believe, Pam, that you felt some erotic feelings towards your instructor. Is that correct?*

PAM AYRES *I did. I took a shine to the instructor. I think that's why I jumped out the aircraft, really, 'cause I wanted to impress him.*

JOHNNY VEGAS *I often do that. If I like a woman, I jump out the window. Just to show 'em I really care.*

Why shouldn't you touch a meteorite?

It's not because you might burn your fingers.

A *meteorite* is an object that has fallen to Earth from space. *Meteors*, or 'shooting stars', are objects passing through the Earth's atmosphere. Hundreds of tons of meteors bombard the Earth every day, but most of them are smaller than a grain of sand and burn up on entry.

Both words come from the Greek for celestial phenomena, *ta meteora*, which translates literally as 'things suspended high up'. In films and comics, meteorites are hot – they hiss and sizzle as they land in the snow. In reality, they're usually cold: some are even covered in frost.

This is because space is extremely cold. Although the friction of entering the atmosphere heats meteorites up, it also slows them down. They can take several minutes to fall to the ground: quite long enough for them to lose all the heat their outer surface has temporarily gained.

Meteorites are either stony or metallic – metallic ones ring like a bell when struck with another piece of metal. Most of them are as old as the Earth itself. A few are found immediately after their fall, many have lain in the ground for tens of thousands of years before being discovered. You are most unlikely to come across one. In the whole of the USA between 1807 and 2009, only 1,530 verified examples were found – that's fewer than eight a year. Actually seeing a meteorite falling, and then finding it, is even rarer. In the same period, it only happened 202 times – by coincidence, exactly once a year. The latest edition of the Natural History Museum's *Catalogue of Meteorites*, published since 1847 and listing every known meteorite, records just twenty-four as ever being found anywhere in the British Isles. Meteorite experts get hundreds of calls from the public every year: they rarely turn out to be the real thing.

The reason for not touching one is that you may contaminate any organic matter it might carry. If you do find a fresh one, you should put it in a sealed plastic bag (without touching it) and send it to your nearest research group.

The 'Bolton Meteorite' was found in the backyard of a house in the high street of the Lancashire town in 1928. It caused great excitement, which was rather dampened by the verdict of the British Museum in London – that it wasn't a meteorite at all, just a piece of burnt coal. Even so, it's still on display at the Bolton Museum.

When the first Europeans came to northern Greenland, they were amazed to find the local Inughuit, or polar Inuit, people using metal knives, despite having no idea how to either mine or smelt metal. They had chipped iron flakes off a meteorite using volcanic stones, and set them into handles made of walrus tusks.

The meteorite was one of three that were the centrepieces of their religion. They were 4.5 billion years old and the largest weighed 36 tons. In 1897, the American explorer Admiral Robert E. Peary stole them, selling all three to the American Museum of Natural History in New York for $40,000.

STEPHEN *Around 50,000 meteorites larger than 20 grams fall from space to Earth every year. But more have been found on which continent than any other?*

RICH HALL *Antarctica.*

STEPHEN *Antarctica, yes.*

ALAN *Bit tough on the penguins really, isn't it.*

PHILL JUPITUS *That's why they always stand up, because there's less of a surface area.*

What is a 'brass monkey'?

It's got nothing to do with cannonballs.

The phrase 'cold enough to freeze the balls off a brass monkey' is often said to refer to a metallic grid with circular holes in it, set under a pyramid of cannonballs on a ship's deck to keep it stable. When this 'brass monkey' got cold enough, the metal contracted and the cannonballs all popped out.

In fact, the phrase means exactly what it says; the fake nautical euphemism is an attempt to make its rude humour more acceptable.

First of all, it doesn't make any sense to stack piles of cannonballs on the deck of a pitching warship. And they weren't: they were kept in long thin racks running between the gunports, with a single hole for each cannonball.

Second, these frames were called 'shot-racks' or 'shot garlands' and they were made of wood, not brass.

Third, for one of these imaginary 'brass monkeys' to contract even 1 millimetre (0.4 inch) more than the iron cannonballs it was supposed to hold, the temperature would have to drop to −66 °C, 8 degrees colder than ever recorded in Europe.

Fourth, naval slang from the days of sail abounds in expressions that involve the word monkey, but the phrase 'brass monkey' is nowhere among them. *The Sailors Word Book of 1867*, the comprehensive dictionary of nautical terms compiled by the naval surveyor and astronomer Admiral W. H. Smyth (1788–1865), records monkey-block, monkey-boat, monkey-tail, monkey-jacket, monkey-spars, powder-monkey and monkey-pump (an illegal device for illegally sucking rum through a hole drilled in the cask). The only entry under brass reads: 'BRASS. Impudent assurance.'

Fifth, according to Dr Stewart Murray, a professional metallurgist and Chief Executive of the London Bullion

Market Association, the difference in thermal contraction between brass and iron in such a situation is 'absolutely tiny', even at extreme temperatures, and 'far too insignificant to have that kind of effect'.

'Cold enough to freeze the balls off a brass monkey' began life demurely as 'cold enough to freeze the tail off a brass monkey'. It was first recorded in mid-nineteenth-century America and variants of it were used as often about extremes of heat as they were of cold. In Herman Melville's novel *Omoo* (1850) one of the characters remarks that 'It was 'ot enough to melt the nose h'off a brass monkey'.

Michael Quinion of www.worldwidewords.org suggests that the 'monkey' element originated in the popular nineteenth-century brass ornaments featuring the three monkeys that 'hear no evil, see no evil, speak no evil'.

Clustering round a roaring Dickensian fire on a winter's night, far inland from the sea, what better reminder could there be of how cold it is outside than the line of cheeky brass monkeys sitting on the mantelpiece?

What would you find on the ground at the northernmost tip of Greenland?

You will struggle to find any snow or ice at all. You are most likely to bump into a large, malodorous beast known as the musk ox.

Peary Land is a mountainous peninsula extending from northern Greenland into the Arctic Ocean. It is the most northerly ice-free land on Earth. Lying 725 kilometres (450 miles) south of the North Pole and covering 57,000 square kilometres (22,000 square miles), it is bigger than Denmark.

It was first mapped in 1892 by the American explorer Robert E. Peary (1856–1920), who modestly named it after himself.

Dry enough to be counted as a desert, it is frost-free for three months in the summer, when temperatures often exceed 10°C and can reach 18°C. Winter is very cold, though: usually around −30°C. Rain is rare and the very occasional snow that falls is so dry it simply drifts away and never forms into ice.

Vegetation covers only 5 per cent of the total area but thirty-three species of flowering plant have been recorded and this is enough to support the population of 1,500 musk oxen.

Despite their names, musk oxen are actually large, shaggy members of the goat family. They get their name from the intense smell the males secrete from glands under their eyes when aroused. Musk-ox hair can grow almost 60 centimetres (2 feet) long, covering them in a thick-fringed pelt that reaches to the ground. This keeps them warm but it also means they aren't particularly fast on their feet.

Their defensive strategy is to form a circle around the younger and more vulnerable members of the herd and try to stare down any predators.

Historically, this worked well with Arctic wolves and bears, but wasn't much use against men with rifles. At the turn of the twentieth century, they had been hunted to the brink of extinction. They are now a protected species and the Arctic population has recovered to 150,000 individuals.

Musk oxen are ancient. They evolved over 600,000 years ago and were contemporaries with the woolly mammoth, the giant ground sloth and the sabre-tooth tiger. They are one of very few large mammal species to have survived the last Ice Age, which reached its peak 20,000 years ago.

How cold is 'too cold to snow'?

It's never too cold: at least, not in this world.

Anyone who lives in a country where it snows in winter will have heard people say, 'It's been trying to snow all day, but it's just too cold!'

This is never the case. Snow has been recorded in Alaska at below −41 °C and there are reports of snow falling at the South Pole at an incredible −50 °C. Flakes have even been made in the lab at −80 °C, which is as cold as the coldest parts of Antarctica ever get. It is true that, at temperatures below −33 °C very little ordinary 'snow' is produced. Instead, individual ice crystals fall to Earth in a phenomenon known as 'diamond dust'. These are so cold they can't clump together to form the familiar snowflakes, but they are still snow.

The reason why it doesn't always snow when it's cold is that, in northern Europe, very cold weather is usually associated with high pressure. In an area of high pressure, there is little air movement, so the cold air gradually sinks, warming as it falls. This means that any water in the air evaporates completely rather than forming into clouds. In summer, this produces hot, clear weather. In winter, it allows heat from the ground to rise upwards, because there is no insulating cloud layer. This lowers the ground temperature, particularly at night, when there is no sun to warm it. Although it's bitterly cold, there are no clouds to produce snow.

Not that this means it is necessarily warmer when it's snowing.

The coldest temperature ever recorded in England was −26.1 ° C at Newport, Shropshire on 10 January 1982 − a day also notable for its heavy snowfall.

Where do you lose most of your body heat?

Not necessarily, as Mummy warned you, from the top of your head.

The amount of heat released by any part of the body depends largely on how much of it is exposed. On a cold day, you could easily lose more body heat from a bare arm or leg.

That myth about the head is not only persistent, it's official. The current field manuals for the US Army recommend a hat in cold weather, stating: '40 per cent to 45 per cent of body heat' is lost through the head. The idea is thought to stem from the 1950s, when military scientists put subjects in Arctic survival suits (that didn't cover the head) to measure heat loss in extremely low temperatures.

According to Professor Gordon Giesbrecht, at the University of Manitoba, the world's leading expert on cold-weather survival, the head and neck are only 10 per cent of our body surface area and are no more efficient at losing heat than the rest of our skin.

If our heads *seem* to get colder it's because the concentration of nerve cells in our head and neck makes them five times as sensitive to changes in temperature as other areas. But information from our nervous system (feeling cold) isn't a direct indication of heat loss. This depends on the circulation of the blood – and there isn't a corresponding increase in blood vessels in the head and neck.

Our bodies respond to cold by closing the blood vessels in exposed skin and reducing blood flow to the extremities. This makes the fingers, toes, nose and ears susceptible to frostbite, while the brain and vital organs are unaffected. The other response to cold is shivering: our muscles shake involuntarily to generate heat by using up energy. Both responses are automatic, controlled by a cone-shaped part of the brain called the hypothalamus, which also governs other instinctive processes such as hunger, thirst and tiredness.

Professor Giesbrecht is no armchair theorist. Since 1991, he has put himself into states of hypothermia at least thirty-nine times to study the effects of cold on the human body. Hypothermia (from Greek *hypo* 'under'. and *therme*, 'heat') is the point at which our internal temperature drops below 35 °C, and the body's key processes start to slow down. This has led the redoubtable Dr Giesbrecht to plunge repeatedly into frozen lakes and hurtle a snowmobile at night into freezing seas. This, and the survival guides he has published, has earned him the nickname 'Professor Popsicle', after North America's favourite iced lolly.

Dr Giesbrecht advises that the key to survival if you suddenly find yourself in an icy lake is to master your breathing in the first minute. Once your breathing is steady, you have ten minutes before the cold starts affecting your muscles and an hour before hypothermia sets in. Other tips: hot drinks do not help beat the cold (though sugary drinks do, as they provide fuel for the body to generate heat). And don't blow on your hands to keep warm. The moisture in your breath makes them colder and increases the risk of frostbite.

DAVID MITCHELL *Is it not just a fact that your head is a bit of you that is more naked than the rest of you?*

STEPHEN *Well, that's right, if your arm was exposed, more would escape from your arm than from your head.*

DAVID *If people went around with bare buttocks a lot, they would say: 'Well, in the cold you really should put on a buttock hat.'*

What colour should you wear to keep cool?

We're all told at school that white reflects sunlight and black absorbs it, so that the paler your clothes are, the cooler you'll be.

But it's not quite that simple.

In many hot countries, locals often wear dark colours. Peasants in China and old ladies in southern Europe, for instance, traditionally wear black, and the Tuareg, the nomadic people of the Sahara, favour indigo blue.

Dark clothes are effective because there are two thermal processes happening at once. Heat is coming downwards from the sun but it is also going outwards from the body. Though light clothes are better at *reflecting* the *sun*'s heat, dark clothes are better at *radiating* the *body*'s heat. Given that no one born in a hot climate willingly stands in direct sunlight, the dark clothing has the edge because it keeps you cooler when you're in the shade.

Then there's the wind factor. People who live in really hot places don't wear tight jumpers or tailored suits. They wear loose robes that enable maximum air circulation. In 1978 a study examining the significance of colouring in birds' plumage found that, in hot and still conditions, white feathers were best at letting heat escape; but as soon as the wind got above 11 kilometres per hour (7 miles per hour), black feathers – provided they were fluffy – were the most efficient coolers. Experiments on black and white cattle have reached similar conclusions.

Applying this to humans, given even a modest breeze, loose black clothes will carry heat away from your body faster than they absorb it.

In less extreme climates, one of the best ways to keep cool is to learn how to use windows properly. Physicists at Imperial College, London have shown that optimum air flow in a room comes from opening both the top and bottom sections of a sash window.

If the two openings are of equal size, colder, heavier air coming in through the lower gap pushes the warmer, less dense air out of the top, much as a cooling gust ventilates a Tuareg's flowing garment, known as a *k'sa*.

The equivalent robe in French-speaking West Africa is called a *Grand Boubou*.

Is there any land on Earth that doesn't belong to any country?

Yes, there are two such places.

The first is Marie Byrd Land in western Antarctica, which is so remote that no government seems to want it.

It's a vast swathe of the Earth's surface, spreading out from the South Pole to the Antarctic coast and covering 1,610,000 square kilometres (622,000 square miles). This is larger than Iran or Mongolia, but it's so inhospitable that it supports only one permanent base, which belongs to the USA. Marie Byrd Land is named after the wife of US Rear-Admiral Richard E. Byrd (1888–1957), who first explored it in 1929. The remote research station was the inspiration for John Carpenter's classic horror film, *The Thing* (1982).

The rest of Antarctica is administered by twelve nations under the Antarctic Treaty system established in 1961, which made the continent a scientific preserve and banned all military activity there. The biggest territories belong to the nations that first explored the continent (Britain, Norway and France) and those that are closest (New Zealand, Australia, Chile and Argentina). The ocean beyond Marie Byrd Land stretches up into the empty reaches of the South Pacific, where no one nation is close enough to claim it as their own.

The legal term for a territory outside the sovereign control of any state is *Terra nullius,* literally 'no-man's-land'. Although Marie Byrd Land is the biggest remaining example, there is one small tract of Africa that can claim the same status.

The Bir Tawil Triangle lies between Egypt and Sudan and is owned by neither. In 1899, when the British controlled the area, they defined the border between the two countries by drawing a straight line through a map of the desert. This put Bir Tawil in Sudan and the piece of land next door, called the Halai'b Triangle, in Egypt. The boundary was redrawn (using wigglier lines) in 1902. Bir Tawil ('water well' in Arabic) went to Egypt, and Halai'b to the Sudan.

Bir Tawil is the size of Buckinghamshire – 2,000 square kilometres (770 square miles) – and you'd think both countries would be fighting over it, but they're not. What they both want is Halai'b. Whereas Bir Tawil is mostly sand and rock, Halai'b is fertile, populated, on the Red Sea coast and ten times larger. Egypt currently occupies it, citing the 1899 boundary. Sudan disputes the claim, citing the 1902 amendment. Both disown Bir Tawil for the same reason.

The world's most disputed territory is the Spratly Islands, an archipelago of 750 uninhabited islets in the South Pacific: 4 square kilometres (1½ square miles) of land spread over 425,000 square kilometres (164,000 square miles) of sea. Rich fishing grounds and potential oil and gas fields mean that six nations claim them: the Philippines, China, Taiwan, Vietnam, Malaysia and Brunei. Apart from Brunei, all maintain a military presence in the area. To strengthen their claim, the Philippines pay a rotating team of public sector employees to live on one of the Spratlys. It isn't a popular posting: the charm of a tiny tropical rock that can be walked round in thirty minutes soon fades.

Which country is the river Nile in?

Despite its timeless association with Egypt, most of the Nile is in Sudan.

The Nile rises in Rwanda, in the Great Lakes area of Central Africa, and flows through Ethiopia, Uganda, the Democratic Republic of Congo and Egypt, but the largest section traverses Sudan. The river's two great tributaries – the Blue and White Niles – meet in Khartoum, the country's capital.

Sudan is the largest country in Africa, covering 2,505,813 square kilometres (967,500 square miles), making it bigger than Western Europe and a quarter of the size of the USA. It is also the largest country in the Arab world. Because of its political and military precariousness, no one is quite sure what its current population is, but most estimates suggest 40 million, with four times as many living in the Arabic-speaking Muslim north as in the largely Christian south.

The northern Muslim population is descended from Arab invaders and the indigenous Nubian people, one of black Africa's earliest civilisations. The name 'Nubia' comes from the Egyptian *nbu*, 'gold', as the region was famous for its gold mines. From the seventh century AD, waves of Arab invaders spread out from Damascus and Baghdad, establishing Islam throughout north-west Africa. The first Nubian Muslim ruler ascended to the throne in AD 1093 and northern Sudan has been a part of the Islamic world ever since.

'Sudan' means 'black' in Arabic. It comes from the Arabic *bilad as-sudan* meaning 'land of the black people' and southern and western Sudan contains a complex mix of almost 600 black African tribal groups, speaking over 400 different languages and dialects. Many of them are Christian, or practise traditional African religions. The Dinka – whose name means 'the people' and who are, at over a million strong, Sudan's largest tribal group – practise both.

For over thirty years, the northern government and the southern tribes like the Dinka were locked in civil war. Ending in 1989, the war cost the lives of more than 2 million people and displaced another 4 million. It is estimated that 200,000 southern Sudanese have been forced into slavery in the north. Most of them are Dinka. In 2005 Southern Sudan was finally granted autonomy and this is being implemented by the United Nations.

In the meantime, the Northern Islamic government has been accused of genocide by using terrorist militias to destroy three tribal groups in the western region of Darfur. In 2008 the International Criminal Court (ICC) issued an arrest warrant for President Omar al-Bashir, charging him with war crimes and crimes against humanity. This is the first time the court has brought charges against a serving head of state.

Sudan is 150th out of 182 nations on the UN's human development index. One in five Sudanese lives on less than £1 a day. In the 2009 Happy Planet Index, which measures well-being and environmental impact, Sudan is ranked 121 out of 143, though this beats both Luxembourg and Estonia.

What was Cleopatra's nationality?

She was Greek.

Cleopatra (literally meaning 'renowned in her ancestry') was a direct descendant of Ptolemy I (303–285 BC), the right-hand man to Alexander the Great. On Alexander's death in 325 BC, Ptolemy's loyalty was rewarded with the governorship of Egypt. Like Alexander, Ptolemy came from Macedon, north of Greece. The Macedonians had hereditary, all-powerful kings and despised the newfangled ideas of the south, crushing democracy in Athens in 322 BC. In keeping with his heritage, Ptolemy appointed himself Pharaoh of Egypt in 305 BC, founding a dynasty that would last 275 years.

The Ptolemaic court spoke Greek and behaved as an occupying foreign power, rather like the British in India. The Ptolemies, like all Pharoahs in Egypt, were also gods and they were a close-knit bunch. All the male heirs were called Ptolemy and the women were usually either Cleopatra or Berenice. Brothers and sisters often married each other, to keep things in the family and reinforce their aloofness from their subjects. This makes the Ptolemaic family tree almost impossible to follow.

For example, the Cleopatra we know is Cleopatra VII (69–30 BC), but her mother might have been either Cleopatra V or VI. Our Cleopatra's father, Ptolemy XII (117–51 BC), married his sister, who was also his cousin. It was a tiny gene pool: Cleopatra had only four great-grandparents and six (out of a possible sixteen) great-great-grandparents. The sculptures and coins that survive make clear that she wasn't as beautiful as Shakespeare painted her, but nor did she have the classic Ptolemy look – fat with bulging eyes – that resulted from centuries of inbreeding. And, though no one knows exactly which of her relatives gave birth to her, ethnically she was pure Macedonian Greek.

Despite this, she identified strongly with Egypt. She became queen at eighteen and ruled the country for more than two decades. She was the first Ptolemy to learn the Egyptian language and had herself portrayed in traditional Egyptian dress. She was ruthless in removing any threats to her power, arranging for the murder of two siblings and plunging the country into civil war to take on the third, her brother (and husband), Ptolemy XIII.

When senior courtiers backed Ptolemy, she responded by seducing Julius Caesar, recently elected as *dictator* (senior magistrate in the Roman Senate), and commander of the most powerful army in the world. Together they crushed all opposition. When Caesar was assassinated, leading to civil war in Rome, Cleopatra seduced his second-in-command, Mark Antony. In the midst of all this, she still found time to write a book on cosmetics.

The war ended when the Roman fleet under Octavian (later the Emperor Augustus) defeated Mark Antony at the battle of Actium (31 BC). Antony committed suicide in the belief that Cleopatra had already done so and she poisoned herself (though the latest research suggests no asps were involved). She was the last pharoah. The Romans made off with so much Egyptian gold that the Senate was immediately able to reduce interest rates from 12 per cent to 4 per cent.

STEPHEN *Donkeys' milk is very nutritious indeed; it contains oligosaccharides, which are very, very good for you and have all kinds of immuno-helpful things, don't they, Dr Garden?*

GRAEME GARDEN *I'm sure they do, yes. Very good for bathing in, too. Wasn't Cleopatra in ass's milk?*

STEPHEN *She was in ass's milk, absolutely, and Poppaea, the wife of Nero: 300 donkeys were milked to fill her bath.*

GRAEME *Big girl, was she?*

Why did Julius Caesar wear a laurel wreath?

Not victory, but vanity.

According to the Roman historian Suetonius in *On the Life of the Caesars* (AD 121), Julius Caesar 'used to comb forward his scanty locks from the crown of his head' and was thrilled when the Senate granted him the special privilege of being able to wear a victor's laurel wreath whenever he felt like it.

Caesar's baldness bothered him a lot. During his affair with Cleopatra, she recommended her own patent baldness cure, a salve made from burnt mice, bear grease, horse's teeth and deer marrow, rubbed on the head until it 'sprouts'. Clearly, it wasn't very effective.

Caesar wasn't the only general with hair-loss problems. According to the Greek historian Polybius, the Carthaginian commander Hannibal (247–183 BC) found a way to get round this: 'He had a number of wigs made, dyed to suit the appearance of persons differing widely in age, and kept constantly changing them.' Even those closest to Hannibal had trouble recognising him.

Before the establishment of the Empire, Roman hair was worn simply. Only afterwards did hair styles become more elaborate and wigs more popular. The Empress Messalina (AD 17–48) had an extensive collection of yellow wigs, which she wore when moonlighting in brothels. (By law, Roman prostitutes had to wear a yellow wig as a badge of their profession.) Wigs continued to be worn after Rome became Christian in AD 313 but the Church soon condemned them as a mortal sin.

The tradition of a laurel wreath being given to the victor began at the Pythian Games in Delphi in the sixth century BC. These were held in honour of the god Apollo, usually portrayed wearing a wreath of laurels in memory of the nymph Daphne, who turned herself into a laurel tree to escape his amorous advances.

As well as indicating victory, the laurel had a reputation as a healing plant, so doctors who graduated also received a laurel wreath. This is the origin of the academic expressions baccalaureate, Bachelor of Arts (BA) and Bachelor of Science (BSc). They all come from the Latin *bacca lauri*, 'laurel berries'.

No one knows where the Latin surname Caesar comes from.

Pliny the Elder thought it was because the first Caesar (like Macduff) was 'cut from his mother's womb' – *caesus* means 'cut' in Latin. Pliny's idea is the origin of the term 'Caesarian section'. But this can't be true: such operations were only ever performed to rescue a baby whose mother had died, and Caesar's mother, Aurelia, is known to have lived for many years after his birth.

The most likely meaning of 'Caesar' is that it's from the Latin *caesaries*, which means 'a beautiful head of hair'.

What was Caesar talking about when he said 'Veni, vidi, vici'?

Most of us think *'Veni, vidi, vici'* ('I came, I saw, I conquered') – Julius Caesar's second most famous line after *'Et tu, Brute'* – refers to his invasion of Britain.

In fact, as every schoolboy knows, he was summing up his victory over King Pharnaces II of Pontus at the battle of Zela in 47 BC.

At the time the Roman civil war was at its height, with Caesar leading the Senate's modernisers and Gnaeus Pompeius Magnus (better known as Pompey) commanding the traditionalist forces.

The kingdom of Pontus, on the southern coast of the Black Sea, had proved a troublesome enemy to Rome over the years. Knowing Caesar was preoccupied fighting Pompey in Egypt, King Pharnaces spotted his chance to regain some lost territory and invaded Cappadocia, in what is now northern Turkey. He inflicted a heavy defeat on the depleted Roman defence, and rumours spread that he had tortured Roman prisoners.

When Caesar returned victorious from Egypt, he decided to teach Pharnaces a lesson. At Zela he defeated the large, well-organised Pontic army in just five days and couldn't resist crowing about it in a letter to his friend Amantius in Rome: hence the quote. Suetonius even claims Caesar paraded the famous phrase around after the battle itself. It was to prove a decisive moment in the civil war against Pompey and his supporters, and in Caesar's career.

Caesar's attempted invasion of Britain was a much less satisfactory affair. He invaded twice, in 55 and 54 BC. The first time, he landed near Deal in Kent. The lack of a natural harbour meant his troops had to leap into deep water and wade towards the large British force that had gathered on the shore. Only the on-board Roman catapults kept the blue-painted natives at bay. After a few skirmishes, Caesar decided to cut his losses and withdrew to Gaul.

The following year he returned with 10,000 men and sailed up the Thames, where he tried to establish a Roman ally as king. He left shortly afterwards, complaining there was nothing worth having in Britain and that the locals were an ungovernable horde of wife-swapping, chicken-tormenting barbarians. No Romans stayed behind.

The whole invasion was staged for the Senate's benefit: conquering the 'land beyond the ocean' made Caesar look good at home. This set the pattern for Rome's involvement with Britain: trade and Roman influence continued to grow without the need for full occupation. When that finally happened, ninety-six years later under the Emperor Claudius, it took four legions – 15 per cent of the whole Roman army – to do the job.

The phrase *'veni, vidi, vici'* lives on today in the scientific name of the Conquered lorikeet, an extinct species of South Pacific parrot discovered in 1987. A member of the *Vini* genus, its full name is *Vini vidivici*.

How many men did a centurion command in the Roman Empire?

Eighty.

The actual number of soldiers in each Roman legion changed over time and in different places, and the army was always short of men. Legions were at first divided into ten cohorts, each consisting of six centuries of a hundred men, or 6,000 men in all. But well before Julius Caesar came along, and right through the Roman Empire that followed him, the full strength of a legion had settled at 4,800 men. Each cohort was made up of 480 men and each of its six centuries comprised eighty soldiers, led by a centurion.

The smallest division of the Roman army was the *contubernium*, originally a unit of ten men who lived, ate and fought together. The word is from Latin *con*, 'together' and *taberna*, 'a hut' – military tents were made from boards, or *tabulae*. Such intimacy had the effect of transforming the soldiers into comrades, or *contubernales*, and it was the basis of the Roman army's legendary *esprit de corps*. We know there were ten of them in each tent, because the man in charge was called the *decanus*, meaning 'a chief of ten, one set over ten persons'.

Each century was made up of ten *contubernii*.

By Caesar's time, though, the number of men in each *contubernium* had shrunk to eight, although their leader was still called a *decanus*. It seems that, although a fighting unit of ten men worked well enough when near to home, as the Romans expanded far beyond Italy military experience in distant, dangerous and unfamiliar places found that an eight-man unit was the ideal size for close bonds between soldiers. So, because army rules had always decreed ten *contubernii* in a century, a century became eighty men.

Another Roman official, who might have been in charge of 100 men but wasn't, was the *praetor hastarius*, or 'president of the spear'. Praetors were judges, and the spear was the symbol of property. The *praetor hastarius* presided over a court that dealt with property disputes and resolving wills. Court members were drawn from a pool of *centumviri*, or Hundred Men. But there were never exactly 100 of them. Originally there were 105 – three from each of the 35 Roman tribes – and this later grew to 180.

A hundred of anything is rarer than you might think. The English language has, buried within it, a numbering system that used twelve rather than ten as a base. That's why we say eleven (*endleofan*, which meant 'one left') and twelve ('two left') instead of *tenty-one* and *tenty-two*. The Old English word for 'a hundred' was *hund*, but there were three different kinds – *hund teantig* (a hundred 'tenty' is 100); *hund endleofantig* (a hundred 'eleventy' is 110) and *hund twelftig* (a hundred 'twelfty' is 120). These lasted for many centuries. The expression 'a great hundred' meant 120 well into the sixteenth century and a 'hundredweight', today meaning 112 pounds, was once 120 pounds.

By coincidence, each legion of Roman infantry had a detachment of (much less important) cavalry. There were 120 of them in each legion.

What language was mostly spoken in ancient Rome?

It was Greek, not Latin.

A *lingua franca* is a language used between two people when neither is using their mother tongue. Rome was the capital city of a fast and expanding empire, a commercial hub of over a million people. Although the native language of Rome (capital of Latium) was Latin, the *lingua franca* – the language you would use if you were buying or selling or generally trying to make yourself understood – was *koine* or 'common' Greek.

Greek was also the language of choice for Rome's educated urban elite. Sophisticated Romans saw themselves as the inheritors of Greek culture. Virgil's *Aeneid* – the epic poem that tells the story of Rome's foundation – makes it explicit that contemporary Rome grew directly out of the mythical Greece that Homer had written about. Speaking Greek at home was essential. Most of the literature that upper-class Romans read was in Greek; the art, architecture, horticulture, cookery and fashion they admired was Greek; and most of their teachers and domestic staff were Greeks.

Even when they did speak Latin it wasn't the classical Latin that we recognise. For speaking native Romans used a form of the language called 'Vulgar Latin'. The word vulgar simply meant 'common' or 'of the people'. Classical Latin was the written language – used for law, oratory and administration but not for conversation. It was the everyday version that the Roman army carried across Europe and it was Vulgar, not classical Latin that spawned the Romance languages: Italian, French and Spanish.

But Vulgar Latin was only the daily language of Latium, not the Empire. Greek was the first language of the eastern Empire, based around Constantinople, and of the cities in southern Italy. The name Naples (*Neapolis* in Latin) is actually

Greek (*nea*, new, and *polis*, city). Today, the local dialect in Naples, Neopolitana, still shows traces of Greek and the Griko language is still spoken by 30,000 in southern Italy. Modern Greek and Griko are close enough for speakers to be able to understand one another. Greek, not Latin, was the popular choice for the Mediterranean marketplace.

Lingua Franca was originally an Italian – not a Latin – term for the specific language that was used by people trading in the Mediterranean from the eleventh to the nineteenth century. Based on Italian, it combined elements of Provencal, Spanish, Portuguese, Greek, French and Arabic into a flexible lingo everyone could speak and understand.

Lingua Franca doesn't mean 'French language', but 'Language of the Franks'. It derives from the Arabic habit of referring to all Christians as 'Franks' (rather as we once referred to all Muslims as 'Moors'). *Franji* remains a common Arabic word used to describe Westerners today.

Where is English the official language?

There are many countries in which English is the official language, but England, Australia and the United States aren't among them.

An official language is defined as a language that has been given legal status for use in a nation's courts, parliament and administration. In England, Australia and over half the USA, English is the *unofficial* language. It is used for all state business, but no specific law has ever ratified its use.

Bilingual countries such as Canada (French and English) and Wales (Welsh and English) do have legally defined official languages. National laws often recognise significant minority languages, as with Maori in New Zealand. Sometimes, as in Ireland, an official language is more symbolic than practical: fewer than 20 per cent of the population use Irish every day.

English is frequently chosen as an alternative 'official' language if a country has many native languages. A good example is Papua New Guinea where 6 million people speak 830 different languages. In the USA the campaign to make English the official language is opposed by many other ethnic groups, most notably the Hispanic community who account for more than 15 per cent of the population.

Perhaps the most interesting case of an English-speaking country that doesn't have English as its official language is Australia. As well as large numbers of Greek, Italian and South-East Asian immigrants, Australia is home to 65,000 native Maltese speakers. There are also 150 aboriginal languages which are still spoken (compared to the 600 or so spoken in the eighteenth century). Of these, all but twenty are likely to disappear in the next fifty years. Attempting to declare English the official language risks looking insensitive.

The Vatican is the only country in the world that has Latin as an official language.

When did Parliament make slavery illegal in England?

6 April 2010.

With a few minor exceptions, slavery was abolished throughout the British Empire in 1833, but it wasn't thought necessary to outlaw it at home.

In 1067, according to the Domesday Book, more than 10 per cent of the population of England were slaves. The

Normans, perhaps surprisingly, were opposed to slavery on religious grounds and within fifty years it had virtually disappeared. Even serfdom (a kind of modified slavery) became increasingly rare and Queen Elizabeth I freed the last remaining serfs in 1574.

At the same time, Britain was becoming a colonial power and it was the height of fashion for returning Englishmen to have a 'black manservant' (who was in fact, of course, a slave). This unseemly habit was made illegal by the courts in 1772 when the judge, Lord Mansfield, reportedly declared: 'The air of England is too pure for any slave to breathe', with the result that thousands of slaves in England gained their freedom.

From that moment, slavery was arguably illegal in England (though not in the British Empire) under Common Law, but this was not confirmed by Parliament until the Coroners and Justice Act.

Previous acts of Parliament dealt with kidnap, false imprisonment, trafficking for sexual exploitation and forced labour, but never specifically covered slavery. Now, Section 71 of the Coroners and Justice Act (which came into force on 6 April 2010) makes it an offence in the UK, punishable by up to fourteen years' imprisonment, to hold a person in 'slavery or servitude'.

'Servitude' is another word for serfdom. A serf is permanently attached to a piece of land and forced to live and work there, whereas a slave can be bought and sold directly like a piece of property. It's a fine difference: in fact, the English word 'serf' comes from the Latin word *servus*, 'a slave'.

Until now, the lack of a specific English law has made it hard to prosecute modern slave-masters. There's a difference between 'abolishing' something and making it a criminal offence. Although slavery was *abolished* all over the world many years ago, in many countries the *reality* only changed when laws were introduced to punish slave owners.

You might think slavery is a thing of the past and isn't relevant to modern Britain, but there are more slaves in the world now – 27 million of them – than were ever seized from Africa in the 400 years of the transatlantic slave trade. And forced labour, using migrant workers effectively as slaves (and also outlawed by the Act), is widespread in Britain today.

Under the Criminal Law Act 1967, a number of obsolete crimes were abolished in England including scolding, eavesdropping, being a common nightwalker and challenging someone to a fight.

It is odd to think that, in the year England won the World Cup, eavesdropping was still illegal but slavery wasn't.

ALAN *I bet it was one of these odd little New Labour laws in about 1996, 7, 8 . . .*

STEPHEN *What an odd law, to outlaw slavery. It's political correctness gone mad!*

Why doesn't Britain have a written constitution?

It does have one.

The idea that Britain has an 'unwritten constitution' has been described by Professor Vernon Bogdanor, the country's leading constitutional expert, as 'misleading'.

The rules setting out the balance of power between the governors and the governed *are* written down. They're just not all written down in *one place*.

The British constitution is composed of several documents, including Magna Carta (1215), the Petition of Right Act (1628), the Bill of Rights (1689), the Act of Settlement (1701), the Parliament Acts (1911 and 1949) and the Representation of the People Act (1969). Between them, they cover most of the key principles that, in other countries, appear in a single formal statement: that justice may not be denied or delayed; that no tax can be raised without parliament's approval; that no one can be imprisoned without lawful cause; that judges are independent of the government; and that the unelected Lords cannot indefinitely block Acts passed by the elected Commons. They also say who can vote, and how the royal succession works.

There's also 'case law', in which decisions made by courts become part of the constitution. An important example is the Case of Proclamations (1611), which found that the king (and thus his modern equivalent, the government) cannot create a new offence by merely *announcing* it. In other words, nothing is against the law until proper legislation says it is.

The reason why Britain doesn't have a single written document (and almost every other parliamentary democracy does) is to do with its age. The British state has evolved over a millennium and a half. It had no founding fathers, or moment of creation, so its constitution has continued to develop bit by bit.

This has left some surprising gaps. The Cabinet has no legal existence; it is purely a matter of convention. The law established neither of the Houses of Parliament and, although the office of Prime Minister was formally recognised in 1937, British law has never defined what the PM's role actually is.

But that's not as unusual as it might sound. There is no constitution anywhere whose authors have thought of everything. The US Constitution does not contain one word on the subject of how elections should be conducted.

Whether that would surprise many US citizens is hard to say. In 2002 a survey by Columbia Law School found that almost two-thirds of Americans identified the phrase 'From each according to his ability, to each according to his needs' as a quotation from the US constitution rather than coming from the pen of the founder of communism, Karl Marx (1818–83).

What does a British judge bang to keep order in court?

British judges do not, and never have, used gavels – only British auctioneers.

Actors playing judges on TV and in films in Britain use them because their real-life American counterparts do. After decades of exposure to US movies and TV series, they have become part of the visual grammar of the courtroom. Another self-perpetuating legal cliché is referring to the judge as 'M'Lud'. Real British barristers never do this: the correct form of address is 'My Lord'.

The origin of the word *gavel* is obscure. The original English word *gafol* dates from the eighth century and meant a 'payment' or 'tribute', usually a quantity of corn or a division of land. The earliest known use of the word *gavel* to mean 'a chairman's hammer' dates from 1860, so it's hard to see a connection. Some sources claim it might have been used earlier than this among Freemasons (as a term for a mason's hammer), but the evidence is faint.

Modern gavels are small ceremonial mallets commonly made of hardwood, sometimes with a handle. They are used to call for attention, to indicate the opening (call to order) and closing (adjournment) of proceedings, and to announce the striking of a binding bargain in an auction.

The US procedural guidebook – *Robert's Rules of Order Newly Revised* (1876) – provides advice on the proper use of the gavel in the USA. It states that the person in the chair is never to use the gavel in an attempt to drown out a disorderly member, nor should they lean on the gavel, juggle or toy with it, or use it to challenge or threaten, or to emphasise remarks.

The handleless ivory gavel of the United States Senate was presented by the Republic of India to replace one that had been in continuous use since 1789. The new one was first used on 17 November 1954. The original had been broken earlier in 1954, when Vice-President Richard Nixon brandished it during a heated debate on nuclear energy. Unable to obtain a piece of ivory large enough to replace the historic heirloom, the Senate appealed for help to the Indian embassy, who duly obliged.

The gavel of the United States House of Representatives is plain and wooden and has been broken and replaced many times.

STEPHEN *British judges have never had gavels. Never.*
JACK DEE *Sometimes, if they're conducting an auction at the same time, they do.*

What does European law force British fishermen to do?

If you read the British popular press, your answer is bound to be: 'wear hairnets'. This isn't true.

Under EU rules only people who work in fish-processing factories must have their heads covered, to prevent their hair ending up in our fish fingers.

This particular Euro-myth is unusual in having an identifiable beginning. Former Euro MP Wayne David told the House of Commons in July 2002 that he had overheard a group of British journalists joking about it in a Brussels bar: 'They had invented the story about fishermen's hairnets and sent it back to the UK, and to their amazement, it hit the front pages.'

One of the 'myths' most quoted by pro-Europeans is the belief that the EU has banned bent bananas. Their Eurosceptic counterparts point out that rules governing banana shape certainly do exist. Commission Regulation (EC) 2257/94 decrees that bananas must be 'free from malformation or abnormal curvature', even though no bananas have ever been 'banned' as such.

Unhelpfully this rule does not define or quantify 'abnormal curvature', whereas Commission Regulation (EEC) 1677/88 does specify that the permissible bend of Class I cucumbers may be up to 10 mm per 10 cm (0.4 of an inch per 4 inches).

Nevertheless, many of the myths are entirely unfounded. In 1997 British newspapers announced that it was to be made compulsory for motorway bridges to carry works of art glorifying leading EU figures. The *Daily Mail* voiced the concerns of Tory MEP Graham Mather that, if the scheme were to get off the ground, Britain could be inundated by more statues and busts of former EU Commission President Jacques Delors than there were of Winston Churchill. 'It's a terrifying prospect,' said Mr Mather, 'and might frighten people.' The actual proposal was entirely reasonable. It was to set aside 1 per cent of the EU public works subsidy to spend on art that would 'bring people together and promote human dignity and a spirit of tolerance'.

There was also a notorious *Daily Telegraph* report that official notices would have to be displayed on mountains warning climbers that they were 'in a high place'. The Commission explained that this was a misinterpretation of safety rules. It applied only to people *working* at heights, such as scaffolders – not to those engaged in leisure activities.

Perhaps the strangest example of a genuine EU regulation is the ambiguous message printed on tins of nasal snuff: 'EEC Council Directive (992/41/EEC) CAUSES CANCER', which suggests that it's the directive itself that is deadly, rather than the snuff.

DAVID MITCHELL *Well, it makes practical sense as well, of course, because the hairnet could also catch any smaller fish, like, you know, whitebait or scampi that might get in the hair of the fisherman, and then at the end of the day . . . 'Oh, that's dinner!'*

Why have firemen's poles been banned?

They haven't. 'Health-and-safety-mad' bureaucrats still allow fire stations to be built with the traditional poles in them.

Firefighters on the night shift spend their time in dormitories or rest rooms. When the call to action comes, they leap out of bed and dash to their engines. To get there from the upper floor of the station, sliding down a pole is quicker (and safer) than hurtling down stairs. But, either way, a bunch of half-asleep people trying to get down in a tearing hurry can still lead to a twisted ankle – which isn't much use in an emergency.

The obvious solution is not to use poles *or* stairs, but to build the fire station entirely on the ground floor, and this is now standard practice. However, in built-up areas where land is scarce, new stations are still multilevel. In those, poles are generally installed and old stations have mostly retained their poles.

The 'poles banned' myth can be traced to a flurry of misleading newspaper reports published in the summer of 2006, about a refurbished, pole-free station that had opened in Plymouth. The *Daily Mail* began its shock exposé with the words: 'Barmy fire chiefs came under a blaze of criticism today after they banned the traditional fireman's pole – because it posed a "health and safety hazard".' Meanwhile, the *Mirror* found a 'local pensioner' eager to provide the voice of common sense: 'It's barmy. Can't they just put a pile of cotton wool at the bottom of the pole?' The truth was less sensational: the shape of the renovated building had simply made a pole impractical. The Devon Fire Brigade had not adopted a 'no-pole' policy.

Some basic safety measures arrived surprisingly late in firefighting history. The London Fire Brigade continued using brass helmets until 1936, when it occurred to someone that a non-conductive material might be less of a risk when electric cables were flailing around the firemen's heads. (New York firemen, by contrast, had worn leather helmets for over a century.) Yellow helmets and trousers (for visibility) weren't issued in the UK until the 1970s, and fireproof jackets only replaced woollen ones in 1989.

You may have heard that the fire brigade – and fire insurance – was invented by the US founding father, Benjamin Franklin (1706–90). It's not true: when he started Philadelphia's first fire brigade in 1736 (and the first fire insurance scheme in 1751) such things had long existed in Britain and other countries, and were already established in several US cities. Nor did Franklin invent the fireman's coat; when called to fires, his men wore whatever was to hand. They were well equipped, though: with leather buckets, hoses, fire hooks, ladders and water-pumping engines – all of them imported from Britain.

STEPHEN *What happened to the fireman's pole?*
ROB BRYDON *He tiled the fireman's bathroom.*

Why was absinthe made illegal?

It was never illegal in Britain and it doesn't send you mad.

Few drinks have attracted the hysteria that surrounded absinthe at the end of the nineteenth century. Known as the 'Green Fairy', it was supposed to have enslaved and then destroyed the minds of a whole generation of artists and writers. Vincent van Gogh, Arthur Rimbaud, Charles Baudelaire, Paul Gauguin, Henri de Toulouse-Lautrec, Oscar Wilde and Aleister Crowley were all dedicated *absintheurs* and every kind of depravity was ascribed to its hallucinogenic effects. Alexander Dumas (1802–70) even claimed that absinthe had killed more French soldiers in North Africa than Arab bullets.

The high point of 'absinthe madness' came in 1905, when a Swiss alcoholic called Jean Lanfray shot his wife and two young daughters while drunk (he said he did it because his wife had refused to clean his shoes). He had drunk copious amounts of wine, cognac, brandy and crème de menthe that day, but it was the two glasses of absinthe he'd also had that got the blame. A storm of temperance-led moral outrage followed, which led to absinthe being banned in the United States and across most of Europe (though never in the UK). The prohibition has only recently been lifted.

The crack-cocaine of its day was (and is) made from daisies. Wormwood, or *Artemisia absinthium*, is a member of the daisy family and was prized as a medicinal herb from ancient times. Among many other things, it was used as a cure for intestinal worms, though this wasn't the origin of the name 'worm' wood. It comes from the Old English *wermod* – literally 'man-courage' (it was once also used as an aphrodisiac). Before absinthe came along, wormwood was already a popular flavouring for alcoholic drinks. Vermouth, invented in Italy in the late eighteenth century, took its name from the German for wormwood (*wermut*) and many contemporary brands (Punt e Mes, Green Chartreuse, Bénédictine) still include wormwood in their recipes.

The active ingredient in wormwood is thujone (pronounced 'thoo-shone'), so called because it was first found in the aromatic Thuja tree, a sort of cedar also known as Arborvitae ('tree of life'). Similar in chemical structure to menthol, thujone can be dangerous in high doses and does have a mild psychoactive effect, but not at the 10 milligrams per litre concentration that most absinthe contains. Sage, tarragon and Vicks VapoRub all contain similar levels of thujone, but no one has yet linked them to depraved behaviour.

The legendary effects of absinthe are almost certainly due to its high alcohol content, which, at 50–75 per cent by volume, comfortably exceeds most other spirits (usually 40 per cent). Preparing a glass of absinthe involved an elaborate ritual in which water was poured into the spirit through a special perforated spoon holding a sugar cube. This diluted it, and took the edge off any bitterness.

The clouding effect the water produces was known as the louche, It isn't certain that it is connected to the Old French word *lousche* which originally meant 'to squint' and gave us the modern louche, meaning shady or disreputable. But whether used to mean squinting, cloudy or dubious, louche is the perfect adjective for a dedicated *absintheur*.

ALAN *I had some absinthe in a bar in Manchester, and they made it over a hot spoon. And it was trannie night. And I enjoyed it much more after the absinthe than before.*

STEPHEN *What was it Ernest Dowson said? 'Absinthe makes the tart grow fonder.'*

How many countries are represented in the G20 group of leading economies?

It's not twenty, but it is The Answer.

The G20 group was created after the financial crises of the late 1990s, in an attempt to bring stability to the global economy. Previously known as the G33 and, before that, the G22, its formal title is 'The Group of Twenty Finance Ministers and Central Bank Governors'. The representatives are drawn from nineteen countries: Argentina, Australia, Brazil, Canada, China, France, Germany, India, Indonesia, Italy, Japan, Mexico, Russia, Saudi Arabia, South Africa, South Korea, Turkey, the UK and the USA.

The twentieth seat is held by the European Union.

There are currently twenty-seven members of the EU, but France, Germany, Italy and the United Kingdom are already in the original list of nineteen. So, adding the remaining twenty-three countries of the EU to the original nineteen members, gives us the total number of countries represented by the G20.

Rather pleasingly, it is forty-two.

According to Douglas Adams in *The Hitchhiker's Guide to the Galaxy*, forty-two is The Answer to Life, the Universe and Everything. Whether or not that is true, it's definitely the answer to The Number of Countries in the G20.

And forty-two is also the number of dots on a pair of dice, the number of years winter lasts on Uranus and the length in centimetres of the penis of the Argentinian Lake duck.

Fully extended and relative to its size, this is the longest of any vertebrate.

Which European country has the lowest age of consent?

Vatican City. You can legally have sex there with a twelve-year-old.

This bizarre situation goes back to the time when the Vatican was established as a sovereign state (separate from the papal diocese of the Holy See) under the Lateran Treaty of 1929.

Until 1930 the age of consent in the whole of Italy was twelve. The fact that it still is in the Vatican has more to do with death than sex. The death penalty had been abolished in Italy in 1889, but Mussolini reintroduced it in 1926. When the Vatican City State was born three years later – and had to choose a legal system – it decided against capital punishment and adopted the laws in force in Italy on 31 December 1924. From then on, as an independent country, the Vatican had no further connection with Italian law. When Italy raised its age of consent from twelve to fourteen in 1930, the Vatican saw no need to follow suit. Over half its population consisted of celibate Catholic priests and no children lived there at all, so it can't have seemed particularly relevant.

Today, outside Europe, the age of consent in Angola is also twelve, as it is in parts of Mexico. In most Arab states sex is illegal outside marriage, but children can be married at younger than twelve. An exception to this is Tunisia, which has the world's oldest age of consent (twenty). North Korea has no age of consent at all.

The Vatican has its own banking system, coinage, telephone network, post office and radio station. Banking operations are shrouded in secrecy. There is no income tax and no restriction on the export or import of money. Its small size results in several statistical anomalies. For example, it has the highest crime rate in the world: with a population of barely 800, more than 1,000 offences are recorded each year. (Fortunately, this is mostly pick-pocketing and purse-snatching rather than sex crimes.) The Vatican also has the highest number of helipads and TV stations per capita in the world, and also the most restricted voting system (you have to be a cardinal under eighty years of age). It is also the only country in the world that has no hotels.

English law first imposed a legal age of consent in 1275. It, too, was set at twelve, but the law was muddied by the anti-witchcraft frenzy of the sixteenth century. Men accused of underage sex could plead 'bewitchment'. The mere mention of the word was often enough for them to escape conviction. In 1875 the age of consent was raised to thirteen and it reached its present level of sixteen ten years later.

An age of consent for homosexual sex was first proposed in 1957, after a three-year inquiry headed by Sir John Wolfenden (1906–85). He suggested twenty-one as a suitable age but it took another decade before this was finally made law in 1967. In 1994 the age of same-sex consent was lowered to eighteen and it was reduced again in 2001 to sixteen, bringing it into line with the consensual age for everyone else.

The 1994 bill was also the first British legislation ever to mention lesbian sex, setting the age of consent between two women at sixteen.

Who lives in Europe's smallest houses?

We do.

According to a survey by the *Commission for Architecture and the Built Environment* (CABE), the British build the pokiest homes in Europe. The UK has both the smallest new houses and smallest average room size.

The average size of a room in a new house in France is 26.9 square metres. The equivalent in the UK is 15.8 square metres – only a smidgeon larger than a standard parking space (14 square metres).

In terms of overall floor space, the UK average for new homes is a miserly 76 square metres, less than a third of the size of the average tennis court. This compares to: Ireland (88 square metres); Spain (97 square metres); France (113 square metres) and Denmark (137 square metres).

Outside Europe, the comparisons are even less flattering. Australian homes cover an average area of 206 square metres and American homes are nearly three times as big as ours at 214 square metres.

There have been attempts to alter things for the better. In 1961 Sir Parker Morris (1891–1972), an urban planner and founder of the Housing Association's Charitable Trust, chaired a government report called *Homes for Today and Tomorrow*. Out of this came a set of specifications, called the 'Parker Morris' standards. These went though each room in a standard house, laying down what the minimum floor space per inhabitant should be, the number of flushing toilets required, the acceptable standard of heating to be installed and a sensible amount of space for each essential piece of furniture. By 1967 the specifications had been adopted by all new towns, all local authority housing departments and most private developers.

The Parker Morris standards were abolished in 1980. Under Mrs Thatcher's iron rule, local authorities were urged to give priority to market forces instead. There are still no national minimum space standards for the UK, though in 2008 Boris Johnson, the Mayor of London, pledged to reintroduce them for the capital in an updated, 10 per cent more generous form.

Today almost three-quarters of UK residents say there's not enough space in their kitchen for three small recycling bins, while half complain they don't have enough space to use their furniture comfortably. More than a third claim their kitchens are too small even for a toaster or microwave and almost half say they don't have enough space to entertain visitors.

The expression 'not enough room to swing a cat' does not, as some people think, refer to the space needed to brandish a 'cat o'nine tails' whip. The first recorded use of the phrase (1665) is three decades earlier than the first use of the term 'cat o'nine tails' (1695).

In Britain, when we say 'not enough room to swing a cat', we mean it literally.

Which country is the most successful military power in European history?

France.

If you enter 'French military victories' on Google, a cheeky bit of software pops up with the message: 'Did you mean French military defeats?' This, plus the 'cheese-eating surrender monkeys' tag immortalised by *The Simpsons*, plays on the enduring reputation of the French army as cowardly losers. *Mais, ce n'est pas vrai!* France has the best military record in Europe.

The French have fought more military campaigns than any other European nation and won twice as many battles as they have lost.

According to historian Niall Ferguson, of the 125 major European wars fought since 1495, the French have participated in fifty – more than both Austria (forty-seven) and England (forty-three). And they've achieved an impressive batting average: out of 168 battles fought since 387 BC, they have won 109, lost forty-nine and drawn ten.

The British tend to be rather selective about the battles they remember. Our triumphs at Waterloo and Trafalgar and in two World Wars easily make up for losing at Hastings. But the school curriculum never mentions the battle of Tours in 732, when Charles the Hammer, king of the Franks, defeated the Moors and saved the whole of Christendom from the grip of Islam. While every English schoolboy was once able to recite the roll-call of our glorious wins at Crécy (1346), Poiters (1356) and Agincourt (1415), no one's ever heard of the French victories at Patay (1429) and (especially) at Castillon in 1453, where French cannons tore the English apart, winning the Hundred Years War and confirming France as the most powerful military nation in Europe.

And what about Duke of Enghien thrashing the Spanish at Rocroi late on in the Thirty Years War in 1603, ending a century of Spanish dominance? Or the siege of Yorktown, Virginia, in 1781 in which General Comte de Rochambeau defeated the British and paved the way for American independence? Under Napoleon, France crushed the might of Austria and Russia *simultaneously* at Austerlitz in 1805, and, at Verdun in 1916, the French pushed the Germans back decisively in one of the bloodiest battles of all time.

The British always prided themselves on superiority at sea, but this was only because they realised they could never win a land war on the Continent. The French army has, for most of history, been the largest, best equipped and most strategically innovative in Europe. At its best, led by Napoleon in 1812, it achieved a feat that even the Nazis couldn't repeat: it entered Moscow.

These remarkable achievements help explain another French military victory. Whether it is ranks (general, captain, corporal, lieutenant); equipment (lance, mine, bayonet, epaulette, trench); organisation (volunteer, regiment, soldier, barracks) or strategy (army, camouflage, combat, esprit de corps, reconnaissance), the language of warfare is written in one language: French.

In which country was Alexander the Great born?

It depends who you're asking. The simple answer is Greece. After that it gets complicated.

Before the fourth century BC, Macedonia (or Macedon, meaning 'land of the tall') was a small kingdom in the north-east corner of the Greek peninsula. When Alexander the Great (356–323 BC) succeeded his father Philip II in 336 BC, Macedonia had already conquered all the other city-states and kingdoms of ancient Greece. The town of Alexander's birth, Pella, then in the kingdom of Macedonia, is now in the area of Greece still known as Macedonia. But, by the time of his death, aged thirty-three, Alexander ruled more of the world than anyone before him, and the Macedonian empire had spread beyond Europe, into the Middle East and Asia. This is where the problems start.

After Alexander's empire disintegrated, Greece and the southern Balkans were ruled by the Romans, invaded by Slavs and conquered by the Ottoman Turks. Ethnic identities became entangled and rarely coincided with national boundaries. Nowhere was this more complicated than in Macedonia. Pella, Alexander's home town, became Turkish, then Bulgarian, and then, in 1926, it was returned to Greece. Today, an estimated 4.5 million people claim to be

Macedonian. They are spread across Greece, the Former Yugoslav Republic of Macedonia (FYROM), Bulgaria, Serbia and Kosovo.

Nineteenth-century diplomats called this 'The Macedonian Question' and you might think the answer to it would be the establishment of a Macedonian state. In fact, you might think that that's what FYROM was. If only it were that simple. 'Ethnic' Macedonians are split into three main groups: Greek Macedonians (about 2.5 million, most of whom live in Macedonia in Greece); Macedonian Slavs (1.3 million, who live in FYROM); and Macedonian Bulgarians (about 370,000, who are also Slavs, but speak a different language from 'Macedonian Slavs', and live in the Bulgarian province of Pirin Macedonia). All three groups are Orthodox Christians, but there is no love lost between them.

The Greeks refuse to accept the name FYROM, suggested as a compromise by the United Nations. They claim the only 'true' Macedonia is in Greece and that Macedonian culture, the legacy of Alexander the Great, is Greek and the Slavs can't 'steal' it. The Macedonian Slavs say they can call their own country what they damn well please. The Bulgarians are more pragmatic. They recognise FYROM but claim that most of 'their' Macedonians are proud Bulgarians first. In the meantime, they busily grant citizenship to thousands of immigrants from FYROM who want to live in Bulgaria since it joined the European Union in 2007.

It's an ironic legacy for Alexander, revered in his time as a great unifier. But his legend nonetheless endures. If you happen to be sailing in the Aegean when a mermaid stirs up the sea, don't worry. Do as Greek fishermen still do. When she calls out, *'Where is Alexander?'* just shout back, *'He lives and reigns and keeps the world at peace,'* and you'll get home safely.

STEPHEN *What did Alexander the Great do with the banana and the ring-necked parakeet?*

JEREMY HARDY *Partied all night long.*

JO BRAND *Was he like those people that go into casualty and say: 'I was just hoovering, and I slipped, and it went up my arse'?*

JEREMY *'I put the parrot in to get it out.'*

STEPHEN *Well, no, the answer is actually that, er, Alexander the Great introduced them to Europe.*

Who killed Joan of Arc?

It was the French, not the English, who executed the 'Maid of Orléans'. They burnt her for being a cross-dresser.

Jeanne d'Arc (1412–31) was a peasant girl from Domrémy in north-east France who inspired a remarkable series of victories during the Hundred Years War – England's long and doomed attempt to conquer France.

By 1420 the King of France, Charles VI (known as 'Charles the Mad' because he suffered from the delusion that he was made of glass) was too ill to rule. His queen, Isabeau of Bavaria, took charge. She agreed to the marriage of her daughter Catherine to the English king, Henry V, transferring the French succession to their offspring and declaring her own son Charles illegitimate.

The French king Charles VI and the English king Henry V died within weeks of each other in 1422, and the infant son of Henry V and Catherine, Henry VI, was declared king of both England and France. The disinherited Charles of France still had the support of a group of French nobles, but his coffers were empty and he had fallen out with the powerful Duke of Burgundy, who threw in his lot with the English. By 1428, the Anglo-Burgundian alliance controlled all of northern France, including Paris, and had ventured as far south as the Loire, where they began laying siege to the city of Orléans.

Then fate intervened. An eighteen-year-old illiterate farm girl presented herself to the future Charles VII. She said God had spoken to her and that she would drive out the English and install Charles as king. Whether it was divine will that was on her side (an old French prophecy said that a young maid would save France) or her tactical nous (she favoured pre-emptive attacks) her impact was immediate. Dressed as a man, with cropped hair and wearing white armour, she broke the five-month English siege at Orléans in a week. More triumphs followed. Charles VII was crowned at Reims seven weeks later.

In early 1430 Jeanne fell into the hands of Burgundian troops. They sold her to the English for a ransom (worth £4.5 million today) and the English persuaded a French ecclesiastical court to bring charges of heresy against her.

When she came to trial eight months later, she had suffered torture and probably rape at the hands of her captors. She confessed, but then recanted, claiming she'd only done so 'out of fear of the fire' and reappeared dressed in men's clothes. Given that the most serious charge against her was dressing as a man – an 'abomination unto the Lord' (Deuteronomy 22:5) – this was all the French judge, Pierre Cauchon, the Bishop of Beauvais, needed.

On 30 May 1431 Joan was burnt at the stake at Rouen. She was nineteen. To prevent people from building a shrine in her honour, her remains were dumped in the Seine. In 1453 Charles VII avenged her memory by expelling the English from France and ending the Hundred Years War. Soon afterwards Pope Callixtus III ordered a retrial in which Joan of

Arc was found 'not guilty'. Sadly, it was too late to find her 'not dead' as well.

How tall was Napoleon?

He wasn't short.

The universal belief that Napoleon Bonaparte (1769–1821) was tiny came about from a combination of mistranslation and propaganda.

Napoleon's autopsy, carried out in 1821 by his personal physician Francesco Antommarchi, recorded his height as '5/2'. It is now thought this represents the French measurement '5 pieds 2 pouces', which converts to English measurement as 5 feet 6½ inches (1.69 metres).

The average height of Frenchmen between 1800 and 1820 was 5 feet 4½ inches (1.64 metres), so Napoleon would have been taller than most of the people he knew and taller, in fact, than the average Englishman, who was then 5 feet 6 inches (1.68 metres). Napoleon was only 2½ inches shorter than the Duke of Wellington – tall for his day at 5 feet 9 inches (1.75 metres) – and 2½ inches taller than his other great rival Horatio Nelson, who was only 5 feet 4 inches (1.62 metres).

Shortly after seizing power in 1799, Napoleon imposed height requirements on all French troops. In the elite Imperial Guard, Grenadiers had to be at least 5 feet 10 inches tall (1.78 metres) and his personal guard, the elite Mounted Chasseurs, had to be a minimum of 5 feet 7 inches (1.7 metres). So, for much of the time, the soldiers around him would have been noticeably taller, creating the impression that he was small.

The great British caricaturist James Gillray (1757–1815)

produced the first and most damaging image of a diminutive Napoleon in 'The King of Brobdingnag and Gulliver', inspired by *Gulliver's Travels*. In the cartoon George III holds Napoleon in the palm of his hand, inspects him with an eye-glass and comments, 'I cannot but conclude you to be one of the most pernicious little odious reptiles that nature ever suffered to crawl upon the surface of the Earth.'

The survival of the 'short Napoleon' myth is perpetuated by the widespread use of the term 'Napoleon complex' to describe short people who supposedly make up for their lack of stature by being aggressive.

There isn't much scientific evidence for this commonly held theory, however. It's not an officially recognised psychiatric syndrome and it doesn't seem to occur in the animal kingdom. Although one study found that, in contests between males in some species of swordtail fish, the smaller fish started 78 per cent of the fights, this is very much the exception.

Napoleon may have been aggressive, but he wasn't small.

STEPHEN *Nelson was three inches shorter than Napoleon.*

ALAN *Nelson was five foot four?*

STEPHEN *Yeah.*

ALAN *Like Danny de Vito?*

STEPHEN *Yes. He was a very short chap.*

ALAN *No wonder they put him on such a big column.*

What did Mussolini do?

He certainly didn't make the trains run on time. If anything, he made them less reliable than before.

As early as 1925 European and American fascist sympathisers said of Mussolini, 'At least he makes the trains run on time.' It defused criticism of his despotic policies. Even if all the stories about him were true, only a strong leader could bring order to the chaos in Italy after the First World War.

Today, the cliché is used to belittle a useless person or as a sarcastic complaint about the shortcomings of one's own country: 'Even Mussolini managed to get the trains running on time!'

When Mussolini arrived on the political scene in the early 1920s, the Italian railways were already working as well as any in Europe. The credit for this largely belongs to Cavaliere Carlo Crova, general manager of Italian State Railways in the 1920s, who built an effective, nationalised rail system from the ruins of several private companies. His life's work merely happened to coincide with Mussolini's ascent to power.

Contemporary reports by foreign journalists and diplomats say that, under the Fascist government of the 1930s, the trains didn't operate particularly well, especially on local lines. Fuel and staff were diverted from the railways to mount the invasion of Ethiopia in 1935. Once the Second World War started, coal had to be imported by land instead of sea, and the railways weren't up to the job.

Italian government propaganda – and its banning of any reporting of rail delays – meant that none of the problems were addressed. Italy's railways were officially excellent and no one dared suggest otherwise.

Interestingly, even in his most detailed and boastful biographical writings, Il Duce himself never claimed to have made the trains run on time. But he may have been the origin of the myth. According to his authorised biography, when the king summoned him to form a government in 1922, Mussolini told his local station master: 'We must leave exactly on time – from now on everything must function to perfection!'

A number of railway stations were built or renovated under Mussolini, notably Ostiense in Rome, specially designed so that Hitler could arrive at somewhere suitably 'ancient Roman' when he visited the city.

Among Mussolini's many unfulfilled ambitions was straightening the Leaning Tower of Pisa, which he felt gave the wrong image of the new Italy. On his orders in 1934 tons of liquid concrete were poured into the wonky landmark's foundations. The result was that the concrete sank into the wet clay, and the tower began leaning even more.

Who thought Waterloo was won on the playing fields of Eton?

Apparently, it was Adolf Hitler.

The Duke of Wellington would have been horrified by the suggestion that he thought cricket had anything to do with his famous victory. Wellington hated sport. Furthermore, he was unhappy at Eton and during his time there the school didn't have any playing fields.

According to the historian Sir Edward Creasy, the mis-understanding came about in the following way. Decades after the battle of Waterloo, the Duke passed an Eton cricket match and remarked: 'There grows the stuff that won Waterloo.' But this was purely a general comment about the qualities of the British officer class, not an appreciation of his old school's cricket coaching.

Adolf Hitler, it seems, took a very different view. In 1934, Anthony Eden went to meet him in Berlin. Eden was then the British cabinet minister responsible for the League of Nations and hoped to find common ground with Hitler by reminiscing about the old days (they had fought in opposite trenches at Ypres in the First World War). Eden described him as 'reason-able, charming and affable', but the Führer only wanted to talk obsessively about one thing: Eton.

Hitler was convinced Britain owed its victory in the First World War to strategic skills acquired at Eton. Eden, an Old Etonian himself, disagreed. He pointed out that the Eton College Officer Training Corps was a shambles.

His protests were in vain: one of the first things Hitler did after the outbreak of the Second World War was to arrange for Eton to be bombed.

Two bombs fell on the school. One shattered all the glass in the college chapel; the other narrowly missed a library full of boys studying. There were no reported casualties. When parents asked for the pupils to be moved to a safer location, the Headmaster, Charles Elliott, refused. If London's poor couldn't leave London, he said, Etonians wouldn't leave Eton.

Eton College was founded in 1440 by Henry VI. Called the 'King's College of Our Lady of Eton beside Wyndsor' it was originally intended as a charity school, providing free education for seventy poor students using scholars from the town as teaching staff. Henry VI lavished upon it a substantial income from land, and a huge collection of priceless holy relics – including alleged fragments of the True Cross and the Crown of Thorns.

Today Eton has 1,300 pupils and 160 masters and the annual school fee is £29,682. The Officer Training Corps still exists and the current British Prime Minister is a former member of it. By his own account, David Cameron's favourite song is 'The Eton Rifles' (1978), a scathingly anti-public school composition by The Jam.

STEPHEN *When the railway was being built through that particular part of Buckinghamshire, who was it that said, 'We won't have a station here?' What school is nearby?*

ROB BRYDON *Oo-oh, erm . . . It's Eton.*

STEPHEN *Eton College, of course, is there, and yes, they thought the boys would be tempted to go into London and visit prostitutes and so on.*

BILL BAILEY *'I'd like a Prostitute Super-Saver, please!'*

JIMMY CARR *[baffled expression] 'But this prostitute seems to be a woman.'*

Which revolution ended the First World War?

The German Revolution of November 1918. It's much less well known than the Russian Revolution of 1917, but the repercussions were just as significant.

By the middle of 1918, most Germans knew they had lost the First World War. So when Admiral Franz von Hipper (1863–1932), commander of the German battlecruisers at the Battle of Jutland, proposed a last do-or-die engagement with the British Navy, the reaction was less than enthusiastic and several ships mutinied. Although the revolt was short-lived, it persuaded the German High Command to rescind the battle order and return the fleet to Kiel.

There, convinced they were back in control, the authorities arrested forty-seven of the mutineers. Local union leaders, outraged by the treatment of the sailors, called for a public demonstration. On 3 November, several thousand people marched through Kiel under banners demanding 'Peace and Bread'. The military police opened fire on the march and seven protestors were killed.

Within twenty-four hours there was a mass uprising of soldiers, sailors and workers all over Germany, demanding an end to the war, the abdication of the Kaiser and the establishment of a republic. At this point, most states in the German Federation still had individual royal families but, in less than a week, they had all abdicated in favour of democratically elected Workers' and Soldiers' Councils.

In Berlin Friedrich Ebert (1871–1925), leader of the Social Democrats, the main left-wing political party, was worried that this might spark a communist revolution along Russian lines, plunging the country into civil war. To appease the rebels, he asked the Kaiser to abdicate. By this time even the troops on the Western Front were refusing to fight, but the Kaiser refused. Exasperated, the liberal Chancellor of the Reichstag, Prince Max von Baden, took matters into his own hands and sent a telegram announcing the Kaiser's abdication.

The Kaiser promptly fled to the Netherlands where he remained until his death in 1941. Baden resigned and, on 9 November, Ebert declared a republic with himself as Chancellor. The Armistice was signed two days later.

Ebert then tackled the revolutionaries, who wanted the entire mechanism of the old state abolished. In early 1919 the newly formed German Communist Party provoked armed insurrections in many German cities. Ebert had them brutally suppressed by the army. To the Left Ebert was now a traitor, and the militaristic Right hated him just as much for signing the infamous 'war guilt' clause in the Treaty of Versailles.

On 19 January 1919 Ebert established a new constitutional government, not in Berlin but at Weimar, the base of the great writers Goethe and Schiller and the spiritual home of German humanism. For the next fourteen years the Weimar Republic battled political instability and hyper-inflation caused by punishing war debts. In one year, between 1921 and 1922, the value of the German Mark fell from 60 to 8,000 against the dollar. The German Revolution that had ended the First World War created the chaos out of which Nazism was born.

Which country suffered the second highest losses in the Second World War?

The worst were in the USSR. The second worst were in China.

The Soviet–German war of 1941–45 was the largest conflict in human history. When Hitler sent three million troops into the Soviet Union, he expected a quick victory. Four years later, an estimated 10 million Soviet troops and 14 million Soviet citizens had died. The Germans lost over 5 million men too: it was in Russia that the outcome of the Second World War was really decided.

It was a vast theatre, fought over thousands of square miles. The Red Army were untrained and hopelessly underequipped in the early stages of the war, with infantry often pitted against tanks. The initial German advance was swift, destroying countless towns and villages, and wrecking the infrastructure of agriculture and industry. This left millions of Russians homeless and hungry. As the German advance became bogged down, the troops were ordered to show no mercy, systematically butchering prisoners and civilians alike.

It was a very similar set of factors that produced the war's second largest death toll. Very little is known in the West about the Sino-Japanese War of 1937–45, yet even the lowest estimates suggest 2 million Chinese troops and 7 million civilians died. The official Chinese death toll is a total of 20 million.

The Japanese invaded China in 1937 to provide a buffer between themselves and their real enemy, the USSR. China had no central government: much of it was still controlled by warlords and Chiang Kai-Shek's Nationalists and Mao Zedong's Communists hated each other almost as much as they did the Japanese. Chinese troops were pitifully short of weapons and modern military equipment (some still fought with swords) and they were no match for the disciplined and ruthless Imperial Japanese army.

The invasion turned into the greatest, bloodiest guerrilla war ever fought. Both sides pursued horrific scorched earth policies, destroying crops, farms, villages and bridges as they retreated, so as to deny their use to the enemy. Widespread famine and starvation were the result. As in Russia, a lack of military hardware was made up for by the sheer numbers of Chinese willing to fight and die. And, by the end of the war, 95 million Chinese were refugees.

Early on in the conflict, after capturing Chiang Kai-Shek's capital, Nanking, Japanese troops were sent on an officially authorised, six-week spree of mass murder, torture and rape that left 300,000 dead. Over the course of the war, 200,000 Chinese women were kidnapped to work in Japanese military brothels. Another 400,000 Chinese died after being infected with cholera, anthrax and bubonic plague dropped from Japanese aircraft. But, no matter how appalling the casualties, the Chinese refused to give in.

All Japan's military forces surrendered after the dropping of the atomic bombs on Hiroshima and Nagasaki. In China Mao Zedong's Communist Party swept to power. In 1972 Mao expressed his gratitude to the Japanese prime minister, Kakuei Tanaka. 'If Imperial Japan had not started the war,' he said, 'how could we communists have become mighty and powerful?'

Which nationality invented the 'stiff upper lip'?

It wasn't the British. Unlikely as it may sound, it was the Americans.

To keep a stiff upper lip is to remain steadfast and unemotional in the face of the worst that life can throw at you. Though long associated with Britain – and especially the British Empire – the oldest-known uses of the term are all from the USA, beginning in 1815. Americans were going around with 'stiff upper lips' in Harriet Beecher Stowe's *Uncle Tom's Cabin* (1852) and in the letters of Mark Twain (1835–1910) and it was only towards the end of the nineteenth century that the expression first appeared in print in Britain. By 1963, when P. G. Wodehouse published his ninth Jeeves and Wooster novel, *Stiff*

Upper Lip, Jeeves!, the phrase, if not the concept, had become almost entirely humorous.

The idea behind the expression is that a trembling lip is the first sign you're about to start crying. Why it should be the *upper* lip, in particular, that needs to be stiff is not clear. It may be because the saying originated in an age when most men wore moustaches, which would make shakiness more obvious in the upper lip than in the lower one; or perhaps 'stiff bottom lip' just sounded odd, like some obscure naval flogging offence.

Is a stiff upper lip good for you? That depends on whose research you choose to believe. Cancer Research UK recently published a survey conducted by the University of Leeds that showed that British men were 69 per cent more likely to die of cancer than women. This is due in part, they claimed, to men adopting 'a stiff upper lip attitude to illness': in other words, they ignore persistent symptoms and refuse to have regular check-ups.

On the other hand, psychologists in the USA, studying the aftermath of the terrorist attacks of 11 September 2001, found that — contrary to their expectations, and to popular belief — people who 'bottled up' their feelings suffered fewer negative mental and physical symptoms than those who were keen to talk openly about their experiences.

In Victorian times, the 'stiff upper lip' had a practical application: it was attached to a German contraption called the *Lebensprüfer* ('Life-prover'). This was a device intended to prevent premature burial. Wires were clipped to the upper lip and eyelid of someone who had apparently died. A mild electrical current was sent through their body and, if the patient's muscles twitched, you knew not to bury them quite yet.

What did George Washington have to say about his father's cherry tree?

We don't know. We don't even know if his father *had* a cherry tree.

The story of Washington and the cherry tree was entirely the invention of a man known to Americans as 'Parson' Weems, who wrote and published the first biography of the first US President just months after he died in 1799.

In Weems's tale, the six-year-old George Washington was given a small axe as a present and amused himself with it for hours in the garden of the family's plantation, Ferry Farm in Stafford, Virginia. One day George went too far and hacked the bark off his father's favourite cherry tree, condemning it to death. Though his father, Augustine Washington, was furious, George confessed at once: 'I can't tell a lie, Pa; you know I can't tell a lie. I did cut it with my hatchet.' George's honesty so impressed his father that he gave him a hug and congratulated him on 'an act of heroism that is worth a thousand trees'.

It's a good story, but it appears in no other accounts of Washington's life and was never mentioned by Washington himself. Even Weems was evasive about his sources: 'I had it related to me twenty years ago by an aged lady, who was a distant relative' was as far as he was prepared to go.

Mason Locke Weems (1756–1825) was born in Maryland but studied medicine and theology in London. Ordained by the Archbishop of Canterbury in 1784, he returned to America to take services at Pohick church in Virginia. Both George Washington and his father had once been members of the governing body there and Weems later falsely inflated his role into 'Former Rector of Mount Vernon', Washington's country estate nearly 10 kilometres (6 miles) from Pohick.

In 1790 a shortage of cash forced Weems to leave the ministry and become an itinerant bookseller. He cut an eccentric figure riding through the southern states, peddling his wares at fairs and markets. He was part preacher and part entertainer, talking up the quality of his merchandise as if delivering a sermon, then pulling out his fiddle for a rousing finale.

When Washington died, Weems had been working on his biography for six months. He wrote to a friend that 'millions are gaping to read something about him. I am very nearly prim'd & cock'd for 'em.' The outpouring of grief at the President's death (some people wore mourning clothes for months afterwards) confirmed Weems's view that what the American people needed was a heroic yarn, not a balanced political biography. Washington's modesty, his refusal to join a political party, his adoption of the homely 'Mr President' as his title, his rejection of a third term in office – all needed a mythic context that Weems's fantasy supplied.

A History of the Life and Death, Virtues and Exploits of General George Washington (1800) was one of the first American best-sellers, appearing in twenty-nine editions by 1825, and finding a place next to the Bible in almost every farm in the land. Although it's the source of most half-truths told about Washington, it's also the book that confirmed him as the 'Father of his Country'.

How many men have held the office of President of the United States?

Forty-three. (Not forty-four, as Barack Obama claimed at his inauguration.)

Barack Obama is the forty-fourth president of the USA, but only the forty-third *person* to become president. This is because Grover Cleveland held the position twice – with a four-year break in between – making him both the twenty-second and the twenty-fourth president of the United States.

Stephen Grover Cleveland (1837–1908) was the only Democrat in an otherwise unbroken fifty-year run of Republican presidents from 1860 to 1912. Almost no one has a bad word to say about him. 'He possessed honesty, courage, firmness, independence, and common sense,' wrote one contemporary biographer. 'But he possessed them to a degree other men do not.'

In the 1888 presidential contest Cleveland should have been elected for a second consecutive term. He actually polled more votes than John Harrison, but Republican electoral fraud in Indiana cost him the election. As she left the White House, Cleveland's young wife Frances – at twenty-one the youngest ever First Lady, and the only one to have been married in the White House – told her staff: 'I want you to take good care of all the furniture and ornaments in the house, for I want to find everything just as it is now, when we come back again.' When asked when that would be, she said: 'We are coming back four years from today.'

Which is just what happened. In the 1892 campaign, universally considered the cleanest and quietest since the Civil War, Grover Cleveland beat President Harrison by a landslide. He decided not to fight for a third term, which he was then still allowed to do. (President Roosevelt served for four consecutive terms from 1932–44.) It wasn't until the 22nd Amendment to the US Constitution was passed in 1951 that presidents were limited to a maximum of two terms.

Cleveland died in 1908. His last words were: 'I have tried so hard to do right.'

He is the only president to appear on two different $1 bills.

Despite putting a cross next to the name of the candidates on the ballot paper, the American people do not directly elect their president and vice-president. This is done a month after the popular vote by a 'college' of 538 state electors, allocated according to the size of the state's population: California (55) and Texas (34) have most; Vermont (3) and Alaska (3) the fewest. This system dates back to the beginning of the Union and was adopted because George Washington hoped it would reduce the amount of divisive party politics.

It's not perfect. The 'electors' have no power: they are a constitutional formality, pledged to vote for whichever candidate wins the popular vote in their state. Just as in British general elections, where votes don't always translate into seats, so in America. As long as a candidate wins the eleven biggest states they can be elected president with fewer votes overall. This is how Cleveland lost in 1888 and how George W. Bush defeated Al Gore in 2000.

STEPHEN *Barack Obama is currently known as the forty-fourth, just as Bush was known as the forty-third, but . . . but they aren't. Bush was the forty-second and Obama is the forty-third. Do you know why this is?*
SEAN LOCK *One of them was invisible?*

Which country ritually burns the most American flags?

The USA.

Every year, the Boy Scouts of America and military veteran organisations like the American Legion burn thousands of US flags between them.

This is because Section 176(k) of the US Flag Code (a set of rules on the correct treatment of the Stars and Stripes) provides that: 'The flag, when it is in such condition that it is no longer a fitting emblem for display, should be destroyed in a dignified way, preferably by burning.' Flag burnings (or 'retirements', to use the official term) are usually held on Flag Day, 14 June.

Although the Code allows for burning the flag 'in a dignified way', it also warns sternly against (and lays down the legal penalties for) anyone who 'knowingly mutilates, defaces, physically defiles, burns, maintains on the floor or ground, or tramples upon' the flag for other, possibly nefarious reasons. However, in 1990 the Supreme Court ruled that this was a restriction of 'freedom of speech' and thus violated the First Amendment to the US Constitution. So, even though the US Flag Code says you mustn't, you can legally burn the US flag in America for any reason you like.

The US Flag Code is a comprehensive document. Among other things, it sets out in precise detail how to fold the flag, showing where all of the twelve folds must be made and the symbolic reasons for each fold. It also makes it clear that the flag is not to be embroidered on to cushions or handkerchiefs; not to be 'used as a covering for a ceiling' or as 'a receptacle for receiving, holding, carrying, or delivering anything'; or to be used in advertising; or to form part of a 'costume or athletic uniform'.

Contrary to myth, the flag does not have to be burned if it ever touches the ground, and it's perfectly OK to clean it if it gets a bit grubby, rather than rushing straight to the burning option.

The anxious concern of Americans for the well-being of their flag strikes many foreigners as faintly comical or even fetishistic. But in the USA, where the President serves as both head of state *and* head of the government, there is no symbolic figurehead (such as a ceremonial monarch) to unite the nation. For many Americans, the flag plays that role, providing a non-partisan rallying point for all patriotic citizens, irrespective of their political differences.

That explains why the US Flag Code insists that the Stars and Stripes 'is itself considered a living thing'.

In which country is the Dutch city of Groningen?

The Netherlands.

Groningen is definitely not in Holland and, even if it were, Holland isn't a country.

The city of Groningen is capital of the northern Dutch province of Groningen. It is one of twelve provinces into which the Netherlands is divided. 'Holland' refers only to the two western provinces, North Holland and South Holland, which together represent an eighth of the country's total land mass. To call the Netherlands 'Holland' is like calling the UK 'England' or 'the Home Counties'.

The reason Holland is commonly used in this way is that it punches above its weight in the Netherlands – both in terms of population (40 per cent), and economic and political power (the three largest cities in the Netherlands – Amsterdam, Rotterdam and The Hague – are all in Holland). In the sixteenth century, when the Dutch navy ruled the waves, most Dutch ships came from these three ports, so any Dutchmen found abroad usually came 'from Holland'.

'Holland' is from Middle Dutch *holtland* ('wooded land'). The origin of 'Dutch' is more complicated. Its original meaning was 'of the people': the word 'Dutch' is a corruption of the ancient Indo-European root *teuta* 'people', from which we also get 'Teutonic'. In Old High German this became *duit-isc* ('people-ish' or 'the language of the people') and was used about Germanic languages generally.

The Old English variant of *duit-isc* ('people-ish') was *þeodisc* (pronounced 'thay-odd-ish'). It originally meant 'English' and then, in about the ninth century, came to mean 'German'. As *þeodisc* evolved into 'Dutch' it continued to mean 'German' right up until the early sixteenth century. At that point English rivalry (and frequent war) with the Hollanders or 'Low Dutch' meant the word 'Dutch' was exclusively applied to them, usually as part of a term of abuse. Examples from the time include 'Dutch courage' (bravery brought on by alcohol) and 'Dutch widow' (a prostitute).

For this reason, even as late as 1934, Dutch government officials were advised to avoid using the expression 'the Dutch' in international communications, in favour of the officially sanctioned 'of the Netherlands'.

Confusingly, but entirely logically, the Dutch word for Germans is *duitsch*.

Groningen, the Netherlands's eighth largest city, is the Dutch equivalent of Manchester: a lively university town full of bars. Students make up more than a quarter of its 185,000 population. As Groningen is the only city of any size in the northern Netherlands, locals simply refer to it as 'Stad', which means 'city'. Until Groningen's sugar beet factory closed recently, it gave the city a distinct sweet smell during the summer.

ROB BRYDON *The photo of Groningen that you showed looked like Guildford, didn't it.*

ALAN *Are you suggesting we have more in common with our European neighbours than otherwise?*

ROB *I'm suggesting the world is becoming homogenised and*

indistinct and I for one think that's a bad thing.
STEPHEN *Hear hear hear, quite right, quite right. Very good.*
JIMMY CARR *I think we all think like that, we're all the same.*

What language is the Spanish national anthem sung in?

It isn't.

Despite having one of the oldest tunes of any national anthem, *La Marcha Real* is the only one with no words. They were dropped in 1975 on the death of Generalissimo Francisco Franco, dictator of Spain for forty years. In 2007 the Spanish Olympic Committee, inspired by a performance of 'You'll Never Walk Alone' by visiting Liverpool football fans, held a competition to find new words for the national tune. The winner, called – believe it or not – *¡Viva España!* was dropped after just five days. Several Spanish regions (many of which have their own anthems) denounced the words as 'too nationalistic'.

> *Long live Spain!* (it went)
> *We sing together, with different voices,*
> *and only one heart.*

This seems pretty bland compared to France's bloodthirsty 'La Marseillaise':

> *Do you hear in the countryside*
> *The roar of those ferocious soldiers?*
> *They come right here into your midst*
> *To slit the throats of your sons and wives!*

Or the long-since hushed-up sixth verse of 'God Save the Queen'

> Lord grant that Marshal Wade
> May by thy mighty aid
> Victory bring
> May he sedition hush
> And like a torrent rush
> Rebellious Scots to crush
> God save the King

The oldest (and perhaps the oddest) national anthem of all belongs to the Dutch and dates from 1574. Here it is in its entirety:

> William of Nassau, scion
> Of a Dutch and ancient line,
> Dedicate undying
> Faith to this land of mine.
> A prince I am, undaunted,
> Of Orange, ever free,
> To the King of Spain I've granted
> A lifelong loyalty.

The Dutch seem to have no problem singing about being loyal subjects of Spain, despite not having been so for more than 350 years. Maybe the Spanish should sing the Dutch anthem instead?

Which city has the most Michelin stars in the world?

Not Paris, but Tokyo.

In the 2010 Michelin Guide, Tokyo has eleven 3-star restaurants to Paris's ten. The Japanese capital also has more Michelin stars altogether than any other city in the world – 261 across 197 restaurants – three times more than Paris.

At least some of this is do with scale: Tokyo is a much larger city with 160,000 restaurants. Paris has only 40,000. And France still tops the country listings, with twenty-five 3-star restaurants to Japan's eighteen. (The UK currently has four.)

Though two of Tokyo's eleven 3-starred restaurants are French, most of the 197 starred restaurants in the city specialise in classical Japanese cuisine, including three *fugu* houses, where the deadly poisonous puffer fish is rendered edible by specially trained chefs. The raw ingredients for this (and for all the *sushi* and *sashimi*) come from Tsukiji, the world's largest fish market, which handles 2,000 tons of fish a day. The Japanese are obsessed with good food – about half the output of Japanese television is food-related.

In 1889, two brothers from Clermont-Ferrand, André and Édouard Michelin, founded the Michelin Tyre Company. In 1891 they patented the world's first removable pneumatic tyre. The company is still based in the Auvergne and is the world's second largest tyre manufacturer, with over 109,000 employees and revenues of £12.3 billion.

André published the first Michelin guide in 1900, when there were just 300 cars in France. The guide was intended to stimulate road travel (more cars meant more tyres) and was given away free to motorists to encourage them to explore France by road. As well as listing hotels and restaurants, the first guides had practical tips on how to change tyres and where to find mechanics.

Michelin stars started in 1926. One star is 'a very good restaurant in its category'; two means 'excellent cooking, worth a detour'; three means 'exceptional cuisine, worth a special trip'. Just seventy-five Michelin inspectors cover all of Europe and many fewer the rest of the world. They eat out on 240 days in a year, file over 1,000 reports, and must order the maximum number of courses and always clear their plates. To remain anonymous they never return to the same place for several years, and never reveal what they do – even to their parents.

The Michelin man is over a century old. His name is 'Bibendum'. His inspiration was a stack of tyres that reminded Édouard Michelin of a human torso. In the first poster featuring him, in 1898, he drained a champagne glass full of nails and glass, making the point that 'Michelin tyres drink up obstacles'. His name comes from the strapline on the poster: *'Nunc est bibendum'* ('Time to drink!').

He isn't tyre-coloured because tyres weren't dark grey until 1912, when carbon black was added to preserve them. They were originally grey-white or beige. The Michelin man is not as racy as he was – he gave up cigars in 1929 after a TB epidemic – but he remains much loved. In 2000 he was voted the best-ever corporate logo, just ahead of the symbol for the London Underground.

STEPHEN *Which city has the most Michelin stars?*

REGINALD D. HUNTER *I know for a fact it ain't London. And I'm not just trying to offend London . . . I'm trying to offend the UK in general.*

STEPHEN *Ha ha.*

REG *But I feel like any country that can produce Marmite, they started later than everybody else in trying to make food taste good.*

STEPHEN *This from a country that has spray-on cheese.*

Where was football invented?

Not in England, but in China.

The Chinese played football for over 2,000 years before the English claimed it. *Cuju* or *tsu' chu* – literally 'kick-ball' – began as a military training exercise but was soon popular all over China. It used a leather ball (stuffed with fur or feathers) and two teams trying to score goals at opposite ends without using their hands. According to some accounts, each goal was a hole cut into a sheet of silk hung between bamboo posts. *Cuju* was first recorded in the fifth century BC and was at its peak during the Song Dynasty (AD 960–1279), when *cuju* players became the world's first professional footballers. The sport eventually fell into oblivion during the Ming period (AD 1368–1644).

In twelfth-century Japan *cuju* was adapted into a new game called *kemari*. Essentially a formal version of 'keepy-uppy', it was played in a square with trees at the corners. The eight players, in pairs, had to keep the ball in the air as long as possible, bouncing it off the trees. There was an umpire who gave extra points for particularly stylish play.

There are also claims of a game even older than *cuju*, called *marngrook* ('game ball'), played by the Aboriginal peoples of Western Australia. Involving over fifty players, the aim was to prevent the ball (made of possum-skin) from touching the ground. The long punts and high catches of Australian Rules football may owe something to *marngrook*.

In medieval England football involved so many players, so few rules and so much violence that it was regularly banned: no fewer than thirty royal and local laws were enacted against it between 1314 and 1667. This didn't reduce its popularity among all classes – even the young Henry VIII shelled out 4 shillings for a pair of leather football boots (worth about £100 today).

Modern football started in England in 1863, when rugby football and association football (or 'soccer' for short) diverged and England's Football Association was founded. The world's oldest football club is Sheffield FC, founded six years earlier (in 1857) as an amateur club.

Although the 1863 rules of the English game provided the template for today's international sport, it took a long time to shake off its violent origins. In the nineteenth century you could shoulder-barge players even if they didn't have the ball, and if a goalkeeper caught the ball, he could be shoved over the line to score.

One of the rules proposed in 1863 allowed players to approach the man with the ball and 'to charge, hold, trip or hack him, or to wrest the ball from him'. This was eventually dropped, despite the objections of Blackheath FC who argued that, without it, 'you will do away with the courage and pluck of the game, and it will be bound to bring over a lot of Frenchmen who would beat you with a week's practice'.

How prescient that has proved to be.

What's the most dangerous sport in the world?

Kite-flying.

The kite-flying capital of the world is Lahore in Pakistan, particularly during the spring festival of Vasant Panchami. The kites are used to fight duels: the idea is to use your kite to down your opponent's, so the strings are made of metal coated with abrasive glass.

When one kite brings down another, the cry of 'Bo Kata!' ('Kite down!') goes up, accompanied by drum rolls.

Over the past decade the sport has injured several thousand Punjabis in Pakistan and India – and killed 460 of them. It's so dangerous that it's banned for all but fifteen days of the year.

People chasing the kites are killed falling off roofs or running into the path of traffic. Many have their throats cut by the kite-strings – especially motorcyclists, who are horribly garrotted by the lethal wires draped across the roads.

There are frequent power cuts when the strings foul electricity cables, and the sport is regarded as such a dangerous nuisance that there is agitation for a complete ban, organised by the Kite-flying Effectees Committee.

Other dangerous sports include: base-jumping (hurling yourself from a cliff or building with a parachute), which kills ten to fifteen people a year; cave-diving (scuba-diving crossed with potholing), which accounts for about ten fatalities a year; rock fishing (literally, fishing off rocks), where the sea annually sweeps at least ten Australians to their deaths; and high-altitude mountaineering, which claims one in a hundred.

The single most dangerous officially sanctioned sporting event is the Paris to Dakar rally, which has killed at least fifty-eight people in its thirty-two-year history. This includes twenty-five competitors – and probably many more spectators – mostly in the African leg of the 10,000-kilometre (6,000-mile) race. Official records are notoriously vague but (as well as high-speed crashes) the dangers faced include land mines, kidnapping by bandits, unexpected outbreaks of civil war and extreme sandstorms.

The most injury-prone sport for women, with over 20,000 casualties a year, is cheerleading. The injuries are generally sprains and broken bones caused by bad falls. It isn't an exclusively female sport and didn't become predominantly female until the 1950s. Today only 5 per cent of America's 3 million cheerleaders are men. The former US president George W. Bush was head cheerleader for the high school baseball team at Phillips Academy in Andover, Massachusetts and he continued his distinguished cheerleading career once he got to Yale. As far as we know, he managed to emerge unscathed.

STEPHEN *You have to sever your competitor's kite from its string, and so the string's actually made of metal with glass; sharp, abrading glass. And motorcyclists get garrotted, 'cause hundreds of people do it all over the country.*

JIMMY CARR *Who told you this, Stephen? This is nonsense. This doesn't happen.*

SEAN LOCK *No, I saw it. Channel 5: When Kiters Go Bad . . .*

Who was the first Olympian to score a 'perfect 10'?

It wasn't Nadia Comăneci at the Montreal Games in 1976 – in fact, at the time of the first 'perfect 10', she wasn't even born.

In 1924 in Paris, a French gymnast named Albert Sequin (1891–1979) won the individual Gold in a vaulting event called the Men's Sidehorse, which has only been contested at one other Olympiad (St Louis in 1904). His score was listed as 10.000, which makes him the first to score a perfect 10.

The 1924 Olympics was Albert Sequin's only Games, but he made the most of it: also picking up silver medals for the Men's Team All-Around – and for the Men's Rope-Climbing, which hasn't appeared at the Olympics since 1932.

Rope-climbing Olympians began by sitting on the floor, with the lower end of an 8-metre (26-foot) rope dangling between their outstretched legs. Only their hands and arms could be used in climbing: the use of feet and legs was banned, even in the initial push-off. The key to success was the momentum gained by an explosive, upper-body surge from the floor. In some forms of the competition, the climbers were required to keep their bodies L-shaped – that is, with their legs sticking out horizontally – throughout the climb.

At the top of the rope was a 'tambourine', a flat plate covered with soot. Back on the ground, the competitor would show his stained fingers to prove that he had touched the tambourine. In 1904 the rope-climbing Gold went to the legendary American George Eyser who won six Olympic medals that year, despite his wooden leg.

Nadia Comăneci, the first female Olympian to score a perfect 10, did so at the age of fourteen in 1976. The youngest female gold medallist was Marjorie Gestring of the USA, who took a diving Gold in 1936, aged thirteen.

Sports that are no longer part of the Games include live Pigeon-shooting: nearly 300 birds were killed during the event at the 1900 Paris Olympiad. However, Pistol Duelling at the 1906 Athens Games produced no fatalities: competitors shot at mannequins dressed in frock coats with bull's-eyes on their throats. The Diving Plunge (St Louis, 1904) – which tested how far athletes could travel in the water without actually swimming – and the Long Jump for Horses (Paris, 1900) are other modern non-runners. In 2008 the official Beijing Olympic website announced the introduction of Olympic Poodle-Clipping – but this turned out to be an April Fool's joke, included in the agenda by accident after first being printed by the *Daily Telegraph*.

Perhaps the most unusual Olympic record-breaker of all time was Japanese runner Shizo Kanakuri. In 1912 he began the marathon at the Stockholm Games but, being exhausted after his eighteen-day journey to Sweden, stopped for a rest after 30 kilometres (nearly 19 miles) and asked at a local house for a glass of water. Having drunk it, he fell asleep on the sofa and woke up the next morning. In 1967, aged seventy-six, he was invited to return to the city and complete his run. His finishing time was therefore 54 years, 8 months, 6 days, 32 minutes and 20.3 seconds.

Name an event at the first Olympic games

No – not the discus, javelin, marathon or anything you may've seen on a vase.

The ancient Greeks invented many sports but at the first recorded Olympics, in 776 BC, there was only one contest: a running race, called the *stadion* as it was a stadion long (roughly 192 metres (about 600 feet), the length of the running track at Olympia).

The winner of the first race was Koroibos of Elis, and he was a naked chef. (The games were performed in the nude, but another tradition has it that this only began in 720 BC when the loincloth of the winner, Orsippos of Megara, fell off during the race.)

In later years wrestling, boxing and the pentathlon were added. Women were excluded, and the only item worn by any athlete was a leather thong, sported by the boxers. This was neither an Essex thong (familiar to Brits as a scanty pantie, often partially exposed by low-slung trousers), nor an Australian thong (which is a rubber sandal, also known as a flip-flop). The Olympic thong was a strap of oxhide worn round the knuckles.

The members of the coaching staff were also naked. This tradition began in 404 BC after a widow called Kallipateira broke the rule against female spectators and dressed as a trainer to watch her son Peisirodos. When he won, she leapt over a barrier to congratulate him and all was revealed.

The word 'gymnastics' comes from the Greek for 'naked': the *gymnasion* (our gymnasium) was where the athletes trained.

There were four Panhellenic or 'all Greece' games in ancient Greece, so they didn't have to wait for four years to celebrate athletics, chariot racing and combat. Different symbolic prizes characterised the games: at Olympia the prize was the olive branch; at Nemea it was dried celery. In the fifth century the victory wreath at the Isthmian games in Corinth was changed from pine to dried celery to rival the Nemean games. At Delphi the Pythian games, named for Pythian Apollo, the snake-slayer, the wreath was of laurel. At the Pythian and Isthmian games music contests were also held.

The first Olympics to be held outside Greece took place in Gloucestershire. A lawyer called Robert Dover established his 'Olimpick Games' on a hill above Chipping Camden in 1612. There were 'manly pursuits' – wrestling, cudgel-play and 'spurning the barre' (a kind of caber-toss) – but also, in a nod to the Pythian games, prizes for singing, pipe playing, horseracing and chess.

Another revival at Much Wenlock in Shropshire in 1850 included the excellent sport of jingling, where someone dressed in a costume festooned with bells was pursued by a team wearing blindfolds. There should be a campaign to revive this sport.

The first international Olympic games, held in 1896, was set up by Baron de Coubertin, inspired by seeing the Much Wenlock games; it had a similar mixed flavour, offering medals for sculpture, music, painting, literature and town planning. At the 1900 Paris Olympics they had a 'poodle-clipping' contest, won by a farmer's wife who trimmed seventeen poodles in two hours.

Such non-sporting competitions survived until 1948, when Avery Brundage (the American who presided over the International Olympic Committee from 1952 to 1972) decided that the winners of the fine arts medals might capitalise professionally on their accolades, undermining the rigorous amateurism of the games.

STEPHEN *The winner was a cook. His name was Koroibos of Elis, and he was a cook, and like all the contestants, was naked.*

ALAN *They all ran in the nude.*

JOSIE LAWRENCE *How wonderful! I would like to have seen the triple jump.*

ALAN *What about the pole vault?*

JOSIE *Oh, don't!*

Why did sportsmen start going into huddles?

It had nothing to do with team-building.

The huddle was invented at Gallaudet University, a college for the deaf in Washington DC, as a way of hiding hand signals from other deaf teams.

In American football, the 'line of scrimmage' is an imaginary line across the pitch where the two sides face each other before commencing the next part of the game, or 'play'. Until the 1890s, the signal caller on each team shouted out his team's strategy for the next play. Nothing was hidden from the opposite team's defence.

When the forerunner of Gallaudet College (founded in

1864) started playing American football with an all-deaf team, their quarterback, Paul Hubbard, used American Sign Language (ASL) to call a play at the line of scrimmage. His team therefore had a distinct advantage when they played non-deaf colleges, but other deaf schools could easily read his intentions. So in 1894 Hubbard began concealing his signals by gathering his attacking players into a cluster before each play.

This worked brilliantly and became a regular habit. In 1896 the huddle started showing up on other college campuses and it is now considered an essential part of the game.

Gallaudet was the first University for deaf people, set up by Edward Milner Gallaudet, the son of Thomas Hopkins Gallaudet (1787–1851), the man who brought sign language to America. Because Thomas Gallaudet (who wasn't deaf himself) based American Sign Language (ASL) on the French sign language that he had learned in Paris, American and French sign languages share 60 per cent of the same gestures.

This has the strange result that it is much easier for a deaf American to make himself understood in Paris than in London.

STEPHEN *Do you know where the sports huddle originated?*
JACK DEE *Glenn Huddle?*

What's a bat's eyesight like?

No, they aren't blind at all.

Of the 1,100-odd species of bat in the world, not one is sightless – and many can see very well indeed. The notion that bats don't need eyes because they get about exclusively using echolocation or 'sonar' is complete nonsense.

Fruit bats (also called Megabats) don't use echolocation at all. They have large eyes, which they use both to navigate and to find their food – which is, as you might expect, fruit. Echolocation isn't much help in finding food that doesn't move around. Instead, for fruit-location, they also have a keen sense of smell.

The Common Vampire bat (*Desmodus rotundus*) is the only bat that feeds on the blood of mammals. It is such a very long way from blind that it can see a cow 120 metres (400 feet) away: in pitch darkness, in the middle of the night.

Even microbats – which eat insects and include all British bats, and which *do* use sonar to hunt – use their (much smaller) eyes for avoiding obstacles, for spotting landmarks, and for working out their flying height. Microbats have good night vision. They see in black and white because they're nocturnal, whereas fruit bats see in colour because they're active in the daytime.

In the Americas there are several species of 'fishing bats', such as the Greater Bulldog bat (*Noctilio leporinus*), which lives by using its keen eyesight and immense feet to drag fish out of the water. It is easily identified, not only by its 66-centimtre (26-inch) wingspan, but also by the repugnant odour of its roosts.

Very few humans find bats palatable but, for special occasions like weddings, the Chamorro people of Guam like to boil giant fruit bats or 'flying foxes' in coconut milk and eat them whole – wings, fur and all. This may explain why so many Chamorro suffer from a rare and terrible neurological condition – ALS-Parkinson dementia complex.

The bats feed on poisonous cycad plants, whose dangerous neurotoxins are passed on (now lightly flavoured with coconut) to the unfortunate diners.

What is batology?

It's not the study of bats: that's 'cheiropterology'. It's the study of blackberries, from the Greek *batos*, a bramble.

Blackberry bushes are also known as brambles, from the Anglo-Saxon *brœmbel*, 'a prickly shrub'. 'Bramble', 'broom' and 'briar' were once interchangeable terms for thorny under-growth, though briar is now only applied to the wild rose and broom to a yellow-flowered shrub. All three words are from the ancient Indo-European root *bhrem* meaning 'spike' – as is the German for blackberry, *Brombeere*, and the French for raspberry, *framboise*.

Studying blackberries isn't as one-dimensional as it sounds. More than 1,000 subspecies have been recorded, 400 of them in the UK alone. A member of the rose family and a close relative of apples, pears, plums and strawberries, the basic bramble, *Rubus fruticosus*, interbreeds very easily, and many different versions can often be found growing together in the same bramble patch. That's why ripening times and taste can vary so much, even on the same soil.

Despite their name, blackberries aren't berries. In botanical terminology, they are 'aggregated drupes'. Each little blob or 'drupelet' that makes up a whole blackberry contains a single tiny stone, just like a plum or an apricot.

Blackberries appear in three phases. The first fruits, which ripen in late summer, are the lowest, largest and sweetest and should be eaten raw. The second fruits generally ripen in late September and are less juicy – but good for pies, puddings and jams. In England, there is an old tradition that the Devil has spat (or urinated) on the blackberries gathered after Michaelmas (29 September). Late blackberries are susceptible to frost and mildew, both of which turn the fruit sour, as the legend warns. They are best cooked combined with apples.

As well as being rich in iron and vitamin C, blackberries

have long been used in herbal medicine to counter the effects of venomous bites and dysentery. The sixteenth-century herbalist John Gerard advised: 'They heale the eyes that hang out, and hard knots in the fundament.' In the nineteenth century, dried blackberry leaves were mixed with tea to make it go further.

Blackberries grow faster in Australia than anywhere else in the world. They were introduced there by English settlers in the mid-nineteenth century and now cover an area larger than Tasmania.

Battology (with two 't's) is another matter. It means 'pointlessly repeating the same thing over and over again' – from the Greek *battologia*, 'stammering speech'. *Batophobia* (from a different Greek word, *batos*, meaning 'passable') is the fear of being close to tall buildings. This is not to be confused with *bathophobia*, the fear of depth; *bathmophobia*, fear of stairs; or *batrachophobia*, fear of frogs.

STEPHEN *What is batology?*

ALAN *The study of batteries.*

STEPHEN *No, it's not that, nice thought.*

ALAN *It is! There's no other word in English with 'b-a-double-t' at the beginning.*

STEPHEN *Battle? Batter? It reminds me of the story someone was saying that 'sugar' is the only English word that begins with 's-u' but where the 's' is pronounced 'sh', and someone called out, 'Are you sure?'*

Can you name an animal that only eats bamboo?

Meet the bamboo mite.

Bamboo mites (*Schizotetranychus celarius*) eat bamboo and bamboo alone. They are tiny creatures related to spiders and are only 0.4 mm (1/60 inch) long. They form colonies in dense webs under bamboo leaves and suck the chlorophyll from the leaf cells. This makes the leaves mottled and unsightly and a heavy infestation can kill the plant altogether. The mites live about forty days inside their web, only leaving it to defecate. Radical pruning is the safest way to get rid of them, or you could try importing one of several species of larger, predatory mite to eat them (these cost about 1p each via mail order).

Another parasite that lives uniquely on bamboo is the noxious bamboo mealybug (*Dinoderus ocellaris*). This pest turns the sap of the bamboo into sugary honeydew. This in turn grows a sooty-black mould that looks nasty but which is irresistible to ants. A practical (if fairly slow) way to control bamboo mealybugs is to eat their larvae. In Thailand bamboo borer grubs are a delicacy, often appearing on menus as 'fried little white babies'.

One animal that *doesn't* live entirely on bamboo is the Giant panda (*Ailuropoda melanoleuca*). Admittedly, up to 99 per cent of its diet *is* made up of bamboo, but pandas will happily eat small mammals, fish and carrion if they can rouse themselves to catch any.

The problem is that pandas are built like carnivores but eat like herbivores. Bamboo is available all year round, but it's so low in nutrition that, to satisfy their basic needs, pandas must spend twelve hours a day munching the equivalent of a hay bale of the stuff. This leaves little time (or energy) for hunting or gathering. Nor does it produce enough fat to hibernate in the winter. Instead, it generates a tremendous amount of waste. Pandas defecate more than forty times a day – excreting about half the weight of what they eat – and their droppings are so fibrous that one Thai zoo uses them to make souvenir paper.

Perhaps because of the endless regime of eating and sleeping, pandas aren't very sociable. When it comes to defending their territory, they avoid energy-sapping confrontations. Instead, they keep other pandas at bay by marking their boundaries with scent. They do this in four distinct ways, the most unusual being to leave a mark while doing a handstand. The higher the pee, the more dominant the signal is rated by potential rivals. No other animal in the world does this.

As well as keeping the 2,000 surviving wild giant pandas alive, bamboo has other extraordinary qualities. It is the world's fastest-growing plant: one species in China grows a metre (about 3 feet) a day (that's nearly 8 centimetres, or 3 inches, an hour) and, when fully grown, can reach 60 metres (200 feet) tall. It also has a 'bend-factor' ten times greater than that of steel, making it ideal for construction – almost all the scaffolding in Hong Kong is made of bamboo.

Which is hairier: human or chimpanzee?

Humans may look less hairy than a chimpanzee, but we have the same number of hair follicles – about 5 million – on our bodies, of which only 100,000 (2 per cent) are on our scalps.

Our hair has evolved to be finer and more transparent than in other primates. We lost our fur, and no one knows why. One theory is that it was to reduce lice. Another is that, when our ancestors moved out of the forests on to the savannah about 1.7 million years ago, we needed to lose body hair to stop overheating. As we became less hairy, we became darker-skinned to protect our skin from the sun. But that doesn't explain why the Inuit of the Arctic have less body hair than many sub-Saharan Africans.

Nor does it explain why our scalp hair is programmed to grow for such long periods: left to its own devices, it would grow down past our waists. Other mammalian fur is more like our body hair – it grows to a set length and then is replaced. (Nor can we explain why some men sprout luxuriant hair out of their ears, noses, eyebrows and backs, even as their heads go bald.)

One theory links our loss of fur with increased brain size. A bigger brain creates more heat; in order to keep our temperature under control, we evolved to sweat heavily (sweating is hopeless if you have fur). So, the less fur we had, the more efficient our cooling system became and the bigger our brains grew. Also, as humans walked upright, the only place we still needed hair was on the head, to protect our expanding brains against the sun.

Another more extreme hypothesis suggests we evolved from 'aquatic apes'. This supposes that 8 million years ago the ancestors of modern humans lived a semi-aquatic lifestyle, foraging for food in shallow waters. As fur is not an effective insulator in water, we evolved to replace it, as other aquatic mammals have, with higher levels of body fat. Unfortunately, there isn't any fossil evidence for aquatic humans (or apes) at all.

Yet another idea is that hairlessness, once it had started to evolve, was reinforced by sexual selection – in other words it became attractive to the opposite sex. Charles Darwin went along with this (though, given that, it's odd he chose to have such an enormous beard) and it may be why women are less hairy than men and why smooth, clear skin has become a sign of good health.

Nobody's really sure, though. As leading palaeoanthropologist Ian Tattersall recently remarked: 'There are all kinds of notions as to the advantage of hair loss, but they are all just-so stories.'

What did Neanderthals look like?

A lot like us.

The latest reconstructions of Neanderthals look very similar to humans. If you gave one a haircut and a tracksuit, it wouldn't look out of place on a bus.

The first fossilised remains of humanity's closest cousins were found in 1856 near Düsseldorf in the Neander river valley, hence the word *Neanderthal* (*Tal*, then spelt *Thal*, is German for 'valley'). *Homo neanderthalensis* used tools, wore jewellery, had religious rites, buried his dead and could probably talk. Like us they had the essential hyoid bone (which holds the root of the tongue in place) and recent genetic analysis shows they had exactly the same 'language gene' (FOXP2) that humans do. Using the word Neanderthal to mean 'oafish' or 'unreconstructed' is unfair. In fact, this notion derives from a misinterpretation of the very first reconstruction of a Neanderthal skeleton.

It was the work of a French palaeontologist called Pierre Marcellin Boule (1861–1942) who in 1911 put together a specimen with a curved spine, a stoop, bent knees, and a head and hips that jutted forward. In 1957 the skeleton was re-examined and it became clear that the original owner had suffered from a grossly deforming type of osteoarthritis. Not only did this not represent the average Neanderthal, but Boule had also let his preconceptions affect his work, giving the skeleton an opposable big toe like a great ape, even though the bones didn't provide any evidence for such a conclusion.

Neanderthals had barrel-shaped chests and broad, projecting noses – traits some palaeoanthropologists believe helped them breathe better when chasing prey in cold environments. They had bigger brains than modern humans, but they couldn't run as fast and were shorter and less adept at using tools. What they lacked in height they made up for in strength: Neanderthal females had bigger biceps than the average male human does today.

Humans and Neanderthals diverged into separate species somewhere between 440,000 and 270,000 years ago. Early Neanderthals moved out of Africa into the Middle East and northern Europe much sooner than *Homo sapiens* did, and lived there for four times as long. They became extinct 30,000 years ago (the last recorded Neanderthal community was on Gibraltar), which means that humans and Neanderthals co-existed for at least 12,000 years.

No one knows why the Neanderthals died out. Were they out-competed by humans or did they (for some unknown reason) fail to adapt to the last Ice Age, when Europe became a frozen, sparsely vegetated semi-desert? The oldest known ornaments in Europe (made from shells) were the work of Neanderthals and some researchers now think that humans might have learned ritual and even culture from them during the 120 centuries we shared.

But the most startling fact to emerge from analysis of the genome of the Neanderthals is that they interbred with us. So, unless you are a pure black African, between 1 per cent and 4 per cent of you is Neanderthal.

STEPHEN *How would you spot a Neanderthal if you saw one on a bus?*

JACK DEE *He'd be the one who comes and sits next to me.*

JO BRAND *He's the one already sitting next to me, 'cause I'm married to him.*

STEPHEN *Is this going to be the 'humiliate my husband' show?*

JO *It's all right, he doesn't watch this. He doesn't really understand it.*

Which part of you is evolving fastest?

It's your nose.

It was once impossible to know how our sensory organs evolved because the soft parts of our bodies don't survive in the fossil record. However, genetic analysis at Cornell University has led 'sensory psychologist' Avery Gilbert to believe that the nose is the fastest-evolving human organ.

In mammals the largest single family of genes controls the sense of smell. The study of the human genome shows that ours has altered much more rapidly than those of our closest living relatives, the great apes. This means we sniff less, but taste more, sending aromas from the back of the throat to the nose as we chew. Known as 'retronasal olfaction' or 'back-of-the-nose smelling' (as opposed to orthonasal smelling through the nostrils) this ability to savour food as we are eating is almost unique to humans. In Avery's words: 'The human nose evolved to serve the human mouth.'

Two events may have contributed to this. The first was cooking with fire, first discovered 1.8 million years ago by our ancestor *Homo erectus*, bringing with it the enticing smells of roast meat and caramelised fruit. The second was the domestication of animals around 15,000 years ago, closely followed by the invention of farming. This brought a whole new range of flavours (yogurt, milk, cheese, bread and toast) and the domestication of the dog gave us a companion species with an extremely acute sense of smell. One theory is that our ancestors delegated the practical scent-tracking function of our noses to dogs, while we concentrated on the ever more complex and delicious aromas coming from the cooking pot. Eating together around the campfire transformed human culture: our shared sense of taste helped to civilise us.

The nose may be our fastest-evolving organ, but further analysis of the human genome shows that we are also evolving elsewhere. Our hair is becoming less thick, but our hearing (perhaps as a result of developing language) is much better than that of chimpanzees. More alarmingly, the Y chromosome, the one that makes a person male (men have both an X and a Y chromosome) is shrinking. It's lost 1,393 of its original 1,438 genes over the last 300 million years. The geneticist Steve Jones points out that one consequence of this is that women are now genetically closer to chimpanzees than men are, because the two X chromosomes they possess have changed much less rapidly.

There's a widespread assumption that human beings have stopped evolving, because technological advances have insulated us from the environmental pressures that drive natural selection. However, the latest genome research suggests the rate of evolutionary change among humans is much the same as that observed in the rest of nature.

A good example of this is lactose intolerance (inability to digest milk) in adults, which has arisen in some parts of the world (but not others) as the result of a single genetic mutation that took place no more than 5,000 years ago.

What's the commonest metal in the human body?

Calcium.

Well known as an ingredient of chalk and milk, most people are amazed that calcium is a metal. But, in its pure state, it's as silver and shiny as aluminium.

There is about a kilo (2.2 pounds) of calcium in the average person, 99 per cent of it in the bones. A third of what is left over after a cremation is calcium.

The other 1 per cent is in our blood and we couldn't function without it. It neutralises the acid in our food, controls cell division, triggers the release of hormones and – most important of all – controls muscle contraction and transmission of nerve impulses. Without calcium, our heart muscle wouldn't pump.

About 20 per cent of all the calcium in our bones is replaced in the course of a single year. As children grow, more calcium is added to their bones than is lost. This declines as we age: a fifty-year-old is usually losing 1 per cent of the calcium in their bones each year. An eighty-year-old might have 70 per cent less bone calcium than a thirty-year-old: hence the brittleness of older people's bones.

Non-chemists may be surprised to learn that almost all the elements are metals: a metal is simply defined as something that conducts electricity and heat. Of the 118 elements known, only eighteen are non-metals.

Calcium is the fifth most abundant element and the third most abundant metal in the earth's crust but it is never found in a pure state. Sir Humphrey Davy first isolated it in 1808, the same year he discovered the elements sodium and potassium – which are also metals.

Limestone, marble, chalk, coral, pearls, the limescale in kettles, the lenses in the eyes of fish and the indigestion pills,

Rennies, Settlers and Tums, are all made of calcium carbonate.

Limestone is made from the shells of small marine animals and makes up about 10 per cent of all the sedimentary rocks on earth. Coral is made of a crystalline form of calcium carbonate called aragonite and covers about 2 million square kilometres (770,000 square miles) of the planet (roughly the size of Greenland).

Calcium not only helps keep our bodies upright, it does the same for our buildings. Bricks have been glued together by mortar for at least 7,000 years.

Mortar is made from sand and water mixed with lime (also known as 'quicklime'), which is limestone burned at very high temperatures.

The word calcium comes from the Latin *calx*, 'a stone', from which we also get the word 'chalk'. *Calx* also means 'heel' in Latin. From one meaning, we get the word 'calculation' (*calculus* means a little stone, used for counting); from the other, the word 'recalcitrant'.

RORY McGRATH *Calcium, atomic number 20. Last year, I learned all the atomic numbers of all the elements because I was helping my son to revise.*
STEPHEN *Selenium?*
RORY *It's 34! It's 34. Selenium is 34, arsenic's 33.*
STEPHEN *Very good. Isn't he good? They really should put railings around you and have children come and stare at you!*

What were Bronze Age tools made of?

Stone, mostly.

The Bronze Age, which in Europe is dated at 2300–600 BC, began when mankind first discovered how to make and use bronze, but this would have been a *gradual* industrial revolution. For much of the period, old technology (using stone and bone) would have been more widespread than metal. Bronze would have been rare and expensive, so most everyday tools and weapons would still have been made from flint and other familiar materials.

And, just as stone flourished in the Bronze Age, so bronze-working didn't reach its peak until well into the Iron Age (1200 BC–AD 400).

We still use all three materials today. In the twenty-first century, alongside plastic bags and silicon chips, we still continue to produce iron railings, bronze bearings and statues, gravestones and grinding stones. The last people in Britain to make a living working with flint were the flintknappers who supplied the gunflints for firearms. It was a profession that only died out in the nineteenth century, when the percussion cap replaced the flintlock.

The 'Three-Age System' – in which the Bronze Age follows the Stone Age, and is succeeded by the Iron Age – stems from the early nineteenth century. It was the brainchild of Christian Jürgensen Thomsen (1788–1865), a Danish museum curator, who was looking for a nice neat way of arranging his exhibits. It was never intended to be more than a fairly crude means of placing artefacts in a chronological relationship with each other, by classifying them according to the relative sophistication of their manufacture.

Many archaeologists believe that the Stone Age – which is itself split into three eras (the Old, Middle and New Stone ages) – was probably more of a Wood Age, but that wood's predominant role in pre-history has been hidden by the fact that wooden artefacts rot, while stone ones don't.

What was not Made in China and not made *of* china?

Glass.

Though the Chinese invented the compass, the flushing toilet, gunpowder, paper, the canal lock and the suspension bridge long before anyone else, the scientific revolution that transformed the West between the sixteenth and eighteenth centuries completely passed them by.

The reason for this is that they also invented tea.

The earliest known glass artefacts are Egyptian and date back to 1350 BC, but it was the Romans who first produced transparent glass. They liked the way it enabled them to admire the colour of their wine.

By the time the Egyptians worked out how to make glass, the Chinese had been drinking tea (traditionally they began in 2737 BC) for almost 1,400 years. Its colour was less important to them than temperature, and they found it was best served in their most famous invention of all: fine porcelain, or 'china'.

Since they had no particular use for it, early Chinese glass was thick, opaque and brittle. They mainly used it for making children's toys – and soon gave up on it altogether. For almost 500 years, from the end of the fourteenth century until the nineteenth, no glass was made in China at all.

Meanwhile, in 1291 the Republic of Venice, concerned about the fire risk to its wooden buildings, moved its glass furnaces offshore to the island of Murano. Here, inspired by migrant Islamic craftsmen, the inhabitants learned to make the finest glass in the world, giving them a monopoly that lasted for centuries.

The impact of high-grade glass on Western culture cannot be overstated. The invention of spectacles towards the end of the thirteenth century added at least fifteen years to the academic and scientific careers of men whose work depended on reading. The precise reflection of glass mirrors led to the discovery of perspective in Renaissance painting. Glass beakers and test tubes transformed ancient alchemy into the modern science of chemistry.

The microscope and the telescope, invented within a few years of each other at the end of the sixteenth century, opened up two new universes: the very distant and the very small.

By the seventeenth century, European glass had become cheap enough for ordinary people to use it for windowpanes (as opposed to mere holes in the wall or the paper screens of the Orient). This protected them from the elements and flooded their houses with light, initiating a great leap forward in hygiene. Dirt and vermin became visible, and living spaces clean and disease free. As a result, plague was eliminated from most of Europe by the early eighteenth century.

In the mid-nineteenth century, transparent, easily sterilised swan-necked glass flasks allowed the French chemist Louis Pasteur to disprove the theory that germs spontaneously generated from putrefying matter. This led to a revolution in the understanding of disease and to the development of modern medicine. Not long afterwards, glass light bulbs changed both work and leisure forever.

Meanwhile, new trade links between East and West in the nineteeth century meant that a technologically backward China soon caught up. Today it is the world's third-largest industrial power and its largest exporter, with total exports in 2009 of £749 billion.

It is also the world's largest producer of glass, controlling 34 per cent of the global market.

What's the name of the chemical that's bad for you and is found in Chinese food?

Despite its reputation in the press, monosodium glutamate is much less harmful than ordinary table salt.

The list of charges against MSG is a long one. It has been accused of causing obesity, nerve damage, high blood pressure, migraine, asthma and altering hormone levels. But every concerned public body that ever investigated it has given it a clean bill of health.

For centuries, it was agreed that there were only four basic tastes – sweet, sour, bitter and salty – until in 1908 Dr Kikunae Ikeda of Tokyo University discovered a fifth one: a 'meaty' taste that he named *'umami'*. This is the taste of MSG. Like soy sauce, it just makes your food a little more delicious.

The MSG scare arose out of so-called 'Chinese Restaurant Syndrome'. Dr Robert Ho Man Kwok coined the term in 1968, when a number of his patients complained of palpitations and numbness in their neck and arms after eating a large Chinese meal. Dr Kwok blamed monosodium glutamate, and though all subsequent research has proved that to generate such symptoms would require a concentration of MSG in food that would render it completely inedible, the stigma has somehow remained.

We now know that glutamate is present in almost every natural food stuff (it is particularly high in parmesan and tomato juice) and that the protein is so vital to our functioning that our own bodies produce 40 grams of it a day. Human milk contains lots of glutamate, which it uses as an alternate enhancement to sugar – MSG and sugar are the two things that get babies drinking.

A much more dangerous substance is recklessly sprinkled on food every time we eat. Excessive salt intake increases the risk of high blood pressure, strokes, coronary artery disease, heart and kidney failure, osteoporosis, stomach cancer and kidney stones. We'd be safer replacing it in our cruets with MSG.

In the European Union, monosodium glutamate is classified as a food additive – E621.

The dreaded 'e-numbers' listed on jars and tin cans are almost all completely benign; the 'E' stands for nothing more sinister than 'European'. It is simply an international way of labelling the different substances (by no means all of them artificial) that are found in our foods. If you wanted to avoid E numbers altogether, you couldn't: 78 per cent of the air we breathe is E941 (nitrogen) and even the purest water is made entirely from E949 (hydrogen) and E948 (oxygen).

Salt, apparently, doesn't have an e-number.

JOHNNY VEGAS *This is why I don't wanna do shows like this!*

STEPHEN *Why is that, Johnny?*

JOHNNY *Well, 'cause now, I'm gonna lie awake at night, fearing that I'm lactating poison! I feel like I've already hurt people enough in my lifetime.*

STEPHEN *It's not poison; it's good. We're trying to suggest that MSG is not as bad as it's been painted. You may not like the flavour, in which case, certainly, don't have any.*

JOHNNY *Yeah, but I don't want meaty-tasting breasts!*

Does eating chocolate give you acne?

No. Nothing we eat 'causes' acne (but go easy on the breakfast cereals).

Acne affects over 96 per cent of teenagers at some time during their adolescence.

Each human hair grows in an individual pouch in the skin called a follicle (from the Latin for 'little bag'). Feeding into each follicle is a gland that secretes a waxy substance called sebum (Latin for 'grease' or 'suet'). Next to each follicle is another gland, which carries sweat up to the surface of the skin through a tiny pore (from *poros*, Greek for 'passage').

During puberty, testosterone levels increase in both boys and girls giving rise to an over-production of sebum. This spills out into the sweat pores, clogging them up with oily compost ripe for bacteria. The result is a pimple. A colony of these is called acne vulgaris ('acne' for short). Boys have higher levels of testosterone than girls, which is why they also tend to have worse acne.

So it's not chocolate, but testosterone, that 'causes' acne. But diet is a factor too, and some foods definitely make it worse.

In 1981 Professor David Jenkins, a Toronto-based nutritionist, measured the effects of carbohydrates on blood-sugar levels. He found that starchy foods (like white bread, cereals and potatoes) raised blood-sugar levels dramatically; but sugary foods had much less effect. Starchy foods have a simpler chemical structure and are easier for the digestive system to convert into glucose, the most absorbable form of sugar. Protein, fats and more complex sugars (like chocolate) are harder to absorb. From this, Jenkins devised a scale called the GI, or Glycaemic Index (from Greek *glykys*, 'sweet', and *haima*, 'blood').

Foods with a high GI score – the ones that raise blood-sugar levels most – create a surge in the production of insulin, the hormone that regulates the body's intake of glucose. Insulin is itself controlled by testosterone, and dairy products are in turn thought to stimulate testosterone. So at breakfast, it's the cereal and the milk (a double dose of hormonal stimulants) rather than the sugar that may aggravate the acne.

The English word acne was first used in 1835, but it comes from a 1,500-year-old Assyrian spelling mistake. In the sixth century, Aëtius Amidenus, a physician from the city of Amida (now in modern Turkey), accidentally coined a new word – *akne* – to describe a pimple. He had meant to write *akme* (Greek for 'point').

Munching your favourite chocolate bar produces endorphins, which help relieve pain, reduce stress and lower the risk of heart disease and cancer. But pure cacao doesn't have the same effect. Mere chemicals are not enough to satisfy the craving: we also need taste, texture and memories to set our hearts (literally) racing. In 2007 a research company, The Mind Lab, showed that, for some people – especially women – eating a piece of dark chocolate made the heart beat faster, and for longer, than a passionate kiss.

Who gets over-excited by sugary drinks?

Parents.

There isn't a shred of scientific evidence that children become 'hyperactive' when given sugary drinks, sweets or snacks.

In one test, a group of children were all given the same sugar-rich drink, but the parents of half the sample were told they'd been given a sugar-*free* drink. When questioned afterwards, the parents who thought their children *hadn't* had any sugar (even though they had) reported far less hyperactive behaviour.

In another study, some children were put on high-sugar diets and others sugar-free ones. No difference in behaviour was observed. Not even when (according to the *British Medical Journal* in 2008) the children had already been diagnosed with attention deficit hyperactivity disorder (ADHD). Because parents expect sugar to cause hyperactivity, that's what they see.

It all began in 1973, when a US allergy specialist called Benjamin Feingold (1899–1982) first showed that hyperactivity in children is linked to what they eat, and proposed a diet for preventing it. He recommended cutting out all artificial colourings and flavourings, including sweeteners such as aspartame. The Feingold Diet didn't ban sugar but, as medical opinion gradually came to accept the connection between hyperactivity and diet, sugar somehow became confused in the public mind with 'sweeteners'.

No one has ever come up with a decent theory to explain exactly *how* sugar might have this effect on youngsters. If high blood-sugar levels were the cause, they'd be more likely to go ballistic after a bowl of rice or a baked potato.

Throughout the centuries, food has been blamed for causing the behaviour that people were most worried about at the time. The sixteenth-century herbalist John Gerard warned against the herb chervil, which 'has a certain windiness, by means whereof it provoketh lust'. Buddhist monks are forbidden to eat any member of the onion family, because they, too, are thought to cause lust when cooked – and anger when raw.

In the nineteenth century, moralising Victorians attributed 'degeneracy and idleness' in the Irish to the supposed soporific effect of the potato. Englishwomen, by contrast, were warned off eating meat. Such 'stimulating' food was liable to bring on debilitating periods, nymphomania and insanity.

How many glasses of water should you drink every day?

Eight is too many.

You lose water every second of the day through excreting, sweating or simply breathing, so you need to take in liquid to avoid becoming dehydrated. But the advice that you should drink eight glasses of water a day is just plain wrong.

In 1945 a *British Medical Journal* report advised that adults should consume 2.5 litres of water daily but specified that 'most of this quantity is contained in prepared foods'. In the sixty years since, this important final sentence seems to have fallen by the wayside. A normal diet contains enough embedded water for us, theoretically, not to need to drink anything at all.

Drinking lots of glasses of water on top of your normal consumption of food and drink will only make you urinate more.

It's often said that drinking water is good for flushing out your system and keeping your skin blemish-free, but the evidence is patchy. Your kidneys may be helped to remove excess salt in the short term but unless you've been overdosing on crisps (or alcohol) there is no particular benefit. Chronic dehydration makes your skin drier and less elastic, but taking in extra water won't remove your wrinkles and it's unlikely to stop you from getting spots.

Treating dehydration involves more than just water. You need to replace sugar and salts as well, so try eating watermelons. They're rich in sugar, as well as calcium, magnesium, potassium and sodium. Papaya's good, too, as are coconut, cucumber and celery.

The salts and sugar are necessary because they help transport the water around the body. If you find watermelons spoil the line of your safari suit, you can buy sachets of rehydration powders from chemists and travel agents. These contain glucose and salts – but you'll still need to source your own water to dissolve them in – which is where watermelons win: they're 92 per cent water.

Too much water, on the other hand, can be lethal. 'Water intoxication' or hyponatremia (from Greek *hypo*, 'under', Latin *natrium*, 'sodium' and Greek *haima*, 'blood') is caused by over-dilution of essential body salts. Excess water is expelled from the blood into other cells, which then expand and rupture – leading to nausea, headaches, disorientation and, eventually, death.

What use is a sauna?

Saunas do many things, but 'sweating out the body's toxins' isn't one of them.

Sweat is 99 per cent water, with tiny amounts of salt and other minerals. Its function is to cool the body as the water evaporates from the skin, not to remove waste products. It's the liver and kidneys that deal with any toxins in the body, converting them into something useful, or arranging for them to be excreted.

Nor does a sauna necessarily help you get rid of a hangover. Fifteen minutes in a sauna can lead to the loss of 1.5 litres

(2½ pints) of sweat. Unless you drink lots of water to compensate, sweating heavily will only make you more dehydrated. Dehydration puts your kidneys under stress, which slows down the elimination of alcohol from your system.

What a sauna *can* do well is clean your skin, by opening your pores as you sweat. A fifteen-minute session at a temperature of 70 °C and 40 per cent humidity raises the body's surface temperature by 10 °C and its internal temperature by 3 °C. This increases blood flow to the skin and makes the lungs work harder, increasing the intake of oxygen by up to 20 per cent – which is why endurance athletes often use saunas as part of their training.

A sauna followed by a cold shower generates feel-good endorphins in the brain, and can be used to treat mild depression. Research at the Thrombosis Institute in London has shown that the sauna–cold water combination also strengthens the immune system by increasing the number of white blood cells that fight disease. Saunas can also reduce the pain of arthritis and the Finns swear by them as a cure for the common cold.

Though 'sauna' is a Finnish word, the *idea* of the sauna is an ancient one. Writing in the fifth century BC, the Greek historian Herodotus described how the Scythians, a nomadic tribe from Iran, used small tents for the purpose, in which they burned cannabis on the hot stones – so they got high as well as clean. 'The Scythians', he wrote, 'enjoy it so much that they howl with pleasure.' The Apaches of North America have always used 'sweat lodges' made from willow frames covered with skins, in which up to twelve people sit naked around heated rocks. These are periodically soused with water to make steam, cleansing both body and spirit.

The sauna has a similar spiritual significance for the Finns. Traditionally it was a place for the family to gather, for women to give birth and for the dead to be washed before burial. An old Finnish saying is *unassa ollaan kuin kirkossa* – 'behave in a sauna as in a church'.

Finns who break this rule run the risk of being punished by the only permanent resident of the sauna, the *saunatonttu*, or 'sauna elf'.

The word 'sauna' is one of only two expressions in English borrowed from the Finnish language. The other is 'Molotov cocktail'.

What effect does drinking alcohol have on antibiotics?

It doesn't usually have any effect at all.

The idea that alcohol 'stops antibiotics working' was first put about in the venereal disease clinics set up after the Second World War. Penicillin, identified by Alexander Fleming in 1928, had proved particularly effective at clearing up sexually transmitted infections. It was prescribed with the strict instruction not to drink while taking it. The reason for this was psychological rather than pharmaceutical. Drunken people are more likely to jump at the chance of casual sex. By scaring their patients into not drinking, doctors and nurses were giving the drug a chance to work before the infection could be passed on.

This advice became standard medical practice, and it worked: most people still avoid alcohol when on a course of antibiotics. It's true that it's not a good idea to drink *heavily* on antibiotics, because the alcohol competes with the drug for 'processing time' in your liver. This means the drug may work a little more slowly. What it won't do is stop it working altogether.

Of over a hundred types of antibiotic available for prescription, only five are listed as having serious side effects if taken with alcohol.

Of these, the only one commonly prescribed is Metronidazole, which is used to combat some dental and gynaecological infections and for treating *Clostridium difficile*, a bacterial infection picked up in hospitals. The drug prevents the body from breaking down alcohol properly, leading to a build up in the blood of the highly toxic chemical acetaldehyde – a close relative of formaldehyde, better known as embalming fluid. The effects are similar to an extremely bad hangover: vomiting, increased heart rate and severe headaches.

In 1942 the American microbiologist Selman Waksman (1888–1973) – and his student Albert Schatz (1922–2005) – discovered streptomycin, the first drug to be effective against tuberculosis. Waksman described it as 'antibiotic' (from the Greek *anti* 'against' and *bios* 'life') because it killed living bacteria.

Antibiotics are powerless against colds or flu, which are viral infections. It's not clear what viruses are, or even if they can be said to be 'alive'. They have genes (but no cells) and can only reproduce using a host organism. Scientists tend to refer to them as 'biological entities' or 'organisms at the edge of life'.

What *does* stop antibiotics working is not alcohol but over-prescription. In farming 70 per cent of the antibiotics used are given to perfectly healthy animals. In medicine new strains of bacteria have become resistant to former 'wonder drugs' like streptomycin and the World Health Organisation estimates that a third of the world's population now carries a drug-resistant strain of TB. There are fears that as many as 35 million people may die from it before 2020.

Can you name a narcotic?

LSD, cocaine, speed?

None of the above. Medically speaking, a 'narcotic' is an opium derivative, such as morphine. A slightly looser definition might include any drug that causes unconsciousness – technically known as 'narcosis', from the Greek *narke*, meaning 'numbness' or 'torpor'.

Law enforcement agencies in the USA use the word 'narcotic' as a blanket term to mean *any* illegal drug – even though many of them are anything but narcotic in their effects, and many true narcotics, like codeine, are legal.

To avoid this confusion the medical profession now refers to opium – and its derivatives and man-made substitutes – as 'opioids'. Opium is made from *Papaver somniferum*, a type of poppy which has been grown as a medicinal herb for thousands of years.

Nowadays opioids are mostly used in pain control, a task for which they are unrivalled. Though dependence on opioid painkillers is a common result of long-term use, actual addiction is very rare. In 2001 the American Pain Society defined addiction as 'compulsive and continued use of a drug despite harm'. The most common side effect of prescribed narcotics is constipation.

In the nineteenth century, opioids were freely available over the counter. Heroin, discovered by the same man (Felix Hoffman) in the same year (1897) as aspirin, was originally a brand name and was marketed as a cough mixture. One of its supposed virtues was that it wasn't habit-forming. At the time, the medical authorities were much more worried about green tea, which was believed to cause anaemia, convulsions, hallucinations and suffocation.

Britain is currently aiming to become self-sufficient in home-grown opium poppies to ensure a regular supply of the powerful painkiller diamorphine (otherwise known as heroin) for those suffering from cancer or recovering from surgery. In the past, the UK has depended on imports from the Far East.

Despite a 40 per cent fall in production since 2008, Afghanistan still supplies 90 per cent of the world's opium. More than half of this comes from Helmand province, the main stronghold of the Taliban insurgents. According to the UN, the Afghan government manages to intercept only 2 per cent of the opium that is produced.

In 2009 the British army sprang into action and, shortly afterwards, the Ministry of Defence announced that they had seized 1.3 tons of 'a new strain of super poppy seeds', thus denying the Taliban revenue of some £247 million. The Ministry was later forced to admit that what the army had actually got hold of was 1,100 kilos of mung beans, a staple of the Afghan diet.

What's the best way to restart a stopped heart?

Not by using a defibrillator.

If you think otherwise, you've been watching too many medical dramas on TV. Electricity is only used when the heart is beating irregularly. If it has stopped completely, attempts to re-establish a heartbeat take the form of regular intravenous injections of adrenaline and other drugs. Survival rates for such patients are fewer than one in fifty.

The two main forms of irregular heartbeat are (1) the heart beating too fast or *ventricular tachycardia* (from the Greek *tachys*, 'fast', and *kardia*, 'heart') and (2) the random quivering known as *ventricular fibrillation* (from the Latin *fibrilla*, 'fibre', because the heart is a mass of twitching fibres). Both conditions are usually the result of a heart attack, brought on by a failure in blood supply to the heart muscle. If the flow of blood to the brain becomes so irregular that the patient loses consciousness and stops breathing, the heart attack has become a 'cardiac arrest' and requires immediate medical attention. Brain damage begins four minutes after the flow of blood has stopped.

It is at this point that the electric paddles, or defibrillator, are used to stimulate the heart muscle to return to a regular rhythm. If this takes place within three to five minutes of the onset of an arrest, then there is a 74 per cent chance of a normal heartbeat being restored and a one in three chance of survival. In 2007 the UK Department of Health announced that the 681 defibrillators installed at airports, railway stations and shopping centres had saved 117 lives.

The first defibrillator used on a human was in 1947, under the supervision of Ohio surgeon Claude Beck. Sudden cardiac arrest remains the biggest cause of death in the Western world: more than 70,000 die from it each year in the UK.

Without access to a defibrillator, the chances of survival are much lower — about 1 in 25. Nevertheless, proper use of manual resuscitation techniques saves many lives by keeping the patient's blood flowing until a defibrillator can be found. This is done by pressing rhythmically on the patient's chest to pump blood through the heart (mouth-to-mouth resuscitation is now deemed less effective). A steady beat is important and, for many years, first-aiders were taught to sing the song 'Nelly the Elephant' as they pumped. Now the recommendation is for faster chest compressions, so the 103 beats per minutes of the Bee Gee's 'Stayin' Alive' is preferred.

The face of the dummy still used to teach resuscitation techniques (known as 'Rescue Annie') is that of an unidentified young suicide pulled out of the river Seine in 1900. The pathologist at the morgue was so overcome by her beauty that he made a plaster cast of her face. Her tragic story made her a fashion icon for a whole generation of writers, artists and photographers.

When Peter Safar and Asmund Laerdal designed Rescue Annie in 1958, they had no idea that she would become the most kissed woman of all time.

STEPHEN *The defibrillators: what do you use those for?*
JACK DEE *To start the heart up again when it stops.*
JIMMY CARR *Oh. I use them for making paninis . . .*

Can a living person be a successful heart donor?

Surprisingly, it is possible for a living person to donate their heart to someone else and survive the experience – provided they get another heart in exchange.

This happens when someone with severe lung disease but a healthy heart is assessed as having a better chance of survival if they receive a heart-and-lung transplant. In return, they can donate their heart to someone who needs only a heart transplant.

The cardiac surgeon Magdi Yacoub (now Professor Sir Magdi Yacoub) carried out the first of these so-called 'domino' transplants in the UK in 1987. We don't know the patients' names because they requested no publicity. Later that year a cystic fibrosis sufferer called Clinton House became the first US donor of a living heart. He donated his to John Couch, while he received a new heart and lungs from an unidentified car accident victim.

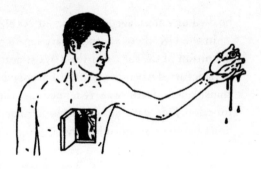

The first successful transplant of any kind made by a living donor took place in Boston in 1954, when one identical twin brother donated one of his kidneys to the other, both of whose kidneys had failed. In theory, everyone can survive perfectly well on one kidney, one lung, one of the two lobes of the liver and only parts of the pancreas and intestines. The liver, uniquely among such organs, has the capacity to grow back almost completely.

In 1896, the English surgeon Stephen Paget (1855–1926) wrote the standard textbook *Surgery of the Chest*, in which he predicted that it would always be too difficult and dangerous to operate on a human heart. But, later that very year, a German surgeon, Ludwig Rehn (1849–1930), successfully repaired the left chamber of a young man's heart after he had been stabbed in the chest. It was the first case of a surgeon operating on a heart and the patient surviving, and Rehn didn't dare try it again. Even in wartime, conventional surgical wisdom stated that shrapnel lodged in the heart should be left there and heart surgery for any reason was almost unheard of before the Second World War.

Things improved rapidly after the war. The South African surgeon Christiaan Barnard (1922–2001) performed the first heart transplant in Cape Town in 1967. Although his patient only lived for eighteen days, two-thirds of transplant patients now survive for more than five years. The longest recorded is Tony Huesman, a sporting goods retailer from Dayton, Ohio who lived for thirty-one years with a transplanted heart until he died of cancer, aged fifty-one, in 2009.

In the UK, these advances have led to a change in the legal definition of death. Until the 1970s, death was considered to have occurred when the heartbeat stopped. After the first heart transplants, death was redefined as the absence of brain function. This gave surgeons the chance to remove a donor heart before it stopped beating.

Which mammal has the most heartbeats in a lifetime?

Thanks to medical science, we do.

Large mammals have slow heartbeats and long lives and small ones have short lives and fast heartbeats. Because of this, no matter what size a mammal is, it has the same average number of heartbeats in a lifetime – about half a billion. This is known as 'the rate of living hypothesis' and it applies to all mammals except humans. Improvements in medicine and hygiene have extended our life expectancy so that we now get through more than five times as many heartbeats in a lifetime than all other mammals.

The world's smallest mammal is the Etruscan shrew (*Suncus etruscus*) of southern Europe, which weighs 2 grams (0.07 ounces) and is 3.5 centimetres (just over an inch) long. Its heart hammers away at an average 835 beats per minute but it only lives for a year, just enough to allow it to reproduce before being eaten.

At the other end of the scale is the Blue whale (*Balaenoptera musculus*), which can reach 30 metres (100 feet) long and weigh 150 tons (thirty times more than an African elephant). It has a heart the size of a small car, which thumps out its stately cadence just ten times a minute for eighty years.

The beats-per-life of the two species are remarkably similar: 439 million for the shrew; 421 million for the whale. In contrast, the average human heart, at seventy-two beats per minute spread over sixty-six years, will beat 2.5 billion times.

The US astronaut Neil Armstrong was so taken by the idea of having a finite number of heartbeats that he joked that he was going to give up exercise because he didn't want to use up his allocation too quickly. But it doesn't quite work like that: though strenuous exercise makes the heart beat faster in the short term, the resultant fitness *decreases* the heart rate in general.

An even better way to slow the heart rate is to take up yoga. Research conducted over thirty days in 2004 in Bangalore, India, showed that yogic breath control and meditation led to an average reduction in the heart rate of 10.7 beats per minute. The control group, who attempted to reduce their heart rate by other means, didn't manage any lasting improvement at all.

A macabre experiment to record the effect of fear on the heart rate was conducted in 1938, when convicted murderer John Deering donated his body to science while he still was alive. Sentenced to death by firing squad in Salt Lake City, Utah, he allowed Dr Stephen Besley, the prison doctor, to wire him to an electrocardiograph. Beneath Deering's calm exterior, Besley recorded his heart rate rocketing from 72 to 120 as he was strapped down, and reaching 180 at the moment of impact. His heart stopped 15.6 seconds later.

Besley commented that, despite having 'put on a good front', the machine had confirmed what he'd expected: Deering 'was scared unto death'.

How long do mayflies live?

The one thing 'everybody' knows about mayflies is that they only live for a day – but their lifetimes are much longer than that.

Depending on species, the adult lives from less than a day to a week, but this is only the final stage of a much longer life-cycle. Most of the mayfly's existence is spent as an aquatic nymph, a period lasting from a few months to four years.

There are 2,500 species of mayfly, fifty-one of which live in the UK. They fly all through the summer – not just in May – and they are not actually 'flies'. True flies belong to the order *Diptera* (Greek for 'two wings'), whereas mayflies belong to the order *Ephemeroptera* (Greek for 'short-lived wings'). Mayflies are much older than true flies. They were one of the first flying insects: there are mayfly fossils that are 300 million years old. Their closest relatives are dragonflies and damselflies – neither of which are 'flies' either.

Mayflies are unique among insects, in that their final skin-shedding takes place after their wings have formed. On first emerging from the water, the immature adult, or nymph, moults and becomes a 'dun', so-called because of its small, dull-coloured wings. It flies a short distance from its pond, and rests for a while on vegetation. Then it undergoes its ultimate transformation, sloughing its final skin and emerging as the much shinier 'spinner'.

Adult mayflies never eat: their only interest is sex. Vast

swarms of males take to the air simultaneously and the females fly among them to pick a partner. Mating takes place in flight, and as soon as the deed is done, the male drops to the water, dead. The female immediately lays her eggs in the water – and *then* drops dead. One species – *Dolania americana* – dies within five minutes of its final moult. In that tiny window of time, it has to dry its new wings, fly, select a partner, mate, and – if it's a female – lay its eggs. A day is a long, long time in the life of a mayfly.

In some countries, it's not only fish that benefit from these huge clouds of protein from the sky. Along the Sepik River in New Guinea, villagers skim masses of post-copulatory mayflies from the surface of the water and cook them in sago pancakes. Apparently, they taste a bit like caviar.

What comes out of a cocoon?

Not butterflies. But most moths do – and so do fleas, bees, worms and spiders.

A cocoon is a kind of silken changing room where a creature metamorphoses into a different stage of its life – such as a spider's egg into a baby spider or a caterpillar into a moth. The word comes from *kokkos*, Greek for 'berry'.

Silkworms are not worms but caterpillars. At about a month old, they spend three days carefully winding a mile-long thread of their own saliva round their bodies that dries into a casing to keep them safe during their transformation into a silkworm moth. Unfortunately for them, it is at this stage that they are picked up by silkworm farmers and shipped off to the factory. It takes 3,000 cocoons to make a pound of silk.

Baby bees develop inside a cocoon made of royal jelly. They

eat themselves out of it. Flea larvae become adults inside cocoons. They can remain in that state, buried in your carpet for months, until vibrations caused by movement nearby announce that a host animal is available for them to jump on.

After mating, an earthworm secretes mucus that hardens into a loose girdle around its body. This sheath slowly slides along the worm's length, collecting eggs and sperm from its genital openings as it goes, finally sliding off its head like a vest, where the ends seal up and it becomes a lemon-shaped cocoon. Inside the cocoon, the eggs and sperm merge into embryos. Spiders, too, place their eggs in a silken sack to hatch. They spin their thickest grade of silk for this purpose. Peasants in Romania use it as an antiseptic wound dressing.

Butterflies don't make cocoons; instead they form chrysalises (from the Greek for 'golden sheath'). A cocoon is an external structure, designed to protect the creature within, whereas the chrysalis *is* the creature. The hard exterior of the chrysalis is the final skin of the caterpillar before it becomes a butterfly.

For many centuries butterflies and moths were thought to be completely unrelated to caterpillars. Then in 1679 the German naturalist and illustrator Maria Sibylla Merian (1647–1717) published a book called *The Caterpillar: Marvelous Transformation and Strange Floral Food* which meticulously detailed the life-cycle and metamorphoses of 186 species of butterflies and moths. Because she published it in German, rather than Latin, it became one of the most talked about science books of the age.

Maria's organised approach to scientific observation and recording was far ahead of most of her contemporaries. Despite this, her discoveries were used by other scientists to justify the old theory of 'preformationism' – the idea that all life was created simultaneously at the beginning of time. They argued that, because the makings of the adult butterfly existed within its pupa form, so Adam and Eve had contained within themselves all the humans who came afterwards, already formed, like a set of smaller and smaller Russian dolls.

What does an amoeba live in?

No, it's not 'soup' or 'dribble' or anything like that. It may surprise you to learn that some amoebae live in houses they design and build themselves.

Amoebae (from Greek *amoibe*, 'change') are minute single-celled organisms. No one knows how many countless thousands of different species there are: anywhere that's damp will provide a home for them – as we know to our cost. The species that causes amoebic dysentery kills over 100,000 people a year and lives in the intestines and livers of 50 million more.

Living beings don't get much simpler than an amoeba: they're just an outer membrane full of a watery fluid surrounding a nucleus containing genetic material. They have no fixed shape, but they do have a front and back, and move by squeezing bits of themselves forward in the direction of food. They eat by surrounding smaller bits of algae or bacteria and absorbing them, and they reproduce by splitting themselves in two.

Which makes it extraordinary that one branch of the amoeba family is able to build themselves portable shelters. They do it by swallowing microscopic granules of sand. Once they have enough on board, they start to glue them together by secreting a form of organic cement. As no one has ever observed this process, we have no idea how they do it.

Each species creates its own distinctive style of home. The des res of *Difflugia coronata* is a globe, with a scalloped entrance at the front, and eight points like the fins of a 1950s spaceship at the back. *Difflugia pyriform* constructs a pear-shaped urn; *Difflugia bacillefera*, a cigar-shaped tube. None of them is bigger than a full-stop.

As with so many domestic arrangements these days, inevitably the time comes to split up. The parent amoeba gets to keep the house; the offspring inherits whatever spare building material is left lying around so it can start knocking up one of its own. How is any of this possible without a brain, or even a nervous system?

In 1757 an Austrian miniature painter and naturalist called Johann Rösel von Rosenhof (1705–59) described and drew an amoeba for the first time. He called it Proteus after the Greek god who could change his shape at will. Since that time, the word 'amoeba' has become universal shorthand for something basic or unsophisticated.

Maybe it's time to revise our ideas. We have recently learnt that the genetic information packed into the single nucleus of *Amoeba proteus* is 200 times greater than our own.

They may be brainless, but you can hardly call an amoeba 'simple'.

What do Mongolians live in?

Don't call it a yurt. They hate that.

Yurt is a Turkish word meaning 'homeland'. Mongolians live in a tent called a *ger*, which means 'home' in Mongolian.

In recent years, 'yurt' has come to be used indiscriminately to refer to any of the portable, felt-covered, lattice-framed structures that are common to many cultures across the Central Asian steppe.

It's a great insult to a Mongolian to call his *ger* a 'yurt'. The English word 'yurt' comes from the Russian *yurta*, a disparaging term for the kind of jerry-built hovels you find in shanty towns. The Russians borrowed it from the Turkic languages where its original meaning was 'the imprint left on the ground by a tent'. Mongolian is a member of an entirely separate language family from Turkic and Russian, and the whole of Mongolian culture is built around the ger. To call their beloved dwelling a yurt is akin to calling a York-shireman's home *un chateau* or *ein Schloss* rather than his castle.

Two-thirds of Mongolians still live in gers – not out of bull-headed national pride, but because they are such practical structures. The walls are circular, made from a lattice of willow held together with leather strips, and topped with a domed roof made from slender, flexible poles. The whole thing is covered in layers of felt and they can be put up or taken down in less than an hour. Their aerodynamic shape makes them very stable in the howling winds of the steppe and their thick felt lining keeps them incredibly warm. Rural Mongolia has the widest temperature range in the world: from a sweltering 45 °C in summer to winter lows of −55 °C. Even those Mongolians who do own houses tend to move into a ger for the winter, just because they are so cosy.

There are strict rules governing layout. To minimise draughts, the door always faces south. The kitchen is to the right of the door and the traditional Buddhist altar is at the back. The beds are to the left and right of the altar. Guests sit at the top left end of the ger; the more honoured you are, the further you sit from the door. Family members sit on the right. In the middle is the wood- or dung-burning stove with its flue poking through the central roof vent. In summer the walls can be rolled up for extra ventilation.

When a Mongolian couple gets married, their families buy or build them a brand-new ger.

The earliest archaeological evidence for the ger only dates back to the twelfth century, but rock carvings, and accounts of ancient travellers like Herodotus, suggest that something similar has been in use on the steppes for at least 2,500 years.

The armies of Genghis Khan (1162–1227) were housed in similar collapsible structures, and the great Khan himself administered the whole of the Mongol empire from a huge ger known as a *gerlug*. It was permanently mounted on a cart pulled by twenty-two bulls.

STEPHEN *What do Mongolians live in?*

ROB BRYDON *They're called something like yak . . . it's like a yult or a yak.*

JO BRAND *Do you mean a yurt?*

ROB *Yes, that's the one.*

KLAXON

ROB *No, that's *not* the one. No, no.*

Can you name a tapestry?

Go to the top of the class if the medieval Apocalypse Tapestry from Angers in north-west France sprang to mind. Or the second-century BC ancient Greek tapestry found in Sampul, western China; or the four fifteenth-century Devonshire Hunting Tapestries hanging in the Victoria and Albert Museum in London.

But it's minus 10 if you said 'Bayeux Tapestry'. This isn't a tapestry at all: it's embroidery. A tapestry is a heavy textile with a design woven in as it's made on a loom, while embroidery is the business of stitching decorations on to a piece of existent fabric – in this case, coloured wool on linen.

The Bayeux *embroidery* is long and thin. It's 70 metres (230 feet) long but only 50 centimetres (20 inches) high. It's a piece of Norman propaganda and the person most likely to have commissioned it is William the Conqueror's half-brother, Odo (1037–98), Bishop of Bayeux and Earl of Kent, who features prominently in the narrative. Today it hangs in France, but the workmanship is English and it was probably made at Canterbury.

Apart from King Harold himself, it's easy to tell who's who: the English are depicted with lavish moustaches while the Normans are clean-shaven. French commentators at the time were shocked by the long-haired English 'with their combed and oiled tresses', calling them 'reluctant warriors' or 'boy-women' (*feminei iuvenes*). The French, on the other hand, look like skinheads.

The battle of Hastings didn't take place at Hastings but several miles away on Senlac Ridge, just outside the helpfully renamed village of Battle. The English king mustered his troops at a vantage point on the crest of the hill known as the 'Hoary Apple Tree' and the Saxon line held until he was lured down to his death by a faked Norman retreat.

Harold is traditionally supposed to be the figure shown with an arrow in his eye, but there are two other figures near where his name is stitched – one with a spear through his chest, and one being cut down by a horseman. He could well be both, or neither, of these people.

In August 1944 Heinrich Himmler, Hitler's second-in-command, ordered the head of the SS in France to bring the Bayeux Tapestry with him as the German Army retreated from

France. Four days later, the SS tried to snatch it from the Louvre, but they were too late – the Resistance had occupied the building.

If Himmler had acted faster, the so-called 'tapestry' of Bayeux would have left France on a Nazi truck – an ordeal it might very well not have survived.

Who became king of England after the battle of Hastings?

WHO HE?

Edgar the Ætheling.   *ED*

There were four kings of England in 1066, one after the other. Edward the Confessor died in January and was succeeded by Harold. When Harold was killed at Hastings in October, Edgar the Ætheling was proclaimed king. He reigned for two months before William the Conqueror was crowned on Christmas Day.

Among many things the Normans brought with them that the English didn't like was the idea that a king's eldest son automatically succeeded him. Anglo-Saxon kings were elected, not born. The duty of organising this fell to a council of religious and political leaders called the Witan (short for *Witangemot*, or 'wise-meeting').

Royal blood was only one of the factors taken into account. The king had to be able to defend the country and a dying king could nominate anyone as his heir. When Edward the Confessor died childless and without naming his successor, there was a constitutional crisis. His reign had ended thirty years of Danish rule (begun with Cnut's conquest of England in 1016) and his mother was a Norman. This gave both Cnut's great-nephew, William, Duke of Normandy, and King

Harald Hardrada of Norway and (in his opinion) Denmark, claims to the English throne.

Edgar was Edward the Confessor's great-nephew. The word *Ætheling* ('prince') marked him out as a potential king, but he was only fifteen. With invasion imminent, the Witan rejected him as too inexperienced and opted instead for Harold Godwinson, Earl of Wessex and Edward the Confessor's brother-in-law.

Harold promptly marched up to Yorkshire where he defeated (and killed) Harald Hardrada at the battle of Stamford Bridge, before having to rush all the way back down again, to lose his own life near Hastings on the Sussex coast. As soon as news of Harold's death reached London, the surviving members of the Witan met to elect Edgar as king. But their heart wasn't really in it. They soon rescinded their decision and surrendered the boy to William. He hadn't even been crowned.

But Edgar, like Harold, was no milksop. Born in Hungary, son of Edward the Exile, he escaped Norman custody and became known as Edgar the Outlaw. He tried several times to recover the English throne, invaded Scotland, attempted to conquer parts of Italy and Sicily, took part in the First Crusade (in 1098) and may even have joined the Byzantine Emperor Alexios I's elite band of axe-wielding, sea-going mercenaries known as the Varangian Guard. Based in Constantinople, feared across the Mediterranean, it was mostly composed of exiled Englishmen.

When Henry I (1069–1135), William the Conqueror's fourth son, married Edgar's niece Matilda, he pardoned the former boy king. Edgar died in Scotland in 1126, at the venerable age of seventy-five. Unmarried and childless, he was buried in an unmarked grave: the last Anglo-Saxon king and the last of the male line of the House of Wessex, England's first royal family.

Who invented Gothic architecture?

Not the Goths. It was the French, if anyone.

The Renaissance artist and historian Giorgio Vasari (1511–74) invented the term 'Gothic' for the now much-admired style of architecture in 1550. He meant it as an insult. In his opinion, pointed arches and huge vaulted ceilings were 'monstrous and barbarous' horrors of bad taste that he blamed on the Goths, the Nordic invaders who had sacked Rome and defiled Italy's classical past.

Best known today for his *Lives of the Artists* – short biographies of contemporary painters, sculptors and architects such as Leonardo and Michelangelo – Giorgio Vasari was also an architect himself. He designed the Uffizi Palace in Florence for Cosimo de' Medici (1519–74). Now world-famous as a museum, it was originally an office block for lawyers (*uffizi* is Italian for 'offices').

Vasari thought the northern French medieval style that reached its peak in the great cathedrals of Chartres, Reims and Lincoln was ugly, fussy and old-fashioned, denouncing it as 'German' as well as 'Gothic'. In fact, it had no connection with either and had evolved out of Romanesque, the simpler, rounder, sturdier style known in Britain as 'Norman' architecture. If you'd asked a medieval cathedral mason what he was doing, he'd have said *opus Francigenum*: 'French work'.

But Vasari's contemptuous nickname stuck, just as the words Baroque, Cubist and Impressionist (all once terms of abuse) would later do. The 'Gothic' style soon spread all over Western Europe, but it wasn't until the late eighteenth century that it lost its negative connotations, as artists and writers looked to the Middle Ages for inspiration. In architecture the 'Gothic Revival' led to buildings like Augustus Pugin's Houses of Parliament (1835) and in literature to a new school of 'gothic' novels, full of ghostly ruins, haunted houses and fainting heroines. It was this literary sense of the word that led (in 1983) to teenagers who wore black clothes, painted their faces white and listened to gloomy music being called Goths.

The original Goths came from southern Sweden (still known today as Götaland) and the name 'Goth' simply meant 'the people' (from Old Norse *gotar*, 'men'). Over four centuries, they migrated east and south to conquer large areas of France, Spain and Italy. In AD 410, Alaric, the military commander of the western branch of Goths (known as Visigoths) attacked and looted Rome – the first time the city had fallen to a foreign power in 800 years. Although the emperor Honorius (AD 384–423) had transferred his capital to Ravenna eight years earlier, it was still a psychological shock and a key moment in the long decline of the Roman Empire.

But the Goths weren't all doom and gloom. They founded cities, converted to Christianity and established a written legal code that was still used in Spain centuries later. By the end of the sixth century, however, defeated by other Germanic tribes in the East and driven out of Spain by Islamic invaders from North Africa, the Goths gradually started to fade from history.

The last traces of the Gothic language were written down in sixteenth-century Crimea. All that survives is a list of eighty words, and a song whose meaning no one now understands.

JACK DEE *I was a Goth for a while.*
STEPHEN *Were you?*
JACK *Yeah. I was asked to leave because I was just too miserable.*

Which country do Huns come from?

Neither Hungary nor Germany. The original Huns were more of an army than a tribe, so no modern country can claim to be descended from them.

The Huns arrived in Europe from Central Asia in the fourth century AD. In just eighty years, they built an empire that stretched from the steppes of central Asia to what is now modern Germany, and from the Black Sea to the Baltic. They rode small, fast horses, and spent almost all their time on them. The Romans said that the Huns fought, ate, slept and carried out diplomacy on horseback – so much so that they became dizzy when they set foot on the ground.

We don't know exactly where they came from or what language they spoke, but most historians now believe the Huns were a multi-ethnic, multilingual army. All they had in common was their loyalty to their great leader, Attila (about 404–53), and their superlative technique as mounted archers.

After Attila the Hun died, his three sons quarrelled and his empire disintegrated almost as rapidly as it had formed. The remnants of his armies were defeated in 454 by an alliance of Goths and other German tribes at the battle of Nedao (now in western Hungary). Since there was no Hun state – no buildings, laws, culture or common language – almost nothing of them has survived except stories. This has allowed many people across Europe and Asia to claim Hun blood (the implication being, of course, that they are related to the heroic warrior-king Attila). Given the racial diversity of the Huns, this is meaningless. If the Huns can be said to live anywhere today, they live everywhere.

In nineteenth-century English, 'Hun' meant much the same as 'vandal': someone given to mindless acts of destruction. It wasn't until the very beginning of the twentieth century that 'the Huns' came to mean the Germans – and it was a German who started it. On 27 July 1900, Kaiser Wilhelm II was addressing his troops on their way to join an alliance of colonial powers putting down an anti-Western revolt in China. He urged them to show no mercy to the 'Boxer' rebels (the sarcastic Western name for the movement who called themselves 'The Righteous Fists of Harmony'). 'The Huns under the leadership of Attila', he told them, 'gained a reputation that is still remembered today. May the name of Germany become equally well known in China, so that no Chinaman will ever again dare to look askance at a German.'

When the First World War began in 1914, Allied propagandists seized on this remark. An editorial in *The Times*, headlined 'The March of the Huns', set the tone. It painted the Germans as even worse than the barbarians of old. Unlike the Kaiser, the article thundered, 'even Attila had his better side'.

By the Second World War 'Kraut' and 'Jerry' had become the popular British nicknames for the Germans, although Churchill (a keen historian) still preferred 'the Hun'. In a 1941 broadcast he described the German invasion of the Soviet Union as the 'brutish masses of the Hun soldiery, plodding on like a swarm of crawling locusts'.

STEPHEN *You'll find Alans on the Russian border in the northern Caucasus Mountains, where the Alan tribe has lived since being driven there by the Huns in the fourth century.*

ALAN *That was a bad weekend.*

STEPHEN *Yeah.*

ALAN *We still talk about that.*

STEPHEN *You, and Alan Coren, and Alan Bennett, and Alan Parsons . . .*

ALAN *We get together. We conference call.*

STEPHEN *Yeah.*

ALAN *And if someone mentions the Huns, quite often there's a lull in the conversation, and we have to gather ourselves.*

How did Attila the Hun die?

Leading his army to victory on the battlefield? Laying waste to a Roman city? Murdered by a scheming henchman? No. Attila the Hun – the greatest warrior of his age, the man the Romans called *flagellum Dei*, 'the scourge of God', died in bed. Of a nosebleed.

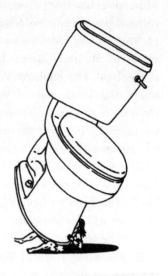

We know this from the Roman historian Priscus, who visited Attila's court in AD 448. According to his account, Attila was celebrating his marriage to a young Gothic woman called Ildico and retired to bed drunk. Next morning his new wife was found weeping over his corpse. The blood vessels in his nose had burst while he slept and he had drowned in his own gore. Attila was about forty-seven years old and he had led the Hunnish army for almost twenty years.

Attila owed much of his success to the devastating speed and manoeuvrability of his troops. Unlike other land armies of the time, they could fight in any weather, not just in summer. In a battle or siege Hun archers could unleash 50,000 arrows in the first ten minutes. But Attila was more than just a ruthless general: he was also a shrewd negotiator. As city after city fell, he liked to pose as a reasonable man, accepting gold in exchange for his victims' future security and building an empire on fear, like a mafia boss or a drugs baron. He didn't want land or power, just obedience and booty. Because of this pragmatic approach, even today his name means barbarism and chaos for some people, but heroic defiance for others.

To manage his set of shifting alliances, Attila had to make sure there was always a plentiful supply of gold (which meant more fighting to acquire it). From his base in Hungary he switched his military focus from the Persians to the Eastern Romans in Constantinople, and then to the Western Romans in Italy and Gaul. Finally, in AD 451, at the battle of Châlons in Gaul, the Huns clashed head-on with the Roman forces of the West. Such was the range of Attila's deal-making skills that almost every tribe in mainland Europe found themselves on one side or the other.

This battle marked the beginning of the end for both the Huns and the old Roman Empire. The Romans and their Gothic allies won, but only just: the Roman legions were decimated and never fought again. Rome was sacked once more in 455 (this time by Vandals) and the Empire relocated to Constantinople, where it stayed for the next 800 years. The complex network of allegiances Attila had built up didn't survive his death two years later and, a year after that, the much-reduced Hun army suffered their final defeat and were scattered, never to return.

Attila's personal style was modest in comparison to the gold-bedecked gangsters around him. He used wooden goblets and plates, dressed simply, and his sword carried no decoration. Not so his funeral. He was buried in a gaudy triple-walled coffin, with a layer each of gold, silver and iron, all of them stuffed full of treasure.

He died somewhere in what is now Hungary, but his grave has never been found. To ensure its location remained secret, all the men in the burial party were killed when they returned to camp.

What should you do when you get a nosebleed?

Don't tilt your head back!

This can divert the nosebleed into the throat. Swallowing blood irritates the stomach and can lead to nausea and vomiting, or if it finds its way into the lungs it can choke you – as Attila the Hun found to his cost. The best treatment is to sit down with your back straight and lean *forward*. Keeping your head above your heart lessens the bleeding. Leaning forward helps drain the blood from your nose.

According to the *British Medical Journal* you can stop the bleeding by using your thumb and index finger to squeeze the soft part of your nose for five to ten minutes. This helps the blood to clot. A cold compress or ice pack placed across the bridge of your nose also helps. If the nosebleed lasts for more than 20 minutes – or if it was caused by a bang on the head – you should go to the doctor.

The scientific term for a nosebleed is epistaxis, which is Greek for 'dripping from above'. The two most common causes of nosebleeds are being punched in the face and nose-picking. The web of blood vessels in your nose can also rupture owing to sharp changes in air pressure or temperature caused by cold weather or central heating, or if you blow your nose too hard.

Almost all nosebleeds occur in the front section of the nose, under the nose bone or septum. This is known as Kiesselbach's area, and it's vulnerable because four facial arteries connect there. Wilhelm Kiesselbach (1839–1902) was a German ear, nose and throat specialist who wrote the definitive textbook on the subject called *Nosenbluten* (German for 'nosebleeds').

High levels of the hormone oestrogen during a woman's period can lead to an increase in blood pressure causing nasal blood vessels to inflate and burst. This is no mere nosebleed.

It goes by the alarming name of 'vicarious menstruation'.

STEPHEN *What are the commonest causes of nosebleeds?*
ALAN *Bouncy castles.*
STEPHEN *A classic, yeah. Another one is being punched in the face.*

What happens if you swallow your tongue?

Nothing. It's physically impossible to swallow your own tongue.

The airway of an unconscious person can sometimes briefly become blocked as the muscle of their tongue becomes limp and it collapses into the back of their throat. However, it will return to its normal position in a few seconds. The tongue is kept in place by a small piece of tissue underneath called the frenulum linguae (from Latin *frenulum*, 'little bridle', and *lingua*, 'tongue'), which stops it being swallowed.

The idea that the tongue is in danger of being swallowed dates back to the early years of first aid in the late nineteenth century. First-aiders were taught that, if someone fainted or was having a fit, they should use forceps to pull the tongue forward, or, if none were available, to grab it with their fingers, using a handkerchief. Some well-meaning (but misguided) people still do this today, inserting pieces of wood – or even their wallets – into the mouths of people who are having fits. This is not a good idea. It stops the patient from being able to breathe.

If someone faints, don't start stuffing the contents of your pockets down their throat, put them into the recovery position: lay them on one side, with their chin tilted up so they can breathe clearly.

Swallowing occurs about 2,000 times a day. Except for the initial conscious decision to do it, it is an automatic process that involves twelve separate muscle movements. Alzheimer's patients and victims of strokes sometimes lose the ability to swallow. They are helped to relearn how to do it by speech therapists. This is because speech uses exactly the same combination of muscles as swallowing.

When someone is close to death, the swallowing reflex often fails. This leads to a build up of saliva and mucus in the back of the throat, causing the so-called 'death rattle'. Before writing the patient off, however, check their airway for wallets.

Which part of your tongue tastes bitter things?

All of it.

The 'tongue map', once widely taught in schools, purported to show how each area of the tongue was solely responsible for one of 'the four basic tastes' – sweet, sour, bitter and salty. In fact, this is quite wrong. Wherever you have taste buds – all over the tongue and the roof of the mouth – you can detect all tastes more or less equally. Plus, there are more than four basic ones.

According to the tongue map, the tip of the tongue tasted sweet things and the back, bitter ones. The sides of the tongue at the front were for tasting salt while the sides at the back did sour. The map was based on German research published in 1901 but an influential Harvard psychologist with the unfortunate name of Edwin Boring (1886–1968) mistranslated it. What the original research had shown was that the human tongue has areas of *relative* sensitivity to different tastes – but Boring's translation stated that each could *only* be tasted in one zone.

What is really mysterious about the tongue map is that it was the official truth for such a long time, even though it's so easily disproved. (Just put some sugar on the part of your tongue that the map says tastes only salt.) It wasn't until 1974 that another American scientist, Dr Virginia Collings, re-examined the original theory. She showed that, though sensitivity to the four main tastes did vary around the tongue, it was only to an insignificant degree. She also demonstrated that all taste buds taste all tastes.

The other myth the tongue map perpetuated was that there are only four basic tastes. There are at least five. Umami is the taste of protein in savoury foods such as bacon, cheese, seaweed or Marmite. It was first identified by Professor Kikunae Ikeda, professor of chemistry at Tokyo University, as long ago as 1908, but was only formally confirmed as the 'true' fifth taste in 2000 when researchers at the University of Miami discovered protein receptors on the human tongue.

'Umami' is derived from *umai*, the word for 'tasty' in Japanese. Professor Ikeda found out that its key ingredient is monosodium glutamate, now known as MSG. Ikeda was shrewd – he sold his recipe for it to the Ajinomoto Company, which still holds one third of the 1.5-million-ton global annual market for synthetic MSG.

Given the importance of protein in our diet, it makes sense for umami to stimulate the pleasure centre of our brains. A robust, mature red wine, for example, has an 'umami' taste. A bitter taste, by contrast, alerts us to the possibility of danger.

'Taste' shouldn't be confused with *flavour*, which is a broader experience involving not just taste, but also smell, sight, touch and even hearing (it's thought that the sound of crunchy food contributes to its flavour).

Lexical-gustatory synaesthesia is a rare condition whereby taste and language are confused in the brain, so that each word has a specific taste. In one experiment a woman tasted tuna whenever she thought of the word 'castanet'.

What does cracking your knuckles do?

Don't worry: it won't cause arthritis. At worst, it might leave you with a limp handshake.

We know this because of the selfless dedication of Dr Donald L. Unger, an octogenarian physician from California. Warned as a child by his mother that if he didn't stop cracking his knuckles he would end up with arthritis, he embarked on an experiment, cracking the knuckles of his left hand (but not those of his right) every day for more than sixty years. His conclusion was that knuckle-cracking had no serious effect. At the end of the experiment, he claims, he 'looked up to the heavens and said: "Mother, you were wrong, you were wrong, you were wrong."' His efforts won him the 2009 IgNobel prize for Medicine, a parody of the Nobel Prize started in 1991 and awarded annually for improbable research that 'first makes us laugh and then makes us think'.

This is not to say that knuckle-cracking is entirely harmless: it can make your joints swell and inflame your ligaments, and, over time, can reduce the strength of your grip.

Our finger joints, like most moving joints in our bodies, are called synovial joints because they contain a strange liquid called synovial fluid whose job is to cushion and lubricate the joint. But it doesn't 'flow' as most bodily fluids do: it has a thick, gel-like consistency, rather like egg white (hence the word *synovial*, from the Greek *syn-*, 'with', and Latin *ovum*, 'egg'). Between each joint is a capsule, filled with synovial fluid and sealed by a membrane. When you pull the bones apart, the membrane stretches. This reduces the pressure inside the capsule and, as the fluid moves to fill the vacuum, bubbles of carbon dioxide form. The 'pop' that we hear is the bubbles *forming* (not bursting) inside the capsule.

If you X-ray a joint just after it has been cracked, the bubbles of carbon dioxide are clearly visible. The joint can't be cracked again until they've dissolved back into the fluid, which explains why you can't crack the same knuckle repeatedly.

The cracking of knuckles (and the creaking of joints) has a scientific name: *crepitus*, from the Latin *crepare*, 'to crack'.

Arthritis comes from the Greek *arthron*, 'joint', and *-itis,* a suffix denoting 'inflammation'. It's been around as long as animals have had articulated skeletons (there is evidence that some dinosaurs' ankle joints were arthritic). The first evidence of human arthritis can be found in ancient Egyptian mummies that date back to 4500 BC.

Arthritis comes in over a hundred different forms and afflicts all ages and ethnic groups. After stress, it's responsible for more lost working days in the UK than any other medical condition, at an estimated annual cost of £5.8 billion. A quarter of all adult Britons consult their GP each year with arthritis-related complaints.

Cracked knuckles are responsible for none of them.

What are the symptoms of leprosy?

In the popular mind, lepers have rotting flesh and parts of their bodies drop off.

It doesn't work like that. Leprosy – or Hansen's disease as it's now called – is an infectious bacterial disease that affects the skin and damages nerve-endings. This means that sufferers can't feel pain and so repeatedly injure their fingers and toes. Over time these wounds become infected and leave disfiguring scars.

It is these injuries, not the disease itself, that cause the deformities leprosy is famous for. People can live into old age with the disease as it doesn't attack vital organs but, left untreated, it can cause crippling disabilities and even blindness.

Leprosy is from the Greek *lepros* ('scaly'). Ironically, it comes from the same root as the word *Lepidoptera* ('scale wings'), the scientific name for butterflies. For many centuries, the word 'leprosy' was used indiscriminately to cover a broad range of disfiguring skin diseases. A 'leper' might just as easily have been someone with a bad case of psoriasis. It wasn't until 1873, when the Norwegian physician Gerhard Armauer Hansen (1841–1912) identified *Mycobacterium leprae* as the cause of leprosy, that its accurate diagnosis was possible. Hansen's discovery was groundbreaking. It was the first time a bacterium had been proven to cause a disease in humans.

Until this point, it had been assumed that leprosy was hereditary because, despite its scary reputation, it's quite difficult to catch. About 95 per cent of people are naturally resistant to the bacterium, and even those who aren't require prolonged close contact to become infected. In 1984, to get this point across, Pope John Paul II kissed a number of lepers in a South Korean leper colony.

The good news is that Hansen's disease has been treatable with antibiotics since 1941. Over the last twenty years, 15 million patients have been cured but there are still some 250,000 new cases a year, and a million people worldwide are receiving, or are in need of, treatment. In 2009 121 countries recorded cases of leprosy. Even the USA recorded 150 and the UK twelve. More than half of all new cases are reported in India. Although 150,000 new cases a year sounds high, this is an infection rate of less than 1 in 10,000. According to World Health Organization standards, this officially qualifies leprosy for 'eliminated' status.

Europe's only remaining leper colony is in Tichilesti in Romania. In 1991 the colony was opened and residents were free to leave. Many of them had known nothing else since childhood and decided to stay on: the colony is more like a village than a hospital, with its own farm, two churches and even a vineyard.

Leprosy is a rare example of a bacterial disease that almost exclusively attacks humans: the only other animals that can catch leprosy naturally are chimpanzees, mangabey monkeys and nine-banded armadillos.

Why did lepers start carrying bells?

Leper's bells were designed to attract people, not to keep them away.

From the earliest times, lepers were forced to live separately. In Europe they were legally forbidden to marry, make a will or appear in court – and were only allowed to talk to a non-leper if they stood downwind. In the Old Testament, God himself instructs Moses to 'put out of the camp every leper'.

This was because leprosy was regarded as a punishment rather than an infectious disease: it was an outer 'uncleanness' caused by inner sin, something that God would smite you with if you harboured lustful or heretical thoughts. It was the priest, not the doctor, who declared you a leper.

In the early twelfth century two things happened to change this attitude. The first was that a number of Christian soldiers returning home from the First Crusade of 1099 were found to have picked up the disease. The second was a shift in the theological consensus concerning a key passage in the Bible. Referring to the Messiah, the prophet Isaiah wrote: 'We did esteem him stricken, smitten of God, and afflicted.' The Hebrew for 'smitten' is *nagua*. When some unknown Biblical scholar realised that everywhere else the word occurs in the Old Testament it means specifically 'smitten with leprosy', the inescapable conclusion was that Isaiah had predicted Jesus would suffer on our behalf by being treated like a leper.

The effect was to rebrand leprosy as a 'holy disease'. The stricken Crusaders, far from being punished, were being marked out by God for special reward. St Francis of Assisi (1182–1226) overcame his revulsion to embrace a leper and made the care of lepers a central part of the monastic order he founded. Henry I's daughter, Matilda (1102–67), established a hospital for lepers at Holborn in London and publicly washed and kissed their feet. All over Europe monarchs and aristocrats competed with one another to endow leper colonies.

Lepers themselves were granted special privileges: the most important being the right to beg. In some places they were entitled to a fixed portion of all the produce sold on market day. For 200 years, although they lived separately, they mingled freely at shrines and travelled on pilgrimages. This was when the practice of lepers carrying bells and rattles started. They were used, not to warn people away, but to attract donations from them: helping a leper was a sacred act.

Attitudes hardened again after the Black Death (1348–50) – the plague was sometimes called 'a leprosy' – but, by the mid-fifteenth century, it hardly mattered: lepers had all but disappeared from Britain.

Lepers were particularly vulnerable to bubonic plague and tuberculosis (the TB bacterium is leprosy's closest bacterial relative). As waves of infectious diseases spread across Europe in the fourteenth and fifteenth centuries, the lepers' already weakened immune systems succumbed first. Their numbers declined; soon there were too few of them left to spread the disease and their bells stopped ringing for good.

STEPHEN *Why did lepers carry bells?*

ALAN *They were doing an act, you know, one of those bell-ringing acts. For 'A Leper's Got Talent'.*

Who wore horned helmets?

Not Viking warriors but Celtic priests.

None of the horned helmets discovered in Europe by archaeologists can be dated to the Viking Age (AD 700–1100). Most are Celtic and were produced during the Iron Age (800 BC–AD 100), including the famous helmet found in the Thames in the 1860s and now displayed in the British Museum. The lightness of its metal and its fine decoration strongly suggest that the Thames helmet must have been worn for ceremonial occasions rather than in battle. To a modern observer, the 'horns' are more like the cones on Madonna's famously pointy bra.

Technically speaking, the only authentic Viking helmet ever found dates from the tenth century AD (though it's in the same style as the pre-Viking Vendel period helmets). Made from iron plate, it was found inside the burial mound of a Viking chieftain and resembles a peaked cap with built in eye-protectors that look like iron-rimmed specs. But there's not even a hint of a horn. It's likely that only senior Vikings wore metal helmets, if they wore them at all. The surviving illustrations from the period show most warriors wearing simple leather skullcaps or fighting bareheaded.

The association of horned helmets with Vikings dates back no further than the nineteenth century, a period when many imperial European nations were re-inventing their mythic heritage. In Britain Druids and the Arthurian legends were all the rage; the Germans were lapping up operas about medieval Teutonic knights; and, not to be outdone, Scandinavians were dusting off their Old Norse sagas. In one of these, a republished edition of *Frithiof's Saga*, a Swedish illustrator called Gustav Malmström included small horns and dragon wings on the hero's headgear.

Frithiof's Saga (1825) became an international hit. Until then the word 'Viking' was virtually unknown in English ('Dane' or 'Norseman' were the usual terms), so the saga literally made the Vikings' name – and their supposed horned helmets created a powerful visual image of them that has lasted to this day.

On the other hand, the tradition of adorning the head with horns for religious purposes seems to have been widespread across the Celtic world. There are several depictions of the god Cernunnos sporting enormous antlers and, in the first century BC, the Greek historian Diodorus Siculus described the Gauls as having helmets with horns, antlers or even whole animals attached. No one knows exactly what Celtic religious rituals involved, but it is likely that the ceremonial antlers were a symbol of fertility and rebirth, because they are shed and regrown each year.

The cern element in Cernunnos means 'horn' in Old Irish and is derived from an Indo-European root that also gives us unicorn, keratin (the substance horn is made from) and corn (a patch of hard, hoof-like skin).

Can you name an animal with horns?

Strictly speaking, not all the pointed projections that stick out of an animal's head are horns.

True horns have a permanent bone core surrounded by compacted strands of a protein called keratin – the same stuff that human hair and nails are made from. Animals that have them include cattle, buffalo, sheep, antelopes and horned lizards.

Animals with pointed projections that *aren't* horns include rhinos (their 'horns' are made of keratin but have no bone core); deer (they have antlers which are made of bone, but covered in velvety skin not keratin, and they drop off and are regrown each year); giraffes (they have ossicones – literally 'big bones' – covered with furry skin but not keratin); and elephants, pigs, walruses and narwhals (they all have tusks, which are overgrown teeth, made of ivory).

Keratin is a remarkable substance. In its softer alpha form, it is what ensures our skin is flexible and waterproof and, as well as producing horn, forms the hair, fur, claws, hooves and nails of mammals. In its harder beta form, it makes the shells and scales of reptiles and the feathers and beaks of birds.

Horns, tusks and antlers have a variety of functions – they can be used as tools, or weapons, or to attract a mate – but only true horns are used to cool down. The blood vessels surrounding the bone core turn the whole horn into a device similar to a car radiator, cooling the liquid by spreading its exposure to the air, in much the same way an elephant uses its large ears. Watusi cattle, a longhorn variety native to central Africa, have enormous horns for this reason. The largest true horns ever recorded belong to a Watusi bull called Lurch: they measured 92.5 centimetres (3 feet) long and weighed 45 kilograms (7 stones) each.

When the keratinous part of a true horn is slid off its bone core, it becomes a useful hollow object. Since prehistory, humans used these for drinking vessels and musical instruments and, later, to carry gunpowder in. The substance known as 'horn' was carved into buttons, handles and combs, made into book bindings or windows (it is translucent if shaved thinly) and boiled down for glue.

There are various accounts of humans growing 'horns' of the non-bony type. One of the strangest concerns Anna Schimper, 'the horned nun of Filzen'. In 1795 her nunnery in the Rhineland was occupied by French troops and the nuns evicted. The shock sent Anna mad and she was committed to an asylum. After years spent banging her head against a table, a horn started to grow from the bump on her forehead. The more it grew, the less deranged she became until she was soon sane enough to return to the nunnery, where she became abbess.

By 1834 her horn had grown to such a length that it was hard to conceal under her wimple, so she decided to have it removed. Although she was eighty-seven and the operation was both bloody and painful, she survived and lived for two more years. By the time she died her mysterious therapeutic horn had started to grow again.

How do you milk a yak?

You don't – any more than you would milk a bull.

Yaks are the males of the species *Bos grunniens* (Latin for 'grunting ox'), and they live in Tibet and Nepal. Westerners who speak of milking yaks are a staple butt of Tibetan jokes.

The female of the species is called a 'dri' or 'nak'. Their milk contains twice as much fat as that of lowland cows. Contrary to some web sources, it is not pink: on the rare occasions it is drunk, blood is sometimes added for flavour. It is golden-coloured and mainly made into yoghurt, cheese and butter. Tibetans put butter in their tea, use it for face lotion and lamp fuel and make it into ritual sculptures.

In Lhasa, fresh yak meat is for sale, draped in slabs over the branches of trees, or stacked in wheelbarrows direct from the slaughterhouse. Butchery is a hereditary trade and all butchers are Muslims. Rancid butter is piled directly on to the paving stones. The whole of Tibet smells of dri butter.

Wild yaks can be 1.95 metres (6 feet 5 inches) at the shoulder; domestic yaks are usually half that height. To operate effectively in the thin air at heights of 5,500 metres (18,000 feet) and temperatures of –40°C (or –40°F – they are the same at that value), yak blood cells are half the size and three times as numerous as those of ordinary cattle.

Yak bones are used to make jewellery and tent fastenings. The horns are carved into knife handles and musical instruments. The tails are exported to India where they are used as fly whisks. The dung is collected and burnt as fuel.

Yaks have the longest hair of any animal. It can grow to be 60 centimetres (2 feet) long on the torso and is used to make rope, clothing, bags, sacks, shoes, tents and coracles. In the seventeenth and eighteenth centuries, it was the most sought-after material (after human hair) for making gentlemen's wigs.

The fashion for wearing wigs began with Louis XIII

(1601–43) – who went prematurely bald in 1624 – and ended with the French Revolution. Wigs were often as expensive as the rest of a man's clothing put together. Today, the BBC can call upon yak-hair wigs from the 10,000 false hair items available to it, and fancy-dress shops offer Santa Claus beards in 100 per cent yak hair.

Dob-dobs were monks from the Se-ra monastery in Tibet who specialised in the collection of yak dung. By the late nineteenth century they'd evolved into a combination of monastic police force and predatory gay mafia. They would occasionally venture down to the nearby city of Lhasa to pick fights and kidnap young boys. They were easily recognised because they kept the skirts of their habits kilted up higher than regular Buddhist monks. This gave them a bulky look round the thighs, which they exaggerated by swinging their buttocks as they walked.

STEPHEN *Whose job is it in Tibet to milk the yaks?*
ROGER McGOUGH *I know who cleans the hooves.*
STEPHEN *Who's that?*
ROGER *Yaksmiths.*

What do you say to get a husky to move?

Just about anything except 'Mush!' You can call 'Hike!', 'Hike on!', 'Ready!', 'Let's go!', or simply 'OK!' – but a sled driver will only shout 'Mush!' when he doesn't want to disappoint the tourists.

'Mush', far from being an authentic Inuit word, is a Hollywood mishearing of the command given by French

Canadian sled drivers: *Marche!* It's most unlikely that any real-life husky handler ever said 'Mush!', but it's certainly not favoured today. It's too soft a sound for the dogs to hear clearly.

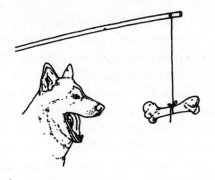

Stopping sled dogs is the problem, not starting them. They are born to run. If they ever get free, they'll just head for the horizon until exhaustion overtakes them and you'll never see them again. While they're in harness, though, yelling 'Whoa!' and standing on the sled's brake pad should be enough to hold them. To get them to turn right, use 'Gee!' and for left 'Haw!' (no, they're not Inuit words either). Only the lead dog needs to understand your commands; the rest just follow the leader.

Huskies, the best known of the many kinds of dog that have been used to pull sleds, were originally bred for winter transport by the Chukchi people of Siberia. In the summer, the dogs ran free, fending for themselves. This combination of tameness and independence made them perfect working dogs.

They're surprisingly small – weighing between 15 and 25 kilograms (35–55 pounds) – but those who race huskies for sport prefer dogs with outsize appetites. After marathon runs, covering as much as 160 kilometres (100 miles) in twenty-four hours, they will need to eat and drink enthusiastically to replace lost calories and prevent dehydration.

If you're thinking of getting a husky as a pet, you might want to take some advice from the Siberian Husky Club of Great Britain concerning the breed's 'bad points'. Siberian huskies have no guarding instinct: they will greet a burglar with the same sloppy kiss they give their master. They howl like wolves when happy. They're notorious killers of pets and livestock: if you take them for walks, they have to be kept on a lead. They must have company: they'll wreck your home if you leave them alone. They'll wreck your garden, in any case – and you'll need a 1.8-metre (6-foot) fence to keep them in it. Also, they moult massively – twice a year. In conclusion, the Club says, the Siberian husky isn't suitable for anyone looking for a 'civilised' dog.

The Swiss polar explorer Xavier Mertz (1883–1913) is remembered today as the first person to die of vitamin A poisoning. He was on a three-man mapping mission to the interior of Antarctica when one of the team, most of the sleds and half the dogs fell into a crevasse. On the 480 kilometre (300-mile) trek home, the two survivors were forced to eat the remaining dogs – a necessity which caused Mertz (who was a vegetarian) great anguish. Both men became ill, but Mertz died.

The polar food chain is based on marine algae that are rich in vitamin A. The further up the chain you go, the more it concentrates. Huskies – like seals and polar bears – have evolved to cope with it. Humans haven't. There is enough Vitamin A in just 100 g (3½ ounces) of husky liver to kill a grown man.

On which day should you open the first door on an Advent calendar?

Advent usually starts in November, not on 1 December.

In the Western Christian tradition, Advent begins on Advent Sunday, the fourth Sunday before Christmas, which also begins the Church's year. This can occur on any day between 27 November and 3 December, so there's only a one-in-seven chance of it falling on 1 December. As a result, Advent varies in length from twenty-two to twenty-eight days. The next time Advent Sunday falls on 1 December will be in 2013. For five of the next seven years, Advent will begin in November.

Not that anyone seems to care. Despite their name, 'Advent' calendars are now firmly established as a secular custom and the first door is opened (or the first chocolate consumed) on 1 December, a date whose main function is to remind us that there are only twenty-four shopping days to Christmas. In the UK and USA, a quarter of all personal spending for the year takes place in December.

Counting down the days to Christmas grew up among German Lutherans in the early nineteenth century. At first, they would either light a candle every day or cross off each day on a blackboard. Then, in the 1850s, German children started to draw their own home-made Advent calendars. It wasn't until 1908 that Gerhard Lang (1881–1974), of the Bavarian publishers Reichhold & Lang, devised a commercial version. It was a piece of card accompanied by a packet of twenty-four small illustrations that could be glued on for each day of the season.

Because it wasn't practical to manufacture a different number of stickers each year, this was the moment that Advent became a standard twenty-four days long and the tradition of starting the calendar on 1 December began. By 1920 Lang had introduced doors that opened, and his invention was spreading across Europe. It was known as the 'Munich Christmas Calendar'.

Lang's business failed in the 1930s – Hitler's close association with Munich can't have helped – but after the war, in 1946, another German publisher, Richard Sellmer from Stuttgart, revived the idea. He focused his efforts on the US market, setting up a charity endorsed by President Eisenhower and his family. In 1953 he acquired the US patent, and the calendar became an immediate success, with Sellmer earning the title of 'the General Secretary of Father Christmas'. His company still produces more than a million calendars a year in twenty-five countries. The first Advent calendars containing chocolate were produced by Cadbury in 1958.

Advent comes from the Latin *adventus*, meaning 'arrival', and it was meant to be a season of fasting and contemplation, in preparation for the feast of Christmas.

Despite this, it often started with the raucous celebration of St Andrew's Day on 30 November. 'Tandrew' customs included schoolchildren locking their teachers out of the classroom, organised squirrel hunts and cross-dressing. An 1851 account describes how 'women might be seen walking about in male attire, while men and boys clothed in female dress visited each other's cottages, drinking hot "eldern wine", the staple beverage of the season'.

How many days are there in Lent?

Forty-six. Or forty-four if you're a Catholic.

Lent runs from midday on Ash Wednesday to midnight on Holy Saturday, the day before Easter Sunday. For Catholics it ends two days earlier, at midnight on Maundy Thursday. The 'forty days' of Lent commemorate the forty days that Jesus (and before him, Moses) spent fasting and praying in the wilderness, but the Sundays don't count because you aren't supposed to fast on them.

The technical term for the period is *quadragesima*, Latin for 'fortieth'. In the late Middle Ages, when preachers in Britain began using English instead of Latin, they cast around for a simple but appropriate word to replace it, and fastened on 'Lent' – which then just meant 'Spring' and was related to the days 'lengthening'.

The reason why penance and fasting are suspended for the six Sundays that fall during Lent is that they are considered celebratory tasters for Easter Day, the most important feast of the Christian year.

Some may consider this weak-willed or against the spirit of the thing, but the terms of the Lenten fast have always been treated as negotiable. Even in the sixth century, when Pope Gregory the Great first came up with the idea of giving up meat, milk, cheese, butter and eggs for forty days, it was loosely interpreted. The Celtic church advised fasting during the day but having a hearty supper of bread, eggs and milk in the evening. In tenth-century England, Archbishop Aelfric went the other way and took a hard-line approach – banning sex, fighting and fish as well.

In general, though, fish have always been the saving grace of Lent. Henry VIII encouraged Lent to support the nation's fishing industry. As hungry Christians carried the Good News to distant climes, the definition of 'fish' became quite flexible. At various times, muskrat, beaver and barnacle geese have all been officially counted as 'fish' – as has the capybara, a kind of giant South American guinea pig that can stay underwater for five minutes. In Venezuela today it forms a magnificent centrepiece for Lenten feasts: it's the world's largest rodent. Perhaps because of all these shenanigans, or perhaps because fasting implies the value of its opposite (feasting), the Puritans abolished Lent completely in 1645.

Easter is a 'moveable feast', calculated according to a complex formula that the Church took centuries to agree. It moves about because it has to fall on a Sunday but must never coincide with the Jewish Passover, which was dishonoured when the Crucifixion was held on the same day. There are thirty-five possible dates for Easter. The earliest in the year, 22 March, last fell in 1818 and won't happen again until 2285. The latest is 25 April, which last happened in 1943 and is next due in 2038. The whole sequence repeats itself once every 5.7 million years.

You might think a fixed date would be simpler. The confectionery industry certainly does – 10 per cent of the UK's annual chocolate sales take place in the run-up to Easter. As long ago as the 1920s, they successfully lobbied Parliament to fix it as the first Sunday after the second Saturday in April. The Easter Act (1928) was even passed but, despite having the support of both main churches, it was never implemented as law. No one knows why.

How did the Church of England react to Darwin's Theory of Evolution?

Rather positively, on the whole.

In 1860, the year after the publication of *On the Origin of Species*, there was a debate at Oxford University between Samuel Wilberforce, Bishop of London, and one of the theory's fiercest supporters, T. H. Huxley (known as

'Darwin's bulldog'). At one point the Bishop sarcastically asked Huxley whether he was descended from a monkey on his grandfather's or his grandmother's side. But this wasn't typical of the Church of England's reaction in general.

Much mainstream biblical scholarship in the nineteenth century viewed the Bible as a historical document backed up by archaeological evidence, rather than as the actual word of God. As a result, many senior Victorian Anglicans already thought of the Bible in the same way moderate contemporary Christians do: as a series of metaphors rather than a literal account.

In the same year as the Oxford debate, Frederick Temple, headmaster of Rugby School and later Archbishop of Canterbury, gave a sermon praising Darwin. He said that scientists could have all the laws in the universe they liked, but that 'the finger of God' would be in all of them. The influential author Rev. Charles Kingsley also congratulated Darwin. 'Even better than making the world,' Kingsley wrote to him, 'God makes the world make itself!'

By the time Darwin himself addressed the debate about human origins directly – in *The Descent of Man* (1871) – there were at least as many leading churchmen who had accepted his theory on similar grounds as those (like Wilberforce) who still opposed it. At the same time, many scientists (Huxley included) continued to support compulsory Bible study in schools.

On the Origin of Species by Means of Natural Selection, or the Preservation of Favoured Races in the Struggle for Life – as it was originally called – was the first genuinely popular work of scientific theory. Published by John Murray, the first print run sold out before it had even been printed and Darwin produced another five revised editions. Many of the initial reviews were hostile, anti-evolution organisations were formed, and Darwin was often ridiculed, but the mockery came as much from politicians and editors as from churchmen. Darwin had to get used to pictures of his head on a monkey's body in newspapers, and when he went to collect his honorary degree from Cambridge University, students dangled a stuffed monkey from the roof.

Sometimes his work was simply ignored. Just before *On the Origin of Species* came out, in 1859, the president of London's Geological Society awarded Darwin a medal of honour for his geological expeditions to the Andes and for his four-volume work on barnacles without even mentioning the book.

Darwin lost his own faith, but he hadn't intentionally set out to subvert religion. He always claimed he was an agnostic, not an atheist. And the Anglican Church certainly didn't abandon him. When he died in 1882, it awarded him its highest accolade. He was buried in Westminster Abbey, next to England's greatest scientists Michael Faraday and Isaac Newton.

Who is the only person on Earth who can never be wrong?

No, not even the Pope is 'always right'. He can still commit sins and not everything he says is 'infallible'.

The First Vatican Council introduced the Doctrine of Papal Infallibility on 18 July 1870. Under the doctrine, certain specific statements by the Pope are preserved forever from any possibility of error by the action of the Holy Spirit. This does not mean that *all* the Pope's private or public statements are beyond argument. Many of the Church's strictest laws (those against contraception, for example) are binding on all Catholics, but are not protected by the doctrine of papal in- fallibility. Nor does the doctrine imply that the Pope himself is 'impeccable', or 'incapable of sin' (*peccare* is Latin for 'to sin').

For a papal statement to be 'infallible' it has to fulfil strict conditions. The Pope must be speaking *ex cathedra* (literally, 'from his chair'), in his official capacity as pastor of all Christians, not as a private individual. He has to make it clear he is pronouncing on a doctrine of faith or morals and that this is the last word on the matter. Finally, he must confirm that the statement binds the whole Church and that everyone must agree to it, on pain of what the Catholic Church calls 'spiritual shipwreck'.

An infallible teaching by a pope can contradict previous Church teachings (as long as they were not themselves issued infallibly) but the Pope cannot use his infallibility to make other people's statements retrospectively infallible by agreeing with them. Nor is the whole of a statement made *ex cathedra* necessarily infallible: the Pope has to make clear which bit is which.

This is quite a tall order, even for a pope, so it isn't surprising that, since 1870, only one infallible papal statement has actually been issued. In 1950 Pope Pius XII stated that the Virgin Mary was bodily taken up to Heaven at the end of her life. This is known as the Assumption of the Blessed Virgin Mary, and it is celebrated on 15 August. The Pope did this because, although the Assumption had been taught and observed since the sixth century, it had no direct scriptural authority. By making it a dogma (from the Greek verb *dokein*, 'to seem good'), all doubt was removed (although theologians still can't agree whether Mary was carried up to Heaven before or after she died).

Though only one pope has ever made only one infallible statement, the Vatican has since decided that the content of Pope John Paul II's 1994 pronouncement *Ordinatio Sacerdotalis* ('Ordination to the Priesthood'), in which it was made explicit that Roman Catholic priests have to be men, *was* infallible even though the Pope had failed to say so at the time.

If the Vatican is correct, any future pope who permits female priests will instantly excommunicate himself.

What are the four main religions of India?

Hinduism, Islam, Christianity and Sikhism in that order. Not Buddhism: although Buddhism was founded in India, its spiritual home today is Tibet.

The figures from the latest available census (2001) are: Hindu 80.5 per cent, Muslim 13.4 per cent, Christian 2.3 per cent and Sikh 1.9 per cent. More than three-quarters of the population of India describe themselves as followers of Hinduism, the oldest continually practised faith in the world, and India's Muslim community, at around 145 million, is the third largest in the world, after Indonesia and Pakistan. There are about 25 million Christians in India (almost as many as the UK's 29 million) and 15 million Sikhs.

Buddhists in India account for only 0.7 per cent of the population. New Zealand has a higher percentage of people professing Buddhism (1.08 per cent) than India does. The members of the influential Indian ascetic sect known as Jainism are even fewer in number – about 0.5 per cent. The number of Indian atheists is smallest of all: only 0.1 per cent of the population are rated 'unspecified' by the census.

Buddhism was founded in India and grew rapidly there for a thousand years. But most of its adherents now live in China (notably in Tibet where, until quite recently, one in every six males was a Buddhist monk) as well as Indochina and Japan. It is also the majority religion in Sri Lanka.

Buddhism disappeared gradually from India from the sixth century AD. Though Hinduism absorbed many of its practices (such as vegetarianism) and accepted Buddha into the pantheon of gods, Buddhism was a monastic religion, based on detachment and meditation. This made it less attractive to the state rulers of India who liked to court popularity by staging lavish and colourful Hindu festivals. With the arrival of Islam in the tenth century, Buddhism was finally relegated to its present 'tiny minority' status.

This is only 'tiny' in relative terms. 0.7 per cent of the population of India is 7.5 million people, making it the ninth largest Buddhist community in the world.

There are also twice as many Buddhists as Jains in India. Mahavira (599–527 BC), whose name means 'Great Hero', founded Jainism in north-east India, in the same area and at almost the same time as the Buddha (563–483 BC), whose name means 'Awakened One'. Both men were born to high-caste families, which they both abandoned at about the age of thirty. Mahavira lived as an ascetic, much of the time naked.

Though Jainism declares that everything in the universe, including non-living things, has a soul, it is atheistic in nature and the existence of God is seen as an irrelevance. They believe the taking of any life is a sin and Orthodox Jain monks wear a net over their mouths to avoid swallowing spiders and gently sweep the street before them as they walk to avoid crushing insects.

Gandhi was greatly influenced by Jainism. The Jains' symbol is the *fylfot*, an old English word for the good luck sign better known as the swastika.

From which country did the Gypsies originate?

The Gypsies, or *Romani*, are not from Egypt, or Rome or Romania. Their ancestral home was India.

There are an estimated 10 million Romani people spread across Europe, Asia and the Americas, of which the biggest concentration are the Roma of Central and Eastern Europe. From their first arrival in Europe in the fourteenth century they have travelled under many different names: 'gypsy' and the Spanish *gitano* are just two, and both derive from the mistaken assumption that they came from Egypt. *Romani*, the name they call themselves, doesn't come from a geographic area at all, but from their word *Rom*, meaning 'man'.

Romani had survived as an oral rather than a written language and it wasn't until the mid-nineteenth century that linguists were able to solve the puzzle of its origin. Analysis of the structure and vocabulary confirmed Romani as an Indo-European language descended from Sanskrit, the ancient language of northern India – just like Hindi, Bengali, Gujarati and Punjabi. Romani also contains elements of Greek, Turkish and Iranian, which suggest that they migrated out of India, through Turkey and eventually into Europe.

A century and a half later, geneticists have come to the same conclusion. In 2003 several hundred Romani were analysed for evidence of five genetic mutations linked to certain diseases. The results confirmed that a founder group of perhaps a thousand Romani emerged from India in AD 1000 and then spread out in smaller units. This explains the complex pattern of Romani dialects that are found all across Europe.

For most of the last thousand years, the ability of the Romani to move and adapt has only been matched by the persecution they have suffered at the hands of the sedentary populations they encountered. Forced into slavery in Eastern Europe, ghettoised in Spain, marked out by head shaving and ear removal in France and England, they have been discriminated against legally and socially in every state they have travelled through.

Their painful history culminated in the Nazi regime's attempt at genocide, known as the *Porjamos* ('the devouring' in Romani). This killed an estimated 1.5 million people between 1935 and 1945. And, as recently as 2008, the Italian govern-ment blamed a rise in city crime specifically on Romani migration, describing their presence as a 'national emergency'.

The Romani have enriched European culture for centuries with music, stories and language. A surprising number of English words are borrowed from them, including pal (from *phal*, 'friend'); lollipop (from *loli phabai*, 'red apple'); gaff, in the sense of a place (from *gav*, 'town'); nark, meaning 'informant' (from *naak*, 'nose') and, most prominently in recent times, chav – which comes from the Romani *chavi* meaning 'young boy'.

What was shocking about the first cancan dancers?

It wasn't young women showing their knickers. The cancan started as a dance for both men and women – and neither was saucily dressed. The familiar line of whooping, high-kicking girls didn't come along till almost a hundred years later.

The cancan originated in the working-class dance halls of Montparnasse in the Paris of the 1830s, where it was first known as the *chahut* (meaning 'uproar'). It was for men and women, dancing in quartets, and it quickly became the rock-and-roll of its day, shocking polite society by the amount of bodily contact it allowed between the couples. A contemporary account makes it sound like a demented tango: 'They mingle, cross, part, meet again, with a swiftness and fire that must be felt to be described.' On a visit to Paris, the German poet Heinrich Heine (1797–1856) called the *chahut* a 'satanic ruction'.

Some of the earliest *chahut* stars were men, whose athletic high-kicks and mid-air splits (or *grand écart*) were copied from stage acrobats of the time. When women began to try the high-kicks, they often revealed more than just their athleti-cism. As the fashion for wider hoop-reinforced skirts brought with it ever-frillier layers of undergarment, the kicking, skirt-lifting and bottom-waggling began to take over. The *chahut* was a dance for everyone, but the *cancan* that evolved from it was the pole dance of the 1860s, performed on stage by semi-professional 'dancers' (often a euphemism for prostitutes).

The cancan's reputation grew increasingly sensational. An attempt to bring it to Moscow in the mid-1850s led Tsar Nicholas I to ban the dance, imprison the promoter and deport the performers under armed Cossack guard. The first 'French Cancan' was staged in England in 1861 by the impresario Charles Morton (1819–1904) in his new Oxford Street music hall. It wasn't particularly French (the cancan quartet were mostly Hungarian) but it was an immediate hit with the audience and the police threatened the theatre with closure for promoting indecency.

By the time the great Parisian cabaret clubs opened at the end of the century, female cancan dancers like Jane Avril (immortalised in Toulouse-Lautrec's famous poster) and La Goulue (who danced in expensive clothes, borrowed from her mother's laundry business) had become Paris's highest-earning celebrities. Their provocative routines at the Folies Bergère and the Moulin Rouge were incorporated into the cancan chorus lines that started in the 1920s and which still attracts the tourists to Paris today.

But high-kicks and skirt twirls weren't invented in Paris in the nineteenth century. A country dance in sixteenth-century Brittany had women doing high-kicks in billowy skirts, and there are reliefs of ancient Egyptians doing something similar at the Tomb of Mehu in Saqqara. They date back to 2400 BC.

The cancan bears out George Bernard Shaw's observation that dance is 'the vertical expression of a horizontal desire, legalized by music'. It probably gets its name from the French verb *cancaner*, which means 'to quack' – ducks are great bottom-wagglers. *Cancaner* also means 'to spread scandal'.

Where does tartan come from?

Tartan isn't particularly Scottish.

Making cloth involves inter-
lacing vertical and horizontal
threads called the *warp* and the
weft. This produces an almost
infinite possibility for bands and
blocks of colour. Patterns similar

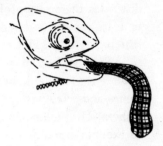

to those we call 'tartan' have appeared in almost every culture
since the invention of weaving in prehistoric times.

Nor is the word itself Scottish. First recorded in English in
1454, it probably comes from the French *tiretaine*, meaning
'strong, coarse fabric'. In medieval Scotland, 'tartan' merely
meant woven (as opposed to knitted) cloth. Plaid, now used
interchangeably with tartan, was originally Gaelic for blanket.
By the late sixteenth century, individual weavers all over the
Highlands were producing their own tartan cloths known as
'setts', much as the weavers of Harris do today with tweed.
And, just as there are 4,000 registered patterns of tweed, what
drove the patterns of the setts was the taste and skill of the
individual weaver, the availability of coloured dyes and the
quality of the local wool. It had nothing to do with any official
'clan' identity.

The original kilt was a much longer, over-the-shoulder
garment, shunned by most lowland Scots and banned by the
British after the defeat of the Jacobite Rebellion in 1745. The
short kilt was the invention of an English industrialist,
Thomas Rawlinson, who opened an ironworks in the
Highlands in the mid-eighteenth century and needed
something practical for his local workers to wear.

At the time English regiments stationed in Scotland were
filled with lowland Scots, loyal to the Crown but keen to
create an identity distinct from other British regiments. What

we now call 'traditional' Scottish dress (short kilt, sporran, dirk) was the creation of these regiments and they were the first to commission regimental tartans such as the Black Watch. A growing sense of 'Scottishness' turned into a full-scale Scottish Revival led by Romantic writers like Sir Walter Scott (1771–1832). By the 1820s kilts, ballads, Highland games and retellings of Scottish legends were the height of fashion. The high point was the state visit of King George IV to Edinburgh in 1822 – the first by an English monarch for 170 years, and expertly stage-managed by Scott himself.

'Clan tartans' were a hoax from the beginning. John and Charles Allen, two brothers claiming to be Bonnie Prince Charlie's grandsons – but who were actually from Egham in Surrey – 'discovered' a late fifteenth-century manuscript called the *Vestiarium Scoticum*. Its authenticity was assured, they said, because they'd asked clan chieftains to 'check' their tartans against the book. In fact, it had happened in reverse. Clan chieftains had chosen tartans they liked and the Allens had turned it into a book. Much like the brothers, it was a complete fake. Even Sir Walter Scott was forced to conclude that the 'idea of distinguishing the clans by their tartans is but a fashion of modern date . . .'

Who wrote 'Auld Lang Syne'?

According to Robert Burns, it wasn't him.

Robert Burns (1759–96) never claimed to have written the song 'Auld Lang Syne'. 'I took it down from an old man's singing,' he wrote in 1793, in a note accompanying the lyric. He sent it to James Johnson, the editor of the *Scottish Musical Museum* (an anthology of traditional Scottish songs) stating that it was 'an olden song' that had never been written down. In fact, Burns was wrong about that – versions of it had been in print several times, including one as recently as 1770.

'Auld Lang Syne' originated in an anonymous fifteenth-century poem that went under various names in various different versions such as: 'Auld Kindries Foryett', 'Old Longsyne' and finally, in 1724, 'Auld Lang Syne'.

Pretty conclusive, you might think – but the song's authorship remains a hot topic among Burns scholars. Only Burns's first verse and chorus bear much similarity to the song's previous incarnations. Some say he claimed the song was a traditional one to give his work extra credibility amongst antiquarians. Others argue that, whether the story of the old man was true or not, Burns had taken a traditional source, as in several other of his most famous poems (such as *My love is like a red, red rose*) and remoulded it into something stronger and more affecting than the original.

If you thought 'Rabbie Burns' wrote 'Auld Lang Syne', you'd be doubly wrong. Burns never signed his name 'Rabbie' or 'Robbie' (or, indeed, 'Bobbie' Burns, as some North Americans insist on calling him). His signatures included 'Robert', 'Robin', 'Rab' – and, on at least one occasion, 'Spunkie'.

Another piece of Burns-related pedantry you might want to bear in mind for New Year's Eve is this: the last line of the chorus isn't 'For *the sake of* Auld Lang Syne'. Since 'auld lang syne' already means 'old times' sake', this is tautologous (from Greek *tautos*, 'the same', and *logos*, 'word'). In Scots, 'for the sake of Auld Lang Syne' is the nonsensical 'for the sake of old time's sake'.

The two extra notes in the line – which is what makes people feel they need to add 'the sake of'' – should be dealt with by singing two extra notes for each of 'for' and 'old'. Try singing 'For-or oh-old la-ang syne' next Hogmanay and be ready with the explanation. And say we sent you.

STEPHEN *What does it mean, Auld Lang Syne?*
DAVID TENNANT *Old long remembrance.*
BILL BAILEY *Old long signs . . .*

Which writer introduced the most words into the English language?

Not Shakespeare, but Milton.

According to Gavin Alexander of Cambridge University, who has trawled the entire *Oxford English Dictionary*, John Milton (1608–74) is responsible for introducing 630 words to the English language, beating Ben Jonson with 558 and John Donne with 342 – all of them way ahead of Shakespeare, who notches up a disappointing 229. Milton's neologisms include *pandemonium*, *debauchery*, *terrific*, *fragrance*, *lovelorn* and *healthy*.

Not that we can say for sure that these any of these authors actually 'invented' all these words; their work simply contains the first *recorded* use, and famous writers are much more likely to be read than obscure ones. If Milton or Shakespeare had filled their books with hundreds of completely new words, their readers and audiences would have struggled to understand them.

But English in the seventeenth century was in a state of creative expansion, rapidly overtaking Latin as the language of culture and science. All you had to do was find a reasonably familiar word in French or Latin and anglicise it: most educated people would quickly guess the meaning. It didn't always work, however. For example, Milton's *intervolve* ('to wind within each other') and *opiniastrous* ('opinionated') never quite caught on.

Readers who struggled with new vocabulary could turn to Robert Cawdrey's *Table Alphabeticall*. Published in 1604, it is generally considered the first English dictionary – although it isn't much more than a list of 3,000 'hard usual English wordes, borrowed from the Hebrew, Greeke, Latine, or French'.

English had to wait more than 150 years to get the dictionary it deserved. Despite being half-deaf, blind in one eye, scarred from scrofula, prone to melancholy and suffering from Tourette's syndrome, Samuel Johnson (1709–84) managed to write 42,773 definitions in nine years, assisted by six copyists. The equivalent French Dictionary took forty scholars fifty-five years.

Johnson's *Dictionary of the English Language* was published in 1755 and cost £4 10 shillings a copy (equivalent to £725 today). It didn't make him rich (it sold 6,000 copies in its first thirty years) but it did make him famous: for the next two centuries it was simply referred to as 'the Dictionary'.

Johnson's lexicographical standards remained unmatched until the *Oxford English Dictionary* appeared in the 1880s. His definitions were so thorough that 1,700 of them were carried over into the first edition of the *OED*. On the other hand, he had no words beginning with X and his etymologies were often dodgy ('May not *spider* be *spy dor*, the insect that watches the dor?').

One of the many pleasures of Johnson's *Dictionary* is discovering obsolete words ripe for revival. For example: *bibacious* (addicted to binge drinking); *feculent* (foul or grimy); *grum* (bad tempered); *keck* (to heave the stomach as if about to vomit); *lusk* (idle or worthless) and *tonguepad* (a great talker).

What were Richard III's last words?

'A horse, a horse, my kingdom for a horse' is one of the best-known lines in English literature, but the real Richard III never uttered them. His last words are among the few things about the battle of Bosworth Field in 1485 that were accurately recorded. They were 'Treason, Treason, Treason!' It was the last time an English king died in battle and it ended the Wars of the Roses in which two branches of the Plantagenet family – the Yorkists and the Lancastrians – effectively snuffed one another out, leading to the founding of a new ruling dynasty, the Tudors.

The last Lancastrian king was Henry VI. When his son Edward was killed at the battle of Tewkesbury in 1471, the Yorkists resumed power under Edward IV – followed by his son Edward V, then Edward IV's brother Richard III.

As a Lancastrian with a tenuous claim to the throne, Henry Tudor, Earl of Richmond, had spent much his life in exile. His arrival at the Welsh port of Milford Haven in August 1485 was at the urging of older exiled Lancastrians like John de Vere, Earl of Oxford, who sensed a chance of turning the tide in their favour with a new candidate for king. When Henry reached Bosworth in Leicestershire he had fewer than 1,000 Englishmen in his army. Most of his troops were French mercenaries or Welshmen. He'd never fought in a battle before, so he left the strategy to his generals.

What he was good at was marketing. After he'd won, he set about rewriting history, painting Bosworth Field as a contest between good and evil: the young idealistic moderniser versus a bitter, misshapen representative of a corrupt regime. This was so successful that definite facts about the battle are scarce. We don't even know where it was fought. In 2009 archaeological evidence suggested it was probably 2 miles south of the present official site. What we do know is that

Richard became detached from his army and was surrounded by Henry's Welsh bodyguards. His supposed allies, Thomas Stanley, Earl of Derby, and his brother Sir William Stanley, chose this moment to switch sides. Hence the king's cry of: 'Treason, Treason, Treason!' as he was skewered by a Welsh poleaxe. Even Henry's official historian was impressed: 'King Richard, alone, was killed fighting manfully in the thickest press of his enemies.'

Richard, at thirty-two, was only four years older than Henry. The idea that he was a hunchback came from John Rouse's *Historia Regius Angliae* (1491), which merely said he had 'uneven shoulders'. He was certainly short but, according to contemporaries, he was good-looking with a strong, sporting physique. He wore heavy armour: an impossible feat for someone with a misshapen back.

Shakespeare was a playwright, not a historian. One of his main sources was the Tudor grandee, Sir Thomas More (1478–1535), who described Richard as 'ill featured of limbs, crook backed, hard favored of visage, malicious, wrathful, envious, from before his birth ever forward'. By no means everyone has bought into this enduring Tudor propaganda. As early as 1813 a plaque appeared at Bosworth putting the alternative version: 'Near this spot, on August 22nd 1485, King Richard III fell fighting gallantly in defence of his realm & his crown against the usurper Henry Tudor.'

When does 'i' come before 'e'?

The 'i before e except after c' rule was abolished in 2009.

The old mnemonic was taught to British schoolchildren for generations, but *Support for Spelling*, a teaching aid published in 2009 as part of the British government's National Primary Strategy, now advises: 'The "i before e" rule is not worth teaching. It applies only to words in which the 'ie' or 'ei' stand for a clear 'ee' sound, so it is easier to learn the specific words.'

In fact, even with 'ee' sounds, there are still plenty of exceptions owing to the proliferation of foreign words in English. Caff*ei*ne, w*ei*rd and Mad*ei*ra all break the rule in one direction; sp*ecie*s, con*cie*rge and ha*cie*nda in the other. Judging solely by the list of official Scrabble words, it turns out that the 'i before e except after c' rule is twenty-one times more likely to be wrong than right. No wonder the government dropped it.

English spelling is hellishly complicated. Many people, particularly in America, have tried to simplify it. In 1768, Benjamin Franklin published a phonetic *alfabet* containing all the familiar letters except c, j, q, w, x and y, and adding six new letters for specific sounds.

Melville Dewey (1851–1931), the inventor of the Dewey Decimal library system, changed the spelling of his Christian name to Melvil and toyed with adapting his surname to Dui. Late in life, he founded a health club in Florida where he put his spelling reforms into action. At one dinner in 1927 the menu featured *Hadok, Poted Beef with Noodles* and *Parsli & Masht Potato with Letis*.

George Bernard Shaw was another passionate advocate of spelling reform, leaving money in his will for a competition to create an easier system. The most extreme example of the way English doesn't always sound the way it's written (although Shaw himself never used it) is the made-up word *ghoti.*

In theory, this could be pronounced 'fish', using 'gh' as in rough, 'o' as in women, and 'ti' as in mention.

In the USA Mark Twain helped draft the Simplified Spelling Board's list of 300 recommended changes, which was accepted in principle by President Theodore Roosevelt in 1906 but rejected by Congress. Nevertheless, many of the simpler spellings did catch on, such as color, defense, mold and sulfate. Others like *profest* (professed), *mixt* (mixed) and *altho* didn't make the cut.

In the UK the Spelling Reform Bill passed its second reading by 65 votes to 53 in 1953 but, after opposition from the House of Lords, it was withdrawn with assurances from the Minister of Education that research would be undertaken into the impacts and benefits of such a change.

The research confirmed the fundamental problem with all new language systems: that, unless they are adopted wholesale, by everyone at once, they lead to more confusion than clarity. The Spelling Reform Bill, like the 'i before e' rule, was relegated to the mists of history.

How many letters are there in Llanfairpwllgwyngyllgogerychwyrndrobwll-llantysiliogogogoch?

Admittedly, it looks like fifty-eight, but there are actually only fifty-one. Both *ll* and *ch* count as single letters in Welsh – along with *dd*, *ff*, *ng*, *ph*, *rh* and *th*. They're called digraphs: two consonants joined together to form a single sound.

Not that it matters, as only tourists (and tourist brochures) call it Llanfairpwllgwyngyllgogerychwyrndrobwllllan-tysiliogogogoch. The village on the island of Anglesey, famous for having the longest officially recognised place name in the UK, is known locally as Llanfair. There are a lot of Llanfairs in Wales (it means 'church of St Mary'), so it's sometimes called Llanfairpwll or Llanfair PG, to distinguish it from the others.

Signposts opt for Llanfairpwllgwyngyll, while the Ordnance Survey map prefers Llanfair Pwllgwyngyll. Even the full name is seen with several variants of spelling, and sometimes with a hyphen between *drobwll* and *llan*. The English translation of the full name is: 'The church of St Mary in the hollow of white hazel trees near the rapid whirlpool by St Tysilio's of the red cave.'

When the first railway station on Anglesey was opened at Llanfair, local businessmen looked for a way to turn the unremarkable former fishing village into a tourist destination and came up with the idea of creating the longest station sign in Britain, made up of the existing names of the village, a nearby hamlet and a local whirlpool.

The local council adopted the imaginary place name, jokingly known as 'The Englishman's Cure for Lockjaw', in 1860. It was a hugely successful publicity stunt. A century and a half later, visitors still come to be photographed beside the station sign and to buy elongated souvenir platform-tickets. The village website also has the world's longest domain name. Llanfair PG has one other claim to immortality: it's the home of the first British branch of the Women's Institute (a Canadian invention), which opened in 1915.

Llanfair PG's full name is the longest in Europe, but the world record is held by the official name for Bangkok. This begins *Krung-Thep-Mahanakhon* . . . and stretches for 167 characters. In second place is a hill in Hawke's Bay, New Zealand, which comes in three lengths of 85, 92 and 105 characters. The most involved of these is: *Taumata-whakatangihanga-koauau-o-Tamatea-haumai-tawhiti-ure-haea-turi-pukaka-piki-maunga-horo-nuku-pokai-whenua-ki-tana-tahu.* Translated from the Maori it means, 'the hill of the flute-playing by Tamatea to his beloved (he who was blown hither from afar, had a slit penis, grazed his knees climbing mountains, fell on the earth and encircled the land).' Understandably, the locals just call it Taumata.

England's longest place name is only eighteen letters long. Blakehopeburnhaugh (pronounced *Black-op-bun-or*) in Northumberland combines elements of Middle English (*blake*, 'black'), Old English (*hope*, 'valley', *burn*, 'stream') and Old Norse (*haugh*, 'flat riverside land').

What's the proper name for the loo?

There isn't one.

The 'smallest room in the house' doesn't have a formal, standard, non-slang name. Whatever you choose to call it, you're using either a *euphemism* (from the Greek *euphemizein*, 'to speak nicely', *eu*, 'well' or 'good') or a *cacophemism* (from its Greek opposite *kakos*, 'bad'). In other words, you are intentionally using either a more polite or a ruder word for what you want to get across.

The JOHN
KHAZI
THE BOWL
PORCELAIN THRONE
DUNNY
The CAN
THE LAV
PRIVY

Lavatory comes from the Latin *lavatorium*, 'place for washing'. A *toilette* was originally a lady's dressing table – from *toile*, the 'cloth' laid across her shoulders when her hair was cut. By extension, the room became her *chambre de toilette*, in which she might attend to all manner of private functions.

No one knows where the word 'loo' originated, but it's probably a corruption of the French *l'eau*, 'water', or *lieu*, 'place'. Most English terms, whether coy, bawdy or comical, are euphemisms – such as restroom, washroom, bathroom, convenience, WC, comfort station, bog, chapel of ease, jakes, john, khazi, thunderbox, the necessary house, lavvy, the lavabo and 'the facilities'. In Edward Albee's play *Who's Afraid of Virginia Woolf* (1962), a dinner-party guest asks if she may powder her nose, to which the host replies, 'Martha, won't you show her where we keep the euphemism?'

This is a perfect demonstration of what linguist Stephen Pinker has called the 'euphemism treadmill', whereby one generation's polite term begins to attract the negative connotations of the object (or place) it is trying to hide, requiring a new euphemism to replace it. Toilet becomes lavatory, lavatory becomes WC, WC becomes restroom and so on.

Fashions change. Plain speaking about defecation and urination hasn't always been considered so ill-mannered. A respectable person in the first half of the eighteenth century might, without giving any offence, announce that they were going out to have a *piss* in the *shithouse*. But, unlike body parts, where we can sidestep both slang and euphemism by reverting to classical terminology – *penis, vagina, anus* – we have never had a single, universally accepted term to describe the place where we go when we ask '*to be excused*'.

This is an extraordinary achievement, given that every single one of us goes there on average 2,500 times a year.

STEPHEN *In Britain in 1994, you might be interested to know, 476 people were injured while on the lavatory. There you are. Underwear hurt eleven people.*

ALAN *How many of those people were drunk?*

How much does your handwriting tell about you?

It reveals who you are, but not what you're like.

We all find it easy to recognise the handwriting of someone we know well: the shape, size and slope of the letters are remarkably consistent. Graphology (from the Greek *graphein*, 'to write', and *logos*, 'study' from its original meaning, 'word') makes a much broader claim: that a person's character can be predicted from their handwriting.

For some reason, it's an appealing idea, but it's as inaccurate as judging a book by its cover, or a person's character from their clothes. All research studies into graphology have shown that it's much less useful in predicting a candidate's personality than, say, psychometric tests like the Meyers-Briggs Type Indicator, which uses ninety-three multiple-choice questions.

For this reason, the British Psychological Society ranks graphology alongside astrology as possessing 'zero validity'. The only reliable results handwriting tests can produce are to show whether you are male or female or have suicidal tendencies. Research published in the *International Journal of Clinical Practice* in 2010 confirmed that when graphological analysis was conducted on a group of forty people who had attempted suicide against a control group who hadn't, the graphological results clearly identified those 'at risk'.

There's a difference between using graphology to detect mental illness and employing it to see if someone has a talent for sales, or is 'trusting' or 'non-trusting'. Despite this, some 3,000 UK businesses regularly use graphology to vet potential employees. The suspicion is that this is used as a cover for illegal discrimination as regards a candidate's age, sex, race or faith. Consequently, in the US it's against the law to use graphology in job interviews. Such tests may be used to authenticate handwriting (when looking for forged signatures) but not to try to ascertain the physical or mental condition of the writer.

In its more reliable role of identifying someone, it was handwriting analysis that sent Al Capone (1899–1947) to prison. Police accountant Frank J. Wilson (1887–1970) found three ledgers recording the business of an illegal gambling operation. The profits were recorded as going, in part, to a man named as 'A' or 'Al'. In an attempt to prove this was Al Capone, over three weeks Wilson collected handwriting samples of every one of Capone's known associates in Chicago. Finally he found a deposit slip from a bank which matched the handwriting in the ledger. Wilson personally traced the bookkeeper who had written the ledgers (a man named Louis Shumway) to a dog track in Miami, and persuaded him to testify against Capone in return for immunity.

The highwayman Dick Turpin (1705–39) was also caught thanks to his handwriting. While in prison under the false name John Palmer he wrote to his brother-in-law asking for help. His brother-in-law refused to pay the sixpence due on the letter and it was returned to the local post office, where the postmaster – Turpin's old schoolmaster – recognised his handwriting. His identity was revealed and he was publicly hanged in York six weeks later.

How can you tell if someone's pleased to see you?

Ignore the shape of their mouth – a true smile is in the eyes.

French physician Guillaume Duchenne (1806–75) discovered the secret of the smile in 1862 by applying electric shocks to the faces of his subjects and photographing the results. He found that an artificial smile used only the large muscle on each side of the face, known as the zygomatic major, while a true smile, induced by a funny joke, involved the muscles running through the eyes, or orbicularis oculi, as well. The effect is a visible wrinkling around the corners of the eyes that is outside voluntary control. In smile research circles, a genuine  smile is still known as a 'Duchenne Smile', while a fake smile is a 'Pan Am Smile' — after the air hostesses in the defunct airline's adverts.

According to Duchenne, a fake smile can express mere politeness, or it can be used in more sinister ways 'as a cover for treason'. He described it as 'the smile that plays upon just the lips when our soul is sad'.

Research has borne out his thesis. In the late 1950s 141 female students at Mills College in California agreed to a long-term psychological study. Over the next fifty years they provided reports on their health, marriage, family life, careers and happiness. In 2001 two psychologists at Berkeley examined their college yearbook photos and noticed a rough fifty–fifty split between those showing a Duchenne or a Pan Am smile. On revisiting the data it was found that those with a Duchenne smile were significantly more likely to have married and stayed married and been both happier and healthier through their lives.

This was reinforced by a 2010 study of 1950s US baseball players. Those with honest grins lived an average of five years longer than players who smiled unconvincingly, and seven years longer than players who didn't smile for the camera at all.

The importance of the eyes in indicating genuine emotions is reflected in the 'emoticons' used in Japan and China. Western emoticons have a pair of fixed dots for eyes but change the mouth shape, like this:

:) meaning 'happy' and :(meaning 'sad'.

Far Eastern emoticons concentrate on changes in the eyes, but leave the mouth the same, like this:

^_^ (happy) and ;_; (sad).

This suggests that the supposedly inscrutable East is better at knowing (and telling) who's pleased to see whom than we are.

STEPHEN *What's the best way to tell if someone is lying?*
SEAN LOCK *What they've said turns out not to be true.*

What's the best way to get to sleep?

Whatever you do, don't count sheep.

In 2002 the Department of Experimental Psychology at Oxford University took a group of fifty insomniacs and got them to try different ways to fall asleep. Those using the traditional sheep-counting method took slightly *longer* than average. What worked best was imagining a tranquil scene such as a beach or a waterfall: this relaxes people and engages their imagination. Counting sheep is too boring or irritating to take your mind off whatever's keeping you awake.

The same study found that 'thought suppression' – trying to block anxious thoughts as soon as they appear – was equally ineffective. This is because of what psychologists call the 'polar bear effect'. Told not to think of polar bears, your mind can think of nothing else. Even the 'the' method many insomniacs swear by – repeating a simple word like 'the' over and over – only works if the repetitions are at irregular intervals, so that the brain is forced to concentrate. As soon you lose focus, the anxiety re-emerges.

The ancient Romans recommended that insomniacs massaged their feet with dormouse fat, or rubbed the earwax of a dog on their teeth. Benjamin Franklin proposed that people finding themselves awake on hot nights should lift up the bedclothes with one arm and one leg and flap them twenty times. Even better, he suggested, was to have two beds, so that one was always cool.

More recently, clinical research has supported Progressive Muscle Relaxation: tensing each group of muscles in turn until they hurt, and then relaxing them. The idea is that an 'unwound' body will eventually lead to an 'unwound' mind.

TATT ('tired all the time') syndrome is one of the most common reasons for visiting a GP – one in five people in the UK report some kind of sleep disorder and a third suffer from insomnia. Sleep deprivation is linked to a quarter of all traffic accidents and to rises in obesity, diabetes, depression and heart disease.

Some sleep research seems to suggest that punctuating long working hours with brief 'power naps' of just a few minutes may actually be good for you. Or you could consider extending your working hours with new eugeroic drugs. (Eugeroic means 'well awake', from Greek *eu*, 'well', and *egeirein*, to awaken.) These are powerful stimulants that double the time people stay awake with no apparent side effects – as well as boosting concentration and memory.

They are unlikely to catch on in Japan at any time soon. The business of *inemuri* – 'to be asleep while present' – is a sign of high status, and Japanese politicians and industrial leaders will openly nod off in important meetings. Their visible need to nap in public indicates how hard they have to work.

STEPHEN *Do you know about Yan Tan Tethera? It's for counting sheep. It actually goes: Yan, Tyan, Tethera, Methera, Pimp, Sethera, Lethera, Hovera, Dovera, Dick, Yan-a-dick, Tyan-a-dick, Tethera-dik, Methera-dick . . . Bumfit suddenly appears, which is fifteen. And it goes all the way up to Giggot, which is twenty.*

ALAN *So one in every fifteen will . . .*

STEPHEN *Will be a bumfit.*

PHILL JUPITUS *Are the last three sheep Cuthbert, Dibble and Grub?*

What happens if you eat cheese before bedtime?

Sweet dreams, it seems.

In 2005 the British Cheese Board organised a study in an attempt to nail the malicious rumour that eating cheese before sleep gives you nightmares. The results were conclusive. More than three-quarters of the 200 volunteers who took part, each of whom ate 20 grams (0.7 ounces) of cheese before retiring, reported undisturbed sleep. They didn't have nightmares (though most of them found they could remember their dreams).

Interestingly, different varieties of cheese produced

different kinds of dream. Cheddar generated dreams about celebrities and Red Leicester summoned childhood memories. People who ate Lancashire dreamed about work, while Cheshire inspired no dreams at all. There also seemed to be a division between the sexes: 85 per cent of women who ate Stilton recalled bizarre dreams involving such things as talking soft toys, vegetarian crocodiles and dinner-party guests being traded for camels.

The overall conclusion was that cheese is a perfectly safe late-night snack. In addition, because it contains high levels of the serotonin-producing amino acid trytophan, it is likely to reduce stress and so encourage peaceful sleep.

It may come as a surprise to find that the British Cheese Board now lists over 700 varieties of British cheese — almost twice as many as are made in France. Having said that, 55 per cent of the £2.4 billion UK cheese market is cornered by just one variety: cheddar. Plus, the definition of 'cheese' has been stretched a bit to include such 'varieties' as Lancashire Christmas Pudding and Cheddar with Mint Choc Chips and Cherries.

The ninth most popular variety of cheese in Britain, Cornish Yarg, may sound ancient, but it only dates back to the 1960s when Allan and Jenny Gray started producing it on their farm near Bodmin Moor. 'Yarg' is 'gray' spelled backwards.

Despite the profusion of new British cheeses, the French still eat twice as much cheese per head as the British, and they sleep well on it, too. No one in France thinks that eating cheese before bed gives you nightmares.

What did ploughmen have for lunch?

Beer, bread, cheese and pickle. Yes, they really did.

The British movie *The Ploughman's Lunch* (1983), written by Ian McEwan and directed by Richard Eyre, claimed that 'the ploughman's lunch' was the spurious invention of an advertising man in the 1960s to encourage people to eat in pubs, and this has become common wisdom. It's since been alleged that the term first appeared in 1970, in *The Cheese Handbook* by one B. H. Axler. In the preface, Sir Richard Trehane, chairman of the English Country Cheese Council & Milk Marketing Board, wrote: 'English cheese and beer have for centuries formed a perfect combination enjoyed as the Ploughman's Lunch.'

Recent research by the BBC TV show *Balderdash & Piffle* found documentary proof that the Cheese Council started using the term 'ploughman's lunch' to publicise cheese in 1960. But there is also evidence that the term ploughman's (or ploughboy's) lunch was used in the 1950s. There's also photographic evidence of ploughmen in the late nineteenth and early twentieth centuries sitting in their fields lunching on what certainly looks like bread, cheese and beer.

What seems most likely is that post-war cheese marketers were determined to remind the public of the long-standing practice of eating bread and cheese in pubs, which had been interrupted by rationing in the Second World War.

So, if ad men didn't invent the lunch, did they invent the phrase? Apparently not: there are anecdotal accounts of the name being used by pubs as early as the 1940s, and there is even a mention in an 1837 *Life of Walter Scott* of 'an extemporised sandwich, that looked like a ploughman's lunch'.

The cheese men certainly *popularised* the phrase as a marketing device, and perhaps on pub menus as well. In doing so, they helped turn a traditional, local name for bread, cheese, beer and pickles into a kind of non-copyrighted super-brand, universally recognised throughout the British Isles.

In the long term, though, only the cheese has benefited. Cheese sales have continued to grow strongly (up 2.8 per cent year on year in 2010), but Britain's last pickled-onion processor, Sheffield Foods, recently described the market as 'flat'. But not as flat as the sales of traditional beer which, despite the efforts of the Campaign for Real Ale, have declined by 40 per cent in the past thirty years.

Iconic though the ploughman's lunch may be, it hasn't saved the institution that most relies on it. Over a hundred traditional British pubs close every month.

Where is Stilton cheese made?

It's not made in Stilton. That would be illegal.

Under European law, Stilton cheese – like Gorgonzola, Camembert and Parmesan – has Protected Designation of Origin (PDO) status. This makes it unlawful to sell it unless it's made in specified areas. In the case of Stilton, this means the counties of Derbyshire, Leicestershire or Nottinghamshire.

The village of Stilton, near Peterborough, is now in Cambridgeshire and was historically part of Huntingdonshire. In 1724, Daniel Defoe noted in his *Tour Through the Villages of England and Wales* that Stilton was 'famous for cheese' and modern cheese historians have shown that a hard cream cheese was certainly made in the village – but no one knows what it was like.

In 1743 the landlord of The Bell, a coaching inn on the Great North Road between London and Edinburgh (now the

AI), started to serve an interesting blue-veined cheese. Because The Bell was in Stilton, travellers took to calling this popular new item 'Stilton cheese'. In fact, the publican, Cooper Thornhill, had discovered it on a farm at Wymondham nearly 50 kilometres (about 30 miles) away, near Melton Mowbray in Leicestershire.

So today Melton Mowbray, not Stilton, is the official capital of the Stilton industry, and has been since 1996. Oddly enough, it wasn't until 2009 that the town was granted protection for its most obvious local product: Melton Mowbray pork pies, under the slightly less stringent Protected Geographical Indication (PGI). In the past, the local pigs that went into the pies were fed on liquid whey, separated out from the milk curd that went into making Stilton. Today, the pork meat in the pie is allowed to come from anywhere in England – but the pies have to be made *in* Melton Mowbray to a particular recipe.

Melton Mowbray pork pies are among thirty-six British regional PDO or PGI products, along with Cornish Clotted Cream, Whitstable Oysters, Jersey Royal Potatoes and twelve other British cheeses apart from Stilton. But not everybody wants one. In 2004 Newcastle Brown Ale became the first product to apply to be *de*-designated by the EU, so that it could move its brewery out of Newcastle across the river to Gateshead. In 2010 it moved out of Tyneside altogether – to the John Smith Brewery in Tadcaster, North Yorkshire. So much for tradition.

One of the British film industry's earliest hits starred a piece of Stilton. *Cheese Mites* (1903) outraged cheese manufacturers and caused screams of terrified delight among audiences. The film was considered the first-ever science documentary and it had been commissioned by its producer, Charles Urban (1867–1942) for a series of popular educational shows running at the Alhambra Theatre in London that were called

'The Unseen World'. It featured a scientist inspecting a piece of ripe Stilton under a microscope – only to discover hundreds of mites 'crawling and creeping about in all directions' (as the film catalogue put it) 'looking like great uncanny crabs, bristling with long spiny hairs and legs'.

Whether this had any effect on sales of Stilton is not recorded – but it did lead to a craze for cheap microscopes. These often came with a free packet of mites.

DAVID MITCHELL *It's basically cheese that's gone off already, hasn't it?*

STEPHEN *Well, that's its point, exactly. It is the celebration of what happens when milk goes off big time stylie.*

SEAN LOCK *You should work for the Milk Marketing Board. 'Get some lovely English milk gone off big time stylie' . . . I'll have a milk gone off big time stylie and tomato sandwich, please.*

Where does the name Milton Keynes come from?

It isn't, as some people think, a combination of the names of the poet John Milton (1608–74) and the economist John Maynard Keynes (1883–1946). The town was built around a village whose name dates back to the thirteenth century.

The original 'Milton Keynes', with its traditional cottages, thatched pub and church, was in the centre of the area designated for development as a new town in 1967. Today it has renamed itself Middleton, after its first mention in the Domesday Book (1067), when it was Mideltone (Old English for 'middle farmstead'). By the thirteenth century this had become

Mideltone Kaynes, after the village's feudal masters, the de Cahaignes. Since all Keynes's are descended from this family, you could say John Maynard Keynes is named after the place, not vice versa. John Milton has no connection with the area at all.

Only two of the twenty-one 'new towns' built in England between 1946 and 1970 take their names from people. Peterlee in County Durham was named after the miners' union leader Peter Lee (1864–1935), and Telford in Shropshire after the Scottish engineer Thomas Telford (1757–1834). Perhaps because of this, when Milton Keynes was founded, a junior minister joked that the name 'combined the poetic with the economic' and an urban myth was born.

The supposedly boring image of Milton Keynes is the butt of many jokes from outsiders, but not from the 235,000 people who live there. The experiment to create a new town on the scale of a city has been a resounding success.

By 1983 34,000 new jobs had been created and 32,000 houses built. At that point, more than 5 per cent of all houses under construction in south-east England were in Milton Keynes. Today the local economy, driven by the rapid expansion of service industries, is one of the strongest in the country and the per capita income is 47 per cent higher than the national average.

Environmentally, the city is one of the greenest in Europe. There are 4,500 acres of parks and woodland containing more than 40 million trees – with a hundred more planted every day. The road grid and roundabout system may confuse visitors but they mean there is almost no congestion for people who live there.

MK (as residents call it) hosted the UK's first multiplex cinema, the first modern hospital to be built from scratch and Europe's first purpose-built indoor skydiving centre. It's also home to Britain's most popular theatre outside London and the Open University.

There's nothing dull about MK's past either. An archaeological survey carried out in advance of building the town uncovered the 150 million-year-old skeleton of an ichthyosaurus, the tusks of a woolly mammoth and Britain's largest collection of Bronze Age gold jewellery, the Middleton Keynes Hoard.

In other countries all this might be a cause for celebration, but not in England.

As Terry Pratchett and Neil Gaiman put it in their novel *Good Omens* (1990): 'Milton Keynes was built to be modern, efficient, healthy, and, all in all, a pleasant place to live. Many Britons find this amusing.'

BILL BAILEY *Satellite navigation, in cars . . . when I was on tour . . . it was useless. You get to Milton Keynes, it just goes, 'Turn left. Turn left. Turn left. Turn left. Turn left. Turn left.'*

Why are vegetarians called vegetarians?

According to the Vegetarian Society, it's not because they eat vegetables.

The society claims that the word 'vegetarian' comes not from 'vegetable' but from the Latin word *vegetus* which means 'vigorous'. The *Oxford English Dictionary*'s earliest recorded use of 'vegetarian' is in 1839 and is defined as someone 'who lives wholly or principally on vegetable foods'. It goes on to state: 'The general use of the word appears to have been largely due to the formation of the Vegetarian Society at Ramsgate in 1847.' Before this, those abstaining from meat had been called many different names: *Vegetalists*, *Phytophagists* ('plant-eaters'),

Anti-creophagists, *Vegitans* but most usually *Pythagoreans* after the fourth-century BC Greek philosopher who, along with Socrates, Plato and Seneca, thought eating animals was inhumane.

The modern vegetarian movement began in Salford near Manchester, England in 1807. It was there that Rev. William Cowherd founded the Bible Christian Church, whose congregation undertook to abstain from eating flesh. One of his followers was Joseph Brotherton, the Salford MP, whose wife wrote the first vegetarian cookbook in 1812. In 1817 part of Cowherd's flock sailed to America to found a branch of the church in Philadelphia. This formed the nucleus of what became America's vegetarian movement.

It wasn't until mid-century that the growing number of English 'Pythagoreans' decided they needed a society to represent them. A meeting was convened at Northwood Villa, the world's first non-carnivorous hospital at Ramsgate in Kent and, on 30 September 1847, the newly named Vegetarian Society was formed. By 1849 their monthly newsletter, *The Vegetarian Messenger*, had a circulation of more than 5,000 copies.

From the beginning there was a vigorous debate about what 'vegetarianism' stood for: did it, for example, also imply abstinence from alcohol and tobacco? Some felt very strongly that it did and in 1888 the society split, with the London Vegetarian Society pursuing the more inclusive approach, leaving the original society based in Manchester. Mahatma Gandhi, architect of Indian independence, joined the London society, whereas the playwright George Bernard Shaw joined the Manchester branch. (Keen though he was, he once excused himself from a vegetarian gala dinner on the grounds that: 'The thought of two thousand people crunching celery at the same time horrified me.')

After eighty years of division, the two societies reunited in 1969, happy that their society's name was more about vigour than veg. They may have a point. Vegetarians tend to be less overweight, with lower levels of cholesterol, lower blood pressure, and less incidence of heart disease, diabetes, osteoporosis and dementia than meat-eaters. A decade-long study published in the UK in 2009 indicated that a vegetarian diet reduced the risk of all types of cancer by 12 per cent.

Vegans eat no animal products at all – not even milk, eggs or honey – and the origin of their name is undisputed. The founder, Donald Watson (1910–2005), explained that he chose the word 'vegan' because it was 'the beginning and end of vegetarian'.

STEPHEN *According to the Vegetarian Society, why are people who don't eat meat called vegetarians?*

JEREMY CLARKSON *So we can identify them as fools and madmen?*

How fast do electrons travel along an electrical wire?

Flick a light switch and the light comes on instantly. So it is surprising to learn that the electrons in any live electric wire are moving *very* slowly: not much faster than the minute hand on a clock.

Discovered towards the end of the nineteenth century, an electron is the negatively charged part of an atom – the one we were taught to think of as whizzing around the nucleus of every single atom on earth. It's the movement of these electrons in the same direction that creates what we call electricity.

How quickly electrons move along a wire in an electric

circuit depends to some extent on what the wire is made of, how big it is, and the strength of the current. If we assume a standard 1-mm diameter copper wire, attached to a battery generating a 10-amp current, the speed at which the electrons are moving is about 0.0008 kilometres per hour (0.0005 miles per hour). To put that in context, a garden snail fairly gallops along at around 0.05 kilometres per hour, or 0.03 miles per hour, 60 times faster.

Although the electrons carrying the charge are slow, the electrical *signal* – say, from a light switch to a light bulb – is travelling at something like the speed of light. That's because the wire carrying the electricity is stuffed full of electrons. Picture a tube completely packed with golf balls: if you push a new one in at one end of the tube, the last golf ball will be forced out at the far end, to make room for the newcomer. It looks like the movement of the last ball has occurred instantaneously – even though, in that time, each of the *individual* golf balls has moved only a tiny distance.

There are two ways in which electricity flows: either alternating current (AC) or direct current (DC). The flow of electrical current in a DC circuit keeps moving forwards. In an AC circuit – the type that comes from our home plug sockets – electrons are continually moving backwards and forwards. It's as if you were pushing a golf ball into one end of the tube while someone was at the other end continually shunting a different one back in.

This 'seesaw' effect means the individual electrons in an AC wire don't actually 'go' anywhere. So, depending on when the wiring was put in, there are probably electrons in your home that have been in residence longer than you have. And most electrons are as old as the universe – about 13.7 billion years.

How big are they? Sometimes scientists say an electron has no size, other times it will be described as a ball about a trillionth of a hair's width, but most of the time, these days, they don't even call them electrons any more but 'probability density charges'.

The particles formerly known as electrons are mere fuzzy clouds of possible electrical energy: in this configuration, the idea of 'size' is meaningless.

STEPHEN *Electrons actually move at point-nought-three miles per hour: a snail's pace along the wire.*

ALAN *Does that work if you get ten snails together? If you push the end snail . . .*

STEPHEN *We'll try that in my dressing room later.*

Which kind of ball bounces highest: steel, glass or rubber?

It's the glass one. Steel balls are the next bounciest and rubber balls come last.

When a ball hits the ground, some of the energy of its downward motion is lost on impact. This energy is either absorbed by the surface of the ball as it compresses, or is released as heat. In general, the harder the ball, the less energy it loses (soft balls squash).

This assumes a hard surface. 'Bounciness' isn't just about the thing bouncing, but also about what it is bouncing off. Drop a marble, or a ball bearing, on to soft sand and neither will bounce at all. All the energy passes into the sand. Drop either of them on to a steel anvil and they will comfortably out-bounce a rubber ball dropped from the same height.

The scientific term for the bounciness of an object is its 'coefficient of restitution' or COR. This is a scale measuring the energy that a material loses on impact. It runs from 0 for all energy lost, to 1 for no energy lost. Hard rubber has a COR of 0.8, but a glass ball can have a COR of up to 0.95.

That's providing it doesn't smash on impact. Astonishingly, nobody really knows why and how glass shatters. The *Third International Workshop on the Flow and Fracture of Advanced Glasses*, a conference held in 2005 involving scores of scientists from all over the world, failed to reach agreement.

Many of the unique qualities of glass are a result of its not being a normal solid, but an amorphous (or 'shapeless') solid. Molten glass solidifies so quickly that its molecules don't have time to settle into a regular crystalline lattice. This is because glass contains small amounts of soda (sodium carbonate) and lime (calcium oxide) that interfere with the structure of the silica (silicon dioxide) atoms as they cool. Without these additions, the silica would cool more slowly. This would form chemically neat and regular – but much less useful – quartz.

Some scientists think that given enough time – maybe billions of years – glass molecules will eventually follow suit and fall into line to form a true solid.

For now, though, they're like cars in a traffic jam – they want to make orderly patterns but can't because their neighbours are blocking the route. The visible result of this underlying chaos is smooth, transparent, mysterious glass.

New entry!

How many horsepower does one horse provide?

It's more than one, up to about fifteen. It depends on the horse and how long you need it for.

James Watt (1736–1819) coined the word 'horsepower' in 1783 as a way of determining the royalties he was due on his steam engines.

Watt didn't invent the steam engine – the credit for the first recorded steam-driven machine goes to Heron of Alexandria in AD 62. In the early eighteenth century, the English engineers Thomas Savery and Thomas Newcomen had produced large steam-driven pumping engines for clearing water from mines. It was while he was repairing a Newcomen engine that Watt made his big breakthrough. He realised that fitting a separate condenser would require a lot less steam to create the vacuum that sucked the piston down. In 1765 he built a prototype of an engine with a separate condenser. It produced more power and used 75 per cent less fuel than the equivalent Newcomen model.

But Watt's genius as an inventor wasn't matched by his business acumen and it was ten years before he was able to turn his machine into a commercially viable proposition. In 1775 he went into partnership with the Birmingham-based entrepreneur Matthew Boulton (1728–1809) and together they built 500 steam engines between 1775 and 1800. In 1781 Watt created a double-action piston that could push as well as pull. This meant his engine could be used to turn a wheel. Almost overnight, it wasn't just large-scale businesses like mines and waterworks that had a use for steam, but mills, breweries, transport and agriculture. The industrial revolution was under way and Watt and Boulton's invention ensured that Britain was at the forefront.

The next challenge was to set a fair price for their ingenuity. Their solution was to charge one-third of the savings that came from using so much less coal than the older engines that they replaced. For customers who still used horses on treadmills as a power source, they invented a standard by which the efficiency of the new engine could be judged. To do this, they deliberately overestimated the power of an average horse, assigning to '1 horsepower' (1hp) a value *less* than the power of one horse. This was a generous move –

and a shrewd one – designed to make businesses feel they were getting their money's worth, and to avoid any potential 'my horse can do better than that' type disputes.

While the average horse steadily produces more than 1 hp, in short bursts it can manage as much as 14.9 hp. Of course, it depends on the horse – some large shire horses can operate at an impressive 1.5 hp for hours at a time.

One horsepower is defined as the power needed to lift 15,000 kilograms (33,000 pounds) to a height of 30 centimetres (1 foot) over a period of one minute.

Humans are only capable of a measly 0.1 hp.

STEPHEN *What can't horses do that almost every other mammal can do?*

JIMMY CARR *I don't think they can vomit.*

STEPHEN *Exactly right. Take some points.*

ALAN *Can't get the old hoof down their throat.*

What's the most economical speed for driving a car?

For many years car manufacturers told motorists that the optimum driving speed for fuel efficiency was about 88.5 kilometres per hour (55 miles per hour). But it's much slower than that.

A fuel-efficiency study carried out in 2008 by *What Car?* magazine tested five cars of various sizes. It found that all of them did best at below 64 kilometres per hour (40 miles per hour), while two of the models reached optimum efficiency at speeds below 32 kilometres per hour (20 miles per hour).

On average, a car uses almost 40 per cent more fuel at 112 kilometres per hour (70 miles per hour) than it does at 80 kilometres per hour (50 miles per hour). It's a simple rule, the report concluded: 'The slower you go with the vehicle running smoothly, the less fuel you will use.'

It's not only driving fast that wastes money. Modern cars are quieter than ever. This gives the impression that the car is running smoothly when it's not, so drivers don't change gear as often as they should. Cruising at 64 kilometres per hour (40 miles per hour) in sixth gear uses 20 per cent less fuel than doing the same journey in fourth.

Air-conditioning can also cut fuel efficiency – by up to a mile a gallon or 1.6 kilometres per 4.54 litres. If you try to get round this by opening the window, you'll use more petrol battling the impaired aerodynamics. Even having the car radio on increases fuel costs.

During the recent football World Cup many England supporters drove around with flags of St George flying from their windows. In 2006 tests at the School of Mechanical, Aerospace and Civil Engineering at Manchester University found that two flags flapping from a medium-sized car travelling at an average of 48 kilometres per hour (30 miles per hour) creates enough wind-resistance to use an extra litre of fuel per hour.

In the USA almost three billion dollars' worth of fuel each year is wasted lugging overweight drivers around. Americans are pumping 938 million (US) gallons more gas a year than they were in 1960. Between 1960 and 2002 the weight of the average US citizen increased by 11 kilograms (24 pounds). Combining these figures, in 2006, researchers at the University of Illinois at Urbana-Champaign worked out that, with gasoline prices at $3 a gallon, transporting all this extra fat about by road cost the country $7.7 million a day, or $2.8 billion a year.

There are other advantages of driving at the right speed. The Energy Research Centre says that, if every UK motorist obeyed the 70 miles per hour speed limit, the saving in carbon dioxide pollution would be equivalent to removing 3 million Ford Focuses from the nation's roads.

What's the best way for the average family to reduce their impact on the environment?

Sell the car? No, get rid of the dog first. A medium-sized dog can have more than twice as much environmental impact as a large car.

An 'ecological footprint' is the amount of land needed to replace resources that someone or something has used and deal with the waste that results. Figures for the aggregate ecological footprint of humankind are calculated by the UN, and currently stand at 1.4 times the whole planet – i.e. we consume raw materials 1.4 times as fast as the Earth can renew them.

'Carbon footprint' is the amount of greenhouse gases produced, measured in tons of carbon dioxide; this is a component of the ecological footprint. There is also a 'water footprint', the amount of fresh water an activity or a person causes to be consumed.

A dog has about the same ecological footprint as two Toyota Landcruisers. This is because they eat so much meat. It takes 43 square metres (463 square feet) of land to produce 1 kilogram (2.2 pounds) of chicken (and much more for other meats), but only 13 square metres (139 square feet) for 1 kilo of cereal.

A recent book (*Time to Eat the Dog? The Real Guide to*

Sustainable Living by Brenda and Robert Vale) calculated that a Landcruiser driven 10,000 kilometres (over 6,200 miles) a year (admittedly run on biofuel) had an eco-footprint of 0.41 hectares (5,000 square yards), compared with 0.84 hectares (10,000 square yards) for a medium-sized dog. For big dogs like German Shepherds, it goes up to 1.1 hectares (13,156 square yards).

Assuming they eat pet food, it would take 400,000 square kilometres (154,000 square miles) of land to feed all the pet dogs in the top ten dog-owning countries; that's one-and-a-half times the size of New Zealand. America alone contains 61 million dogs, plus 76 million cats. Cats have a lesser impact but still about the same footprint as a Volkswagen Golf. Owning two hamsters has about the same impact as a plasma television.

How to reduce the environmental impact of your pet? Feed them on scraps and leftovers. Other 'offset' activity includes giving up golf and taking up tennis (it uses a much smaller area of land); living in sin (the travelling caused by a wedding can take up about ten times the energy your house uses in a year) and, if you do separate, move in as quickly as possible with someone else so you aren't creating a new additional household.

And while you're doing up your new love nest, don't buy a drill — borrow one. The average drill is used for just fifteen minutes in its lifetime.

STEPHEN *Keeping a dog is the equivalent to running two Toyota Landcruisers.*

EDDIE IZZARD *What?*

STEPHEN *Even one little cat is equivalent to a Volkswagen Golf.*

BILL BAILEY *Well, the thing is, I've got four dogs, two cats, birds, fish, rabbit, guinea pig, I could probably get like a . . . like a jet, or something.*

What happens if you leave a tooth in a glass of Coke overnight?

It won't dissolve.

Not only do we know this is untrue, we know the person who first made the spurious claim.

In 1950 Professor Clive McCay of Cornell University told a select committee of the US House of Representatives that high levels of sugar and phosphoric acid in Coca-Cola caused tooth decay. In order to add a bit of drama to his testimony, he went further – claiming that a tooth left in a glass of Coke would begin to dissolve after two days.

It doesn't: as anyone who tries it on a lost tooth can discover for themselves. Even if McCay were correct, nobody holds Coca-Cola in their mouth for two days. The average can of soft drink contains about seven teaspoons of sugar, so it does cause tooth decay – but it does so gradually, not in a matter of hours.

Apart from sugar, the other troublesome ingredient in fizzy drinks is phosphoric acid. This stops the drinks going flat and adds a tangy flavour. It's also used in fertilisers, in detergents and in shipyards to remove rust from aircraft carriers. But it still doesn't 'rot your teeth overnight'. A 2006 study by the American Academy of General Dentistry on the effect of soft drinks on tooth enamel found that high concentrations of citric acid were much more damaging than phosphoric acid. So go easy on the orange juice.

Phosphoric acid also inhibits the digestive acids in the stomach, reducing the absorption of calcium. This means that a serious fizzy drink habit can lead to calcium deficiency, weakening teeth and bones (though not 'dissolving' them).

An occasional glass of Coke is unlikely to do anyone much harm. Coca-Cola was originally marketed as a health drink, growing out of the mid-nineteenth-century European obsession with 'tonic' wine: alcoholic beverages enhanced by herbal infusions. These often included coca, the South American plant extract better known as the source of cocaine.

In 1863 Pope Leo XIII awarded a medal to the Corsican chemist Angelo Mariani (1838–1914) for inventing Vin Mariani, the first coca-based wine. Millions of Europeans enjoyed it, including the Pope himself, Queen Victoria, Thomas Edison, Sarah Bernhardt, Jules Verne and Henrik Ibsen.

John Stith Pemberton (1831–88) of Atlanta, Georgia, soon produced an American version – Pemberton's French Wine Coca. In imitation of their European counterparts, the city's intellectual smart set took it to their hearts. But, in 1885, local prohibition laws compelled Pemberton to produce a non-alcoholic version. He pepped it up with the inclusion of caffeine-rich kola nuts from Africa and Coca-Cola was born.

Coca leaves are still used to flavour Coca-Cola – but only after they've had all the cocaine chemically extracted.

ANDY HAMILTON *My mum used to say to me, because I used to drink a lot of Coke when I was in my early teens: 'You shouldn't drink Coke because it stains the inside of your stomach.'*

HUGH DENNIS *But how do you know that's not true?*

ANDY *No, you don't, but you kind of think, well, if I ever see the inside of my stomach, it's probably going to be a bit late to worry about what colour it is.*

PHILL JUPITUS *I can't wait, Andy. I mean I don't like to talk about a friend's death, but at your post mortem: 'Look at this! Terrible stained intestines.'*

What happens if you cover a beautiful woman from head to toe in gold paint?

She won't die of suffocation.

Many people believe that we 'breathe through our skin', so that anything that blocks all our pores causes rapid asphyxiation. It's not true. We breathe only through our nose and mouth. The pores have nothing to do with it. If they did, scuba diving would be fatal.

Covering a person in gold paint might eventually kill them, if it was left on long enough. They would die from overheating, since their paint-clogged pores would be unable to sweat, which is the human body's chief means of temperature regulation. It would be a very slow and unpleasant way to go.

In the 1964 film of Ian Fleming's James Bond novel, *Goldfinger*, the actress playing the part of the woman murdered by means of body-paint was Shirley Eaton. She published her autobiography in 2000, despite the still persistent myth that she died of skin suffocation during filming. The producers of the film were as taken in by the idea of pore asphyxiation as their audience. Not only was a doctor on standby while Eaton shot her scene, but a 6-inch patch of skin was left unpainted on her stomach, to allow her skin to 'breathe'.

Human skin has about two million pores – about 700 per 6.5 square centimetres (1 square inch), each servicing a sweat gland. The skin is our largest organ, weighing an average of 2.7 kilograms (6 pounds) and covering 1.67 square metres (18 square feet). As well as the pores, a single square inch of skin contains around 4 metres (13 feet) of blood vessels, 1,300 nerve cells and 100 oil glands. Skin cells are constantly being replaced: in an average lifetime, we each get through 900 complete skins.

There is one mammal that *does* breathe through its skin. In

1998 scientists rediscovered the Julia Creek dunnart (*Sminthopsis douglasi*) – an Australian marsupial mouse 12 centimetres (5 inches) long, named after the area in Queensland where it lives, from which it was thought to have gone extinct twenty years earlier.

Julia Creek dunnarts are unusually undeveloped at birth; their gestation period is just twelve days, and the newborn is slightly larger than a grain of rice. As a result, they can't immediately use their lungs, so they exchange oxygen and carbon dioxide through their skin instead: something previously thought impossible for a mammal. Researchers realised this after being puzzled by the fact that the newborn babies were neither breathing nor dying.

Being so tiny, the baby dunnart doesn't need much oxygen and, protected by its mother's pouch, can afford to have extremely thin, permeable skin. Indeed, its skin is *so* thin that its internal organs are visible. By the age of three weeks, however, it is getting half its oxygen from its lungs, and it gradually switches over completely to the conventional mammalian method of breathing.

ROB BRYDON *Do you know how he got the job, Sean Connery? He went for the audition and then he walked away and the producers watched him out of the window and they said he walked like a panther. Which, when you think about it, would be on all fours, and would make him look like a ruddy lunatic. Not the sort of man you want botching up the schedule on an expensive film. Oh, look at him, he's doing it again. Sean, please get up.*

What colour was Frankenstein?

Frankenstein wasn't green, nor was the monster he created. The monster was yellow in the original book and black and white in the film.

James Whale's movie *Frankenstein* (1931) was adapted from the novel written by Mary Shelley in 1818. In the book, the hero, Victor Frankenstein, isn't a doctor but an idealistic young Swiss student, fascinated by science and alchemy. His obsession leads him to create life from inanimate matter, resulting in a 'creature' nearly 2½ metres (8 feet) tall made from the body parts of corpses. In the novel, the way Frankenstein brings him to life is barely described, but in the movie a lightning bolt animates the monster. The spectacular electrical effects were achieved using a Tesla coil built by the brilliant Serbian inventor of AC current, Nikola Tesla (1856–1943). He was then seventy-five years old.

In both the movie and the novel Frankenstein's reaction to his creation is 'horror and disgust'. Here is Mary Shelley's version:

> His yellow skin scarcely covered the work of muscles and arteries beneath; his hair was of a lustrous black, and flowing; his teeth of a pearly whiteness; but these luxuriances only formed a more horrid contrast with his watery eyes, that seemed almost of the same colour as the dun white sockets in which they were set, his shrivelled complexion and straight black lips.

It was to convey this 'corpse-like' effect that Jack Pierce, the make-up artist at Universal Studios, created the famous flat-headed, bolt-through-the-neck version of the monster, as played by Boris Karloff. Though the movie was shot in black and white, all the promotional posters showed him as green.

The film was a huge critical and commercial success, taking

$53,000 (about $750,000 today) in just one New York cinema in its first week and leading to a string of sequels. When *Frankenstein* was adapted into comic book form in the early 1940s, the monster was depicted as green-skinned. This convention continued in the mid-1960s with the TV show *The Munsters*. Though the series was also made in black and white, all the publicity material shows Herman Munster (a comical parody of Boris Karloff) with lurid green skin.

Mary Shelley's creature was very different from the lumbering, inarticulate portrayal made famous by Karloff. He was agile, fast and could talk, albeit in a rather old-fashioned, ponderous way (he'd educated himself by reading Milton's *Paradise Lost*). Like a tragic parody of Adam, the first man, he refuses to eat meat and lives on 'acorns and berries'. He is driven to revenge and murder by Frankenstein's rejection of him, and by the loneliness and sense of shame he feels because of his hideous appearance. His last act is to trudge to the North Pole and burn himself on a funeral pyre to erase all traces of his existence.

Frankenstein, or The Modern Prometheus was written when Mary Shelley was only eighteen years old, and became an immediate sensation. As well as being a landmark in gothic fiction, many now consider it the first science fiction novel.

What colour were Dorothy's shoes in *The Wonderful Wizard of Oz*?

They were silver, not ruby.

L. Frank Baum's novel *The Wonderful Wizard of Oz* was the best-selling book for children in the USA for two years after its publication in 1900. Since translated into more than forty languages, it created one of the most successful publishing franchises of all time: Baum produced a series of thirteen sequels set in the land of Oz and many more were published after his death. He also wrote the script for a musical version, which ran almost continuously on Broadway between 1903 and 1904, and was the first adaptation to use the shortened title, *The Wizard of Oz*.

Under the new name, in 1939 MGM took the famous book and the famous musical and turned them into an even more famous film, directed by Victor Fleming and starring Judy Garland as Dorothy. In 2009 it was named the 'most watched' film of all time by the US Library of Congress. Although it did well at the box office, its huge budget meant it made only a small profit and it was beaten to the Best Picture Oscar by that year's other blockbuster, *Gone with the Wind*. But the immortality of *The Wizard of Oz* was assured by its annual Christmas screening on US television, which began in 1956. It's the most repeated movie on TV of all time.

Dorothy's slippers were changed to red in the film because the producer, Mervyn LeRoy, wanted them to stand out. *The Wizard of Oz* was only the second film made in Technicolor and the new process made some colours easier to render than others. It took the art department over a week to come up with a yellow for the Yellow Brick Road that didn't look green on screen.

The new technology made the six-month shoot hazardous for the actors. The lights heated the set to a stifling 38 °C and eventually caused a fire in which Margaret Hamilton (the Wicked Witch of the West) was badly burned. The cast had to eat liquidised food through straws because their thick colour face make-up was so toxic. The original Tin Man, Buddy Ebsen, nearly died from inhaling the aluminium powder it contained and had to leave the film.

Lyman Frank Baum died in 1919, long before his book

made it to the screen, although he ended his days in Hollywood as a film producer. This was the last in a long line of careers – as a breeder of fancy poultry, a newspaper editor, a theatrical impresario, the proprietor of a general store, a travelling salesman and a writer of over fifty books, many under female pseudonyms such as Edith van Dyne and Laura Metcalf. In 1900, the same year he published *The Wonderful Wizard of Oz* he also brought out *The Art of Decorating Dry Goods Windows and Interiors*, which listed the many marketing advantages of using shop-window mannequins.

But it is *Oz* he will be remembered for and, despite all attempts at interpreting his novel as a political allegory or a feminist tract, it is best read the way he intended, as a home-grown American version of the fairy tales of the Brothers Grimm and Hans Christian Andersen that he had loved as a child.

How do you know if something's radioactive?

No, it doesn't glow in the dark.

Radioactivity isn't detectable as visible light. If it were, the whole earth would glow in the dark, as well as every plant and animal on it. Rocks, soil and living tissue all contain traces of radioactive material.

Radioactivity is not the same as radiation. Radiation is the means by which energy – radio waves, light, heat and X-rays – travels in space. These are all made of photons that spread out (or 'radiate') in waves moving at the speed of light. Though they are all made of the same stuff and travel at the same speed, their waves have different distances between the peaks and troughs, graded along a scale known as the electromagnetic spectrum. At one end are low-frequency waves (with long wavelengths) like radio waves; at the other, high-frequency waves with short wavelengths like X-rays. In the middle is 'visible light', the narrow band of electromagnetic energy that we can see.

All radiation is harmful if we're exposed to too much of it for too long. Sunshine – a mix of wavelengths from infrared (heat), through visible light, to ultraviolet – causes sunburn. At the high-frequency end of the spectrum, the energy is so intense it can knock electrons out of orbit, giving a previously neutral atom a positive electric charge. This charged atom is called an *ion* (Greek for 'going'). One ion creates another in a rapid chain reaction. This can cause terrible damage by changing the molecules in our cells, causing skin 'burns', cancerous tumours and mutations in our DNA.

Substances that do this are called 'radioactive', a term coined by the Polish chemist Marie Curie (1867–1934) in 1898. Although she invented the *word*, the French physicist Henri Becquerel (1852–1908) had accidentally discovered the actual *process* two years earlier, while working with uranium. Following in his footsteps, Marie discovered something a million times more radioactive than uranium: a new chemical element she called 'radium'.

Becquerel, Marie and her husband Pierre shared the 1903 Nobel Prize for their discovery and the 'invigorating' effects of radium salts were soon being hailed as a cure for ailments from blindness to depression and rheumatism. Radium was added to mineral water, toothpaste, face-creams and chocolate and there was a craze for 'radium cocktails'. Added radium to paint made it luminous, a novelty effect that was used to decorate clock and watch faces.

This is the origin of the radioactive 'green glow'. It wasn't the radium glowing, but its reaction with the copper and zinc in the paint, creating a phenomenon called 'radio-luminescence'. The phrase 'radium glow' stuck in the public mind. When the true consequences of exposure to radio-activity were revealed in the early 1930s, glowing and radioactivity had become inseparably linked.

Hundreds of 'radium girls', who had worked in factories applying paint containing glow-in-the-dark radium to watch-faces (and licking the brushes as they did so) were to die from painful and disfiguring facial cancers. And in 1934 Marie Curie herself died of anaemia, caused by years of handling the 'magic' substance she had discovered.

Which part of the food do microwaves cook first?

Microwave ovens don't cook food 'from the inside out'.

Microwaves are a form of electromagnetic radiation that sits on the spectrum between radio waves and infrared light. They are called 'micro' waves because they have much shorter wave-lengths than radio waves. They have a wide variety of uses: mobile phone networks, wireless connections like Bluetooth, Global Positioning Systems (GPS), radio telescopes and radar all rely on microwaves at differing frequencies. Although they carry more energy than radio waves, they're a long way from the dangerous end of the electromagnetic spectrum where X-rays and gamma rays reside.

Microwave ovens don't directly cook food; what they do is heat water. The frequency of microwaves happens to be just right for exciting water molecules. By spreading their energy evenly through food, the microwaves heat the water in it and the hot water cooks the food. Nearly all food contains water, but microwaves won't cook completely dry food like cornflakes, rice or pasta.

The molecules in the centre of your soup aren't heated any quicker than those on the outside. In fact, the opposite is true. If the food is the same consistency all the way through, the water nearest the surface will absorb most of the energy. In this regard, microwave cookery is similar to heating food in a normal oven, except that the microwaves penetrate deeper and more quickly. The reason why it sometimes appears that the middle of microwaved food has 'cooked first' is to do with the type of food. Jacket potatoes, for instance, and apple pies, are drier on the outside than the inside; so the moist centre will be hotter than the outside skin or crust.

Because microwaves work by exciting the water molecules, it also means that the food rarely gets much hotter than the 100 °C temperature at which water boils. Meat cooked in a microwave can be tender, but it is more like poaching than roasting. To break down protein and carbohydrate molecules rapidly and form a caramelised crust as in pork crackling (or to get the crisp exterior of a chip) requires temperatures of 240 °C or higher.

Microwave ovens are a by-product of the invention of radar in 1940. In 1945 Percy Spencer, a US engineer working for the defence systems company Raytheon was building a magnetron (the device at the core of radar that converts electricity to microwaves) when he noticed that a chocolate peanut bar in his pocket had completely melted. Guessing it was caused by the magnetron, he built a metal box and fed in microwave radiation. The first food he cooked in his improvised oven was popcorn; his second experiment, with a whole egg, ended in an explosion. The water in the egg had rapidly vaporised.

Raytheon was quick to introduce the first commercial microwave oven in 1947 and, by the late 1960s, smaller domestic versions had started appearing in American homes. Despite the various myths they have gathered down the years, they now occupy pride of place in 90 per cent of US kitchens.

Where did the British government plan to drop its second atomic bomb?

Yorkshire.

In 1953 British scientists seriously considered detonating a nuclear weapon next to the tiny village of Skipsea, on the East Yorkshire coast road between Bridlington and Hornsea. Home to just over 630 people, it has a medieval church and the remains of a Norman castle but not much else.

It was exactly this isolated, sleepy character – plus its convenient proximity to the RAF base at Hull – that commended the village to the scientists at the Atomic Research Establishment at Aldermaston. They were looking at various coastal sites in the UK for an above-ground atomic bomb explosion following their successful test detonation under the sea off the Monte Bello Islands, north-west of Australia, in 1952. Skipsea ticked all the boxes.

Unsurprisingly, the local community leaders were unanimously opposed to the idea, pointing out that the test site was dangerously close to bungalows and beach huts and that a public right of way ran through it. The Aldermaston team eventually relented and switched their plans back to Australia.

The results of the Maralinga tests in South Australia, in which seven above-ground atomic devices were detonated between 1956 and 1957, show just how close Skipsea – and the rest of the UK – came to total disaster. The interior of the whole Australian continent was severely contaminated, with testing stations 3,200 kilometres (2,000 miles) apart reporting a hundredfold increase in radioactivity. Significant fallout even reached Melbourne and Adelaide.

Maralinga was a site of great spiritual importance to the local Pitjantjatjara and Yankunytjatjara peoples (its name means 'Place of Thunder') and their evacuation was incompetently managed. After the detonations, there was little attempt to enforce site security and all the warnings signs were in English. As a result, many Aboriginals returned to their homeland soon afterwards.

Even more shocking, British and Australian servicemen were intentionally sent to work on the site to gauge the effect of radioactivity on active troops. It is estimated that 30 per cent of the 7,000 servicemen who worked at the location died from various cancers before they turned sixty. The effect on the Aboriginal inhabitants has been even worse – with blindness, deformity and high levels of cancer reported across the local population.

After pressure from the troops' veterans' association and aboriginal groups, the McClelland Royal Commission was set up in 1984. It concluded that all seven tests had been carried out 'under inappropriate conditions' and ordered a comprehensive clean-up of the site, which was eventually completed in 2000. In 1994 a compensation fund of $13.5 million was set up for the local people and limited payments have been made to Australian veterans.

At the time of writing, the UK government has produced no formal compensation scheme for British survivors of its nuclear testing programme.

STEPHEN *Where did Britain originally plan to test their atomic bombs?*

SANDI TOKSVIG *Was it Paris?*

Which two counties fought each other in the Wars of the Roses?

Neither the Yorkists nor the Lancastrians were based in the counties that bear their names, and neither side called the conflict 'the Wars of the Roses'.

The Houses of York and Lancaster were branches of the House of Plantagenet, which had ruled England for 300 years. They were unconnected with either Yorkshire or Lancashire. If anything, more Lancastrians than Yorkists came from Yorkshire and the remainder of the Duke of Lancaster's estates were in Cheshire, Gloucestershire and North Wales. Most Yorkist supporters were from the Midlands, not from Yorkshire, and the Duke of York's estates were mainly concentrated along the Welsh borders and down into south Wales.

The 'Wars of the Roses' weren't wars in the traditional sense. The people involved certainly didn't think of them as such. They were really just an extended bout of infighting between two branches of the royal family. The event that provoked this rivalry was the overthrow of Richard II by Henry Bolingbroke, Duke of Lancaster, who was crowned Henry IV in 1399. There followed half a century of intrigue, treachery and murder, peppered with minor skirmishes, but it wasn't until 1455 that the first real battle was fought. And, even though the throne changed hands between the two sides three times over the period – with Edward IV (York) and Henry VI (Lancaster) getting two goes each – most of England was unaffected by the strife.

After the murder of Henry VI in 1471, there were three Yorkist kings in a row: Edward IV (again), Edward V and Richard III. Although Henry Tudor, the man who wrested the throne from Richard III to become Henry VII, was nominally a Lancastrian, his real intention was to start a new dynasty named after himself. The creation of the red-and-white Tudor rose was a brilliant bit of marketing on his part, supposedly merging the white rose of York and the red rose of Lancaster to symbolise a new united kingdom. In fact, until then, the roses had been just two of many livery signs used by either side. Most of the troops were conscripts or mercenaries who tended to sport the badge of their immediate feudal lord or employer. Even at Bosworth Field in 1485, the climactic battle that finally ended the conflict, the Lancastrian Henry fought under the red dragon of Wales, and the Yorkist Richard III under his personal symbol of a white boar.

But Henry's image manipulation was so successful that, when Shakespeare wrote *Henry VI Part I* in 1601, he included a scene where supporters of each faction pick different coloured roses. This so inspired Sir Walter Scott that – in *Ivanhoe* (1823) – he named the period 'the Wars of the Roses'. So it was 338 years after the conflict ended that the phrase was used for the very first time.

Even if they weren't really wars, or much to do with roses, and didn't involve inter-county rivalries, they were neither romantic nor trivial. The Yorkists' crushing victory at Towton in 1461 remains the largest and bloodiest battle ever fought on British soil. Some 80,000 soldiers took part (including twenty-eight lords, almost half the peerage at that time), and more than 28,000 men died – roughly 3 per cent of the entire adult male population of England.

Who led the English fleet against the Spanish Armada?

It wasn't Sir Francis Drake – he was only second-in-command. The top man was Lord Howard of Effingham, who later led the peace talks with Spain.

The defeat of the Spanish Armada in 1588 was the major engagement in the nine-year war between Protestant England and Catholic Spain that had begun in 1585. The Armada (Spanish for 'fleet' or 'navy') was the largest naval force ever assembled in Europe, with 151 ships, 8,000 sailors and 15,000 soldiers. It sailed from Lisbon in May 1588, with the intention of invading England.

Bizarrely, only thirty years before, Philip II of Spain had been King of England. He had co-ruled the country with his Catholic wife Mary I until her death in 1558. When Mary's younger Protestant sister, Elizabeth, succeeded her, Philip saw her as a heretic and unfit to rule. At first he tried to unseat her by guile, but his best hope ended when Elizabeth executed Mary, Queen of Scots (a Catholic, and the next in line to the throne) in 1587. His patience exhausted, Philip decided to resort to violence. He asked Pope Sixtus V to bless a crusade against the English so he could reclaim the benighted realm for the true faith.

Although it's often described as the greatest English victory since Agincourt, a full-blown battle never really took place. Instead, over several days there was a series of inconclusive skirmishes, in which no ship on either side was sunk by direct enemy action, although five Spanish ships ran aground in August at the minor battle of Gravelines, off what is now northern France. Drake's famous fire ships failed to ignite a single Spanish vessel – although they caused enough panic to break up the Armada's disciplined formation, allowing the smaller and nimbler English ships to get in and scatter them.

Eventually, both sides ran out of ammunition but Effingham had just enough shot left to harry the invaders northwards up the eastern coast of Britain. As the Spanish fleet, thirsty and exhausted, rounded Scotland and sailed down the west coast of Ireland going the long way home, many of their huge ships succumbed to unseasonably fierce storms. Only half of the 'invincible' Armada (and fewer than a quarter of the men) made it back. Although the English lost only a hundred men during the fighting, an estimated 6,000 English troops died in the months afterwards, from typhus and dysentery contracted while on board.

Drake may not have been commander on the day but, to the English, he was already the foremost hero of the age. In 1581, he became the first Englishman to circumnavigate the globe, returning with enough plundered Spanish gold and treasure to double the Queen's annual income. King Philip, of course, regarded him as no more than a common pirate and set a price of 20,000 ducats on his head (£4 million in today's money). The Spanish called the despised Drake by his Latin name 'Franciscus Draco' – 'Francis the Dragon'.

Did Drake really finish his leisurely game of bowls on Plymouth Hoe as the Spanish sailed into the Channel? We'll never know. The story is first mentioned in a pamphlet of 1624, which merely said that various 'commanders and captaines' had been playing; but such was Drake's mythic status that, by the 1730s, the story was told exclusively about him.

What did Cornish wreckers do?

They stole things that were washed up on beaches. There's no evidence to suggest that any Cornish wrecker ever actually caused a shipwreck.

The traditional picture of swarthy Cornish brigands on cliff tops, luring ships to their doom by waving lanterns or lighting signal fires, was invented in the mid-nineteenth century. It seems to have originated with Methodist preachers and then to have been fleshed out in graphic detail by Daphne du Maurier's romantic novel *Jamaica Inn* (1936).

During the great Methodist revival in Victorian times, clergymen used reformed 'wreckers' as living examples of the miraculous transformations that their brand of Christianity could effect; even the most debased sinners could be saved from their criminal pasts and go on to lead decent lives.

But such dramatic propaganda only worked inland. Coastal dwellers knew exactly what the ancient practice of 'wrecking' involved. It meant going down to the site of a wreck and scrounging anything you could get your hands on. It wasn't legal, but it was hardly murderous barbarism either.

Although an Act was passed in 1753 explicitly outlawing the setting out of 'any false light or lights, with intention to bring any ship or vessel into danger', no Cornishman was ever charged with the crime, and no authentic mention of the alleged practice has ever been found in contemporary Cornish documents.

The only such case ever to reach the courts involved the wreck of the *Charming Jenny* on the coast of Anglesey in 1773. Captain Chilcote, the sole survivor, claimed his ship had been lured to shore by false lights, after which three men had stripped his dead wife naked on the beach, and stolen the silver buckles from his shoes as he lay exhausted. One of the men was hanged and another condemned to death, his sentence later commuted to transportation.

The reason why this is the one known example of the crime in English history is because it doesn't make any sense for communities making a living from the sea — including working as pilots, helping ships reach shore safely – to set out to create shipwrecks. They could never be sure that vessels approaching on stormy nights were crewed by outsiders, rather than by sons or neighbours.

The belief that wreckers used false lights (sometimes allegedly tied to the tails of donkeys or cows) probably arose because smugglers used cliff-top lights to signal to their comrades offshore when it was safe to land. Luring fellow mariners to a watery end is no more authentic than the 'traditional Cornish wreckers prayer': *'Oh please Lord, let us pray for all on the sea. But if there's got to be wrecks, please send them to we.'* In fact, these words are part of an original song lyric written by London musician Andy Roberts in 2003.

Today, those who harvest the fruits of the sea in Cornish wrecker style can even avoid breaking the law entirely, provided they report their finds to the Office of the Receiver of Wrecks in Southampton.

How did the USA react to the sinking of the *Lusitania*?

Not by declaring war on Germany, as many people think. The *Lusitania* was sunk in May 1915. America didn't enter the First World War until April 1917.

From the summer of 1914 most of Europe was at war. Germany routinely attacked merchant shipping en route to Britain in an attempt to starve the country into surrender, but the US was determined to remain neutral.

At first, German submarines followed the so-called 'Cruiser Rules' laid down at the 1907 Hague Convention, by which civilian ships could only be sunk after all those aboard had been given an opportunity to evacuate. But when the British started disguising naval vessels as merchantmen and using merchant ships to transport arms, Germany adopted a 'sink on sight' policy. Winston Churchill, First Lord of the Admiralty, actually welcomed this, hoping that the Germans would sink a neutral ship, dragging America into the war. In a now infamous memo to the President of the Board of Trade, he wrote: 'We want the traffic – the more the better; and if some of it gets into trouble, better still.'

The *Lusitania* was a magnificent luxury liner, the jewel of the Cunard line. (She wasn't, as a common misconception has it, the sister ship of the *Titanic*, which was owned by the White Star Line.) As the *Lusitania* prepared to set off from New York to Liverpool, Germany placed adverts in US papers warning that passengers sailing through a war zone did so 'at their own risk'. Captain Turner of the *Lusitania* described this as 'the best joke I've heard in many days,' and reassured his passengers that with a top speed of 26 knots (nearly 50 kilometres per hour or 30 miles per hour) she was too fast for any German U-boat.

Just one torpedo was all that was needed to sink the ship, 13 kilometres (8 miles) off the coast of Ireland, on 7 May 1915. She went down in eighteen minutes with the loss of 1,198 lives – including over a hundred children, many of them babies. One survivor recalled swimming through crowds of dead children 'like lily-pads on a pond'.

On being rescued from the wreck, the hapless Captain Turner remarked, 'What bad luck – what have I done to deserve this?' Only 239 bodies were recovered, a third of whom were never identified. Among the dead were 128 Americans.

The British, and the pro-war faction in America, were delighted by the effect that this proof of Germany's 'frightfulness' had on US public opinion. The Germans, under the pressure of international outrage, promptly abandoned their 'sink on sight' strategy. (It wasn't re-adopted until January 1917, by which time Germany knew that war with the US was inevitable.)

Though President Woodrow Wilson's government refused to be swept into the war by popular anger, the military significance of the atrocity is not in doubt.

Some historians even argue that, by forcing Germany to suspend 'sink on sight' at a crucial stage of the conflict, the sinking of the *Lusitania* gave the Allies a strategic advantage that determined the outcome of the whole war.

When America did finally declare war in 1917, the US army recruited under the slogan 'Remember the *Lusitania!*'

Which radio play first made people think the world was coming to an end?

It was the BBC's *Broadcasting the Barricades* (1926). The work of an English Catholic priest, it inspired Orson Welles to adapt H. G. Wells's *The War of the Worlds* for radio in 1938.

On 16 January 1926 Father Ronald Knox interrupted his regular BBC radio show to deliver a news bulletin, complete with alarming sound effects. Revolution had broken out in London, he announced. The Savoy Hotel had been burned down and the National Gallery sacked. Mortar fire had toppled the clock tower of Big Ben and angry demonstrators were roasting the wealthy broker Sir Theophilus Gooch alive. 'The crowd has secured the person of Mr Wurtherspoon, the Minister of Traffic, who was attempting to make his escape in disguise. He has now been hanged from a lamp post in Vauxhall.'

It should have been obvious it was a spoof. For one thing, Knox was a famous satirist who had once written a scholarly essay claiming that Tennyson's *In Memoriam* was the work of Queen Victoria. Listeners who missed the BBC's announcement of the programme as a 'burlesque' should have guessed it was a joke on hearing that the leader of the uprising was a Mr Popplebury, Secretary of the National Movement for Abolishing Theatre Queues.

But this was only eight years after the Russian Revolution. Many upper- and middle-class people believed a communist takeover of Britain was imminent and took the ludicrous reports seriously. Women fainted and hundreds of people phoned police stations for details of the anarchy. The following day, as luck would have it, snow prevented newspapers reaching many rural areas, confirming the impression that civilisation had, indeed, come to an end.

The BBC rushed to offer its 'sincere apologies for any uneasiness caused' and the press (which for commercial reasons was deeply hostile to radio) lost no time in exaggerating the depth of the 'unease' with headlines like 'Revolution Hoax by Wireless: Terror caused in villages and towns'. The BBC's Director General, Lord Reith, calmly totted up the complaints (249), compared them to messages of appreciation (2,307), and declared the show such a success that he wanted more of the same. Knox later obliged with a programme about an invention to amplify the sounds of vegetables in pain.

Ronald Knox (1888–1957) was the top classicist of his year at Oxford. Though his father and both his grandfathers had been Anglican bishops, he was inspired by G. K. Chesterton to convert to Roman Catholicism and became a respected theologian. Like Chesterton, Knox was also a prolific and successful writer of crime fiction. In 1928, he published 'The Ten Commandments for Detective Novelists'. They included: 'All supernatural or preternatural agencies are ruled out as a matter of course'; 'Not more than one secret room or passage is allowable'; 'The detective must not himself commit the crime'; and, more mysteriously, 'No Chinaman must figure in the story'.

The *New York Times* smugly reported Knox's *Broadcasting the Barricades* with the words: 'Such a thing as that could not happen in this country.' Twelve years later Orson Welles was to prove them entirely wrong.

What did US bankers do after the Wall Street Crash of 1929?

Only two people jumped to their death, and neither were bankers.

The prosperity of the 1920s encouraged millions of Americans to buy stocks and shares by using the value of the stock they were buying as collateral to borrow the money they needed to buy the stock itself. It was a classic economic bubble, and it finally burst on 'Black Thursday', 24 October 1929, when 14 billion dollars were wiped off the value of shares in a single day. Panic selling was so rapid that the New York Stock Exchange was unable to keep pace with the transactions as they were made.

Within hours, the legend had started: reporters were running around Wall Street chasing stories about ruined investors leaping out of skyscrapers. The following day's *New York Times* reported that 'wild and false' rumours were spreading across America, including the popular belief that eleven speculators had already killed themselves, and that a crowd had gathered when they mistook a man working on a Wall Street rooftop for a financier about to jump.

Comedians immediately started telling gags about the supposed jumpers, with Will Rogers tastefully noting that 'You had to stand in line to get a window to jump out of.'

None of it was true. Though there was a lot of panic and uncertainty, a fortnight after the Crash, New York's Chief Medical Examiner announced that suicides for the period were actually *down* on the previous year. John Kenneth Galbraith, the economist, corroborated this in his authoritative history, *The Great Crash* (1954), which concluded: 'The suicide wave that followed the stock market crash is also part of the legend of 1929. In fact, there was none.'

A detailed study of suicide records of the time, carried out in the 1980s, confirmed this. In New York, between 1921 and 1931, jumping from a high place was the second-most frequent method of suicide. Between Black Thursday and the end of 1929, a hundred suicide attempts, fatal or otherwise, were reported in the *New York Times*. Of these, only four were jumps linked to the crash, and only two were in Wall Street.

The two who actually did jump in Wall Street did so in November. Hulda Borowski, a fifty-one-year-old bond clerk, was said to be 'near exhaustion from overwork', while George E. Cutler, a successful wholesale greengrocer, became frustrated when told that his attorney was unavailable to see him, and leapt from the seventh floor of the lawyer's building.

In general, recessions do lead to suicide, though. A 30 per cent rise in the suicide rate was noted in the US and Britain during the Great Depression that followed the 1929 crash, and that pattern has been repeated in more recent downturns.

A study of twenty-six European countries published in *The Lancet* in 2009 found a 0.8 per cent rise in the number of suicides for every 1 per cent increase in unemployment.

In the wake of the financial crash of 2008, American psychologists have even invented a term to describe the phenomenon. They call it 'econocide'.

Who was the first American woman to be buried in Britain?

Pocahontas, as far as we know. She was buried in the church_ yard of St George's Church, Gravesend in 1617, aged twenty-two. She was also the first Native American to be baptised a Christian, to learn English and to marry an Englishman.

Pocahontas was born at Werowocomoco, near what is now Richmond, Virginia. The English translated her name to mean 'Bright Stream between Two Hills' but, in her native language, it seems it was a childhood nickname meaning 'Little Wanton One'. Her real name, like the other children's, was a secret known only to the tribe. Hers was Matoax, 'Little Snow Feather'.

She was the daughter of Wahunsunacawh, the Supreme Chief of the Powhatan Confederacy, an alliance of Algonquin tribes who lived around Chesapeake Bay. This was the area the English first settled when they established the new colony of Virginia in 1607. Pocahontas's father, known as 'The Powhatan', had ten daughters altogether, and he was about sixty when the English arrived.

When Pocahontas was ten, a hunting party led by the Powhatan's brother captured an English soldier and leading colonist called John Smith (1580–1631). According to his account, the little girl intervened to save his life, and he went on to become president of the Virginia colony.

At first, partly owing to Pocahontas's popularity with the settlers, relations with the Powhatans were good. But the situation deteriorated and, in 1610, the first Anglo-Powhatan war broke out. Pocahontas was kidnapped and held hostage.

Four years later, as part of the peace settlement, she was married off to an English widower, John Rolfe (1585–1622), the first man to export tobacco to England from Virginia. It was a political marriage. Rolfe wrote that he was 'motivated not by the unbridled desire of carnal affection but for the good of this plantation, for the honor of our country, for the Glory of God, for my own salvation'. The teenage bride's views are not recorded.

Baptised a Christian and renamed Rebecca, Pocahontas moved to England in 1616, living in Brentford with her husband, their son, Thomas, and a retinue of Powhatans. She appears to have been used as a kind of walking advert for the Virginia Company to show potential colonists and investors how charming the native Americans could be. For the last year of her life, she was famous. The Powhatans were a sensation at court, where Pocahontas was presented as a foreign royal, 'the Indian princess'. The diminutive King James I made so little impression on her that his status had to be explained to her afterwards.

A year later, the Rolfes boarded a ship to return to Virginia, but Pocahontas became gravely ill (possibly of smallpox), was taken ashore, and died. Her last words to her husband were: 'All must die. It is enough that the childe liveth.'

Though the Powhatan were dispossessed of most of their lands within a few years of her death, 'the childe' survived. Thomas's many descendants include Nancy Reagan and Wayne Newton, the Las Vegas entertainer, who is trying to recover Pocahontas's remains from Gravesend for reburial in Virginia.

Is there any part of Britain that is legally American soil?

Yes. It's the John F. Kennedy Memorial overlooking Runnymede, the meadow on the banks of the Thames where King John signed Magna Carta in 1215.

The acre of ground on which the memorial stands was a gift to the United States of America from the people of Britain in 1965. Formerly owned by the Crown, it is the only bit of Britain that is American territory.

Contrary to popular belief, the grounds of foreign embassies are not the sovereign territory of their state, nor are they beyond the law of the land in which they sit. The reason for the confusion is that nationals of the host country may not enter embassies without permission: refugees sometimes use them for this reason. If the authorities believe something illegal is going on inside the building, they have to wait for suspects to leave before arresting them. This doesn't apply to an ambassador or other diplomat, however, who can refuse arrest by claiming diplomatic immunity.

All diplomats in their host countries are immune in this way. The Vienna Convention on Diplomatic Relations states that they can't be arrested or criminally prosecuted by the host country for any violations of local law. The most the host country can do is to expel them, declaring them *persona non grata* (literally 'a person no longer welcome'). However, the diplomat is still covered by the laws of his home country and may be prosecuted under those laws when he returns home. The home country can also waive immunity for its own diplomats, leaving them open to prosecution by the host country.

The US Embassy is currently in Grosvenor Square in London (though it is shortly due to move to a new location in Wandsworth).

When the US government recently attempted to buy the freehold of the Grosvenor Square site from their landlord, the Duke of Westminster, he said that he would let them have it if the Americans returned to him the State of Virginia, confiscated from his ancestors during the War of Independence.

Which was the first film to star Mickey Mouse?

It wasn't *Steamboat Willie*, released on 18 November 1928 – even though the Walt Disney Company still celebrates this date as Mickey's official birthday.

There were two Mickey Mouse cartoons made earlier that year. The first was *Plane Crazy*. In it, Mickey tries to emulate the American aviator Charles Lindbergh (1902–74) by building a plane. He spends much of his first flight trying to force a kiss on Minnie Mouse, eventually causing the plane to crash-land. The second, *The Gallopin' Gaucho*, was a topical parody of *The Gaucho* (1927), starring matinée idol Douglas Fairbanks Junior (1909–2000). The film was set in a bar in the Argentine pampas, where Mickey smokes, drinks, dances a tango and fights the evil outlaw Black Pete to win the affections of the saucy barmaid, Minnie.

Both these films show a much raunchier Mickey than the saintly character he became. But they weren't widely distributed and didn't do well at the box office. Walt Disney (1901–66), and his friend and chief animator Ub Iwerks, had previously enjoyed great success with a series of shorts featuring their first animated character, Oswald the Lucky Rabbit. Universal Studios was the distributor for Oswald, but when Disney asked for a bigger budget, the studio demanded a 20 per cent budget cut instead and Disney walked out – without the rights to Oswald, and without his staff: only Iwerks joined him.

The two men decided to go it alone. They tried out cartoon dogs, cats, horses and cows but eventually Disney found inspiration in the pet mouse he'd once kept, growing up on a farm in Missouri. 'Mortimer Mouse' was renamed 'Mickey' at the suggestion of Disney's wife Lillian. In the first two shorts, Mickey was only slightly different (for copyright reasons) from Oswald the Lucky Rabbit, which may be why he didn't catch the public imagination.

Disney's solution was to make the kind of technical leap forward which would become a hallmark of his films. For his third Mickey Mouse short, *Steamboat Willie*, he recorded a synchronised soundtrack. Given that the first talkie, *The Jazz Singer* with Al Jolson, had been released only a year earlier, this was a remarkably bold move. *Steamboat Willie* was not only the first cartoon with a fully synchronised soundtrack: it was the first use of a soundtrack for a comedy. It was snapped up by a distributor and audiences loved it. Within a year Mickey Mouse was the most popular cartoon character in America.

Walt Disney went on to become the most awarded filmmaker of all time, winning a record twenty-six Oscars from a total of fifty-nine nominations. Mickey Mouse remained his talisman throughout and from 1929 to 1947 he voiced his most famous creation himself. As one employee put it: 'Ub designed Mickey's physical appearance, but Walt gave him his soul.'

Disney's life wasn't the wholesome, happy one he liked to portray. Addicted to sleeping pills and alcohol, he suffered from bouts of compulsive hand-washing, impotence and insomnia, which put his relationship with Lillian under great strain. He once remarked, only half-jokingly, 'I love Mickey Mouse more than any woman I've ever known.'

Can you name a fictional butler?

There are so many to choose from: Beach in P. G. Wodehouse's Blandings Castle stories, for instance, or Alfred from the *Batman* comics, or Stevens in Kazuo Ishiguro's Booker Prize-winning *The Remains of the Day*. Just don't say Jeeves.

In all the Jeeves and Wooster novels by Wodehouse (1881–1975), Bertie Wooster only employs one servant. Since a butler is the head of a household staff, Reginald Jeeves cannot, by definition, be a butler. He is in fact a valet, or gentleman's gentleman. A *butler* was originally in charge of a household's wine, deriving from the old French *boteillier* or 'cup bearer'. This developed into the sense of senior servant. A *valet* was a fifteenth-century French term for a footman, i.e. a horseman's personal assistant. As Bertie Wooster himself clarifies in *Stiff Upper Lip, Jeeves* (1963): 'Jeeves, of course, is a gentleman's gentleman, not a butler, but if the call comes, he can buttle with the best of them. It's in the blood.'

In 2008 the Australian press made much of revelations that Prime Minister Kevin Rudd was served by a 'travelling assistant' on an annual salary of $78,000 (nearly £50,000). John Fisher was nicknamed 'Jeeves' by Mr Rudd's enemies, prompting a government minister to complain that it was offensive to compare Mr Fisher to a butler, given his important role 'assisting with invitations, gifts and travel arrangements'. One opposition senator helpfully pointed out his mistake: 'A valet serves his employer as a person, whereas a butler serves his employer's house – just thought that might be of assistance.'

A valet's intimate duties are many and varied: polishing their charge's shoes, laying out their kit, and arranging their accommodation and food. The 5th Duke of Portland, one of the great landowners in nineteenth-century London, was so keen on his privacy that, when he required the attentions of a doctor, the medical man would be required to stand outside the room while the duke's valet examined his master and called out the results.

The Scottish author, Dr William Gordon Stables, who invented the pastime of caravanning in the 1880s, called himself a 'Gentleman Gypsy'. His household was stripped down to the bare essentials for life on the road: one coachman, a dog named Hurricane Bob, Polly the cockatoo – and Foley, his valet. Foley's main task was to ride ahead of the caravan, on a tricycle, to make sure the road was clear and to look out for interesting stopping places.

The army equivalent of a valet – the batman – was abolished in Britain at the end of the Second World War. Officers had previously been assigned a man from the lower ranks to look after them in much the same way as a gentleman's gentleman would in civilian life.

During the 1997 general election future Tory MP Jacob Rees-Mogg went leafleting the streets of Central Fife assisted by his nanny. Infuriated at the mocking he received, he later told an interviewer: 'I do wish you wouldn't keep going on about my nanny. If I had a valet, you'd think it was perfectly normal.'

STEPHEN *Do you know what Mahatma means?*
ALAN *It means, 'Can I have my hat please, mother?'*
STEPHEN *Funny enough, W. C. Fields almost got there before*

you, because he wrote one of his films under the pseudonym of Mahatma Cane Jeeves, as in 'my hat, my cane, Jeeves!' So, there you are.

What was Dan Dare's original job?

He was a vicar. The legendary comic-strip hero started life as an Anglican priest: Chaplain Dan Dare of the Interplanet Patrol.

From 1950 to 1969, 'Dan Dare' was the lead strip in the *Eagle*. It sold more than 750,000 copies a week – unprecedented for a UK comic both before and since – and Dan Dare merchandise saturated the toy market in a way that wasn't matched until the advent of *Star Wars* and *Harry Potter*.

The *Eagle* was the brainchild of an Anglican priest and former RAF chaplain, Reverend Marcus Morris (1915–89), and a young graphic illustrator called Frank Hampson (1918–85). In 1949 Morris wrote a piece in the *Sunday Dispatch* attacking the importation of horror comics from America: 'Morals of little girls in plaits and boys with marbles bulging in their pockets are being corrupted by a torrent of indecent coloured magazines that are flooding bookstalls and newsagents.' What was needed, he said, was a popular children's comic where adventure is once more 'a clean and exciting business'.

Hampson and Morris's first co-creation was a strip featuring a tough East-End vicar called Lex Christian for the *Empire News*. However, the sudden death of the paper's editor meant it never ran, so Morris conceived a whole comic, which Hampson's wife christened the *Eagle*, after the shape of the traditional church lectern. The first two pages of the new magazine introduced a revised version of Lex Christian, now set in the future. Enter Chaplain Dan Dare of the Interplanet Patrol, complete with dog collar.

With Arthur C. Clarke as scientific adviser, Chad Varah (founder of the Samaritans) as script consultant and Hampson's revolutionary use of a studio of artists working from a huge library of photos, diagrams and 3-D models to create realistic blueprints for each frame, the *Eagle* idea found an enthusiastic publisher in Hulton (owners of the *Radio Times*). It was Hulton's eleventh-hour intervention that spared the children of Britain their first comic strip about a priest. The company felt that 'Dan Dare, Pilot of the Future' was a more commercial proposition and Hampson and Morris eventually agreed. Produced on the dining table of Frank Hampson's council house in Southport, the launch issue sold close to a million copies.

Hampson worked on Dan Dare until 1959, when the relentless pressure and recurring depressive illness became too much for him. He left the *Eagle* and toiled as an anonymous freelance illustrator for the next twenty-five years. In 1975 a jury of his peers voted him the best writer and artist of strip cartoons since the war. His *Eagle* had been a magnet for illustrators: it featured the first published work by David Hockney and Gerald Scarfe.

Dan Dare's Christian past was not without precedent. Superman's adopted parents were committed Methodists, although the Man of Steel never went to church in his tights – unlike Captain America, who was openly Protestant. Spiderman's Peter Parker had regular conversations with God, and The Thing in the *Fantastic Four* is Jewish. Wonder Woman, on the other hand, was explicitly conceived and drawn as an unreconstructed pagan goddess.

Why were postcards invented?

Not as tourist souvenirs – but as a speedy way of keeping in touch.

Postcards were the email of the pre-electronic age and the first medium of personal mass communication. Between 1905 and 1915, about 750 million postcards were sent in Britain each year, more than 2 million a day. The seven daily deliveries of post meant it was perfectly possible to arrange and confirm an appointment in the evening by sending a postcard in the morning.

The postcard era started in the 1870s when government postal services in Europe and the US began issuing pre-paid postal cards. By the 1890s, private printers had produced their own versions, with illustrations on the front and the words 'Post Card' moved to the back.

Between 1901 and 1907 postcard production doubled every six months. At the time, this frenetic activity was known as 'postal carditis' or 'postcard mania' and it was driven by three factors. Technological advances in printing meant that high-quality colour images could be mass-produced cheaply for the first time. Efficient postal services meant they were cheap to send (1 cent in the US; 1 penny in the UK). Finally, better public transport meant people had begun to travel much more regularly and adventurously.

This was the era of the great fairs and exhibitions. If you visited contemporary marvels like the Eiffel Tower, or the 1908 Franco-British exhibition at the White City, or the amusement arcades at Coney Island in New York, a postcard was the perfect way to prove it. On one day in 1906 200,000 of them were sent from Coney Island alone. Postcard collecting (or *deltiology* – from the Greek *deltion*, 'little writing tablet') became the world's number one pastime.

The parallels with email are striking. Advertising quickly

saw the benefits and most of the nineteenth-century postcard traffic was a kind of spam, selling unsolicited goods and services. In 1906 Kodak brought out the 3A folding pocket camera that had postcard-sized negatives and a door that opened allowing a message to be scratched directly on to them. This meant that people could then have their own postcards printed – rather in the way we send attachments.

As with email, postcards had their detractors. The satirist John Walker Harrington wrote of postcard mania in *American Magazine* in March 1906: 'Unless such manifestations are checked, millions of persons of now normal lives and irreproachable habits will become victims of faddy degeneration of the brain.'

As 75 per cent of US postcards were printed in Germany, the advent of the First World War destroyed the German printing industry. This, and the arrival of the telephone, ended the golden age of the postcard.

But still they continue to thrive in the UK, especially from people at the seaside. The Royal Mail estimated that 135 million postcards were sent during the summer of 2009. The top five places they came from were, in order: Brighton, Scarborough, Bournemouth, Blackpool and Skegness.

Who made the first computer?

The key word here is *made*.

The mathematician Charles Babbage (1791–1871) is known as the 'father of modern computing', but more for his ideas than for any concrete achievement. The first full-size Babbage Engine, using his original designs, made exclusively from materials available in his day, wasn't completed until 2002. It is 3.3 metres (11 feet) long, weighs 5 tons, contains 8,000 parts and took seventeen years to build. It can be seen at the Science Museum in London.

In the nineteenth century, the British Empire ran on lists of calculations. From banking to shipping, every aspect of trade was dependent on accurate tables. Mistakes could cost money and lives and the books of tables were notoriously unreliable. It was in 1821 that Babbage decided to build a machine to replace them. Confronted by an error-strewn set of astronomical tables, he exclaimed to a colleague: 'I wish to God these calculations had been executed by steam!'

Babbage was a brilliant mathematician but found human beings difficult to deal with. His intolerance of street musicians led to an organised campaign against him: his London home in Portland Place was bombarded by noise at all hours and abusive placards were hung in local shops. He wasn't much better at handling the politicians whose support he needed to fund his work. Asked by MPs whether his machine would still produce the right answers even if wrong figures were entered, he replied, 'I am not able rightly to apprehend the kind of confusion of ideas that could provoke such a question.'

Despite patenting the cowcatcher for locomotives, and a pair of shears that made the metal tips for shoelaces, Babbage died embittered and forgotten. He had failed to find the money to build his greatest invention, a computer in the modern sense, with a memory and a printer, run by a programme that used punched cards. This first programming 'language' was the work of Ada Lovelace (1815–52), daughter of the poet Lord Byron, who understood the potential of Babbage's work even better than he did, predicting (in the 1840s) that computers would one day play chess and music.

Using Babbage's plans, two Swedish engineers, George and

Edward Schuetz, completed the first prototype of what Babbage called his 'Difference Engine' in 1853. The father and son team not only built the first working computer of modern times, they sold two – one to an observatory in New York and the other to the Registrar-General's office in London. Each was the size of a piano.

But they weren't the *very* first. In 1900 a rusty artefact was discovered off the Greek island of Antikythera. We now know that the 'Antikythera mechanism' was a 2,000-year-old clock-work calculator that could predict astronomical phenomena with striking accuracy and detail.

What we now call 'computers' were originally called 'computing machines'. Until the mid-twentieth century, 'computers' were simply 'people who carried out computations'. So, strictly speaking, the correct answer to the question 'Who made the first computer?' should really be 'the computer's parents'.

What is paper money made from?

Money doesn't grow on trees. Not metaphorically and not actually.

Paper is made from pressed wood pulp. 'Paper money' is made from cotton or linen (sometimes called 'rag paper'). Cotton and linen fibres contain far fewer acids than wood pulp, so they don't discolour or wear out so easily. The cloth is then infused with gelatine to give it extra strength. This material is still used for folding money in the UK, the US and the European Union. The average lifespan of such banknotes is two years.

In 1988, after several years of research and testing by the Commonwealth Scientific and Industrial Research

Organisation (CSIRO), Australia introduced a new set of banknotes made of polypropylene plastic. These last longer and are harder to counterfeit, as they make it easier to incorporate security devices such as holograms. New Zealand, Mexico, Brazil, Israel and the Northern Bank of Northern Ireland have now all switched to plastic notes. In 2005 Bulgaria introduced banknotes using the world's first cotton–polymer hybrid.

The first paper currency *was* made from wood-pulp paper. When gold and silver coins became too heavy to carry around, in the eleventh century during the Song dynasty, 'promissory notes' were issued in China. These were pieces of paper agreeing to pay over to the bearer the equivalent value in gold or silver coins if asked. The notes were made of dried, dyed mulberry bark printed with official seals and signatures. It was called 'convenient money'. It is thought that local issues of non-metal money were made as early as the Tang dynasty in Sichuan. Japanese banknotes still use paper made from mulberry bark.

This state guarantee of paper currency is the principle upon which most money is now issued. In the past, individuals and private banks were also able to issue promissory notes and this led to problems over guarantees. In 1660 Stockholms Banco in Sweden was the first bank in Europe to issue notes but four years later it ran out of coins to redeem them and collapsed.

Times of crisis have often led to emergency currency being issued on material other than cotton or paper. In 1574, when the Dutch were struggling to regain their independence from the invading Spanish, the city of Leyden produced cardboard coins minted from the covers of prayer books. During the Russian administration of Alaska in the late nineteenth century, banknotes were printed on sealskin. In Africa, during the Boer War in 1902, bits of khaki shirt were used.

Sometimes, the value of banknotes falls below the cost of producing them. The hyperinflation in Germany and Austria after the First World War meant that, by 1922, a single gold krone coin was worth 14,400 paper krone (a stack of cash that would weigh about 15 kilograms or 33 pounds). As a result, people improvised their own currency out of playing cards instead.

On a pirate's treasure map, what does X mark?

There are no documented cases of a real pirate ever drawing up a treasure map, let alone putting an 'X' on it to mark where the treasure is buried. Only one pirate, William Kidd (about 1645–1701), is ever recorded as having buried any treasure at all.

There is even some doubt as to whether Kidd was a pirate. Protected by a 'letter of marque' from King William III, he was privately employed by the British governors of New York, Massachusetts and New Hampshire to protect their coastline from genuine pirates or from the French. Legally, this meant he was not a pirate but a 'privateer' (like Sir Francis Drake). His enemies didn't agree; they vilified him as a ruthless, disrespectful and violent brigand. For example, Kidd's sailors once showed their backsides to a Royal Navy yacht instead of saluting it, and Kidd himself killed a disobedient member of his crew in cold blood. He became a political embarrassment and, when he was eventually arrested, the wealthy Englishmen who financed his voyages chose to hand him over to the authorities rather than be accused of piracy alongside him.

It is known that Kidd buried some of his wealth on Gardiners Island, off the coast of Long Island. He had hoped to use it as a bargaining tool to clear his name. However, he'd given the details to one of his backers who then dug it up and sent it on to London to be used in evidence against him. Kidd was tried and found guilty of piracy and murder. He was hanged on 23 May 1701, at 'Execution Dock' at Wapping, in London. His body was hung in a steel-hooped cage over the Thames and remained there for twenty years.

The first treasure map with an X marking the spot appears in the novel *Treasure Island* (1883) by Robert Louis Stevenson. Stevenson also introduced the Black Spot (the pirate's curse) and several piratical expressions including 'Avast', 'Yo-ho-ho' and 'matey' – though 'Shiver my timbers!' came from the pen of another Victorian novelist, Captain Frederick Marryat (1792–1848). It seems that 'walking the plank' was also a literary invention: the only recorded real-life case happened in 1829, well after most piracy had ceased.

Hardly any pirate booty was 'treasure'. The majority was food, water, alcohol, weapons, clothing, ships' fittings or whatever commodity was in the hold. The victims' ship itself might be sold or taken over if it was better than the pirates' own, and the crew and passengers were also valuable – either for ransom or to be sold as slaves. During the seventeenth century, over a million Europeans were captured and sold into slavery by Barbary pirates from Algiers.

Few pirates (or privateers) sailed in galleons. Most used galleys (with banks of oars rather than sails). Unlike the sailing ships that were their prey, these could be rowed against the wind and in any direction, even on a windless day.

Two privateers (though no pirates) are known to have had wooden legs: the sixteenth-century Frenchman François Le Clerc, known as Jambe de Bois, and Cornelis Corneliszoon Jol (1597–1641), nicknamed Houtebeen ('Pegleg').

There is no historical evidence for any pirate ever owning a pet parrot.

STEPHEN *Why would a pirate want to bury treasure?*
PHILL JUPITUS *Well, they can hardly go to the Bradford & Bingley, can they? 'Hello, we've got a chest full of doubloons and booty.' 'Yes, would you like fixed term or extended interest?'*

What did early nineteenth-century whalers use to kill whales?

Not harpoons, but lances.

For the early whalers, the harpoon wasn't a killing weapon; it was used to attach a line to the whale. This was thrown by a specialist harpooner who stood up in a rowing boat with one knee jammed into a cut-out section of thwart called the 'clumsy cleat'. He hurled the harpoon into the whale from up to 6 metres (20 feet) away. The harpoon was attached to a 150-fathom (275-metre or 900-foot) rope impregnated with animal fat to help it run smoothly, coiled in a huge bucket on the deck and kept wet to prevent it catching fire from friction as it paid out.

When it reached its limit, the whalers were treated to a

'Nantucket sleigh ride'. This meant being pulled along by the whale at up to 42 kilometres per hour (26 miles per hour), the fastest speed any man had then reached on water. (Nantucket Island, off the coast of Massachusetts, was the centre of whaling in the North Atlantic in the nineteenth century.) Many hours later, the whale would eventually tire and the boat would row over to it. An officer would then change places with the harpooner to deliver the death blow with a lance (only officers could lance a whale). The cry of 'There's fire in the chimney' meant that blood was spouting from the whale's blowhole and the end was near.

The carcass was then towed alongside the mother vessel and cut up or 'flensed' from the deck using long-handled tools. Often, this exercise was a race against teeming sharks, which tore pieces of blubber from the whale while it was being butchered. Harpooning was such a dangerous profession that the Norwegians allowed only single men to do it.

Things changed in 1868 when Sven Foyn, a Norwegian engineer, invented an exploding harpoon gun. This did kill the whale and could be used from the deck of large, steam-powered vessels. It transformed whaling, allowing the hunting of faster, more powerful species, such as rorquals like the blue whale (from the Norwegian *röyrkval*, meaning 'furrowed whale', after the long pleats in their underbellies). Because rorquals sank when they died, later versions of the exploding harpoon also injected air into the carcass to keep it afloat.

The blue whale became the most profitable of all whale catches: a 27-metre (90-foot) whale yielded 15,900 litres (3,500 gallons) of oil. By the 1930s more than 30,000 blue whales were being killed annually. When the International Whaling Commission banned hunting them in 1966, the population of blue whales had dropped from an estimated 186,000 in 1880 to fewer than 5,000.

The eponymous whale in Herman Melville's *Moby-Dick*

(1851) was named after a real albino sperm whale called 'Mocha Dick' who was often seen near the Chilean island of Mocha and who carried with him dozens of harpoons left embedded in his body from more than a hundred battles with whalers throughout the 1830s and 1840s.

In 2007 Alaskan whalers killed a Bowhead whale that had the tip of a bomb harpoon dated to 1880 embedded in its blubber, which meant it was at least 130 years old when it died.

What makes the Penny Black stamp so special?

It's not their rarity, but their relative commonness that sets them apart.

A staggering 69 million Penny Blacks have been in circulation at one time or other. Many have survived intact. This is because, instead of using envelopes, Victorian letters were written on one side of a sheet of paper, which was then folded and sealed, so the address and stamp were on the reverse of the letter itself. If the letter was kept, so was the stamp.

If you have a Penny Black in your collection, you'll be lucky to get more than £100 for it. Even this is rather a lot considering how many of them there are – their value is kept artificially high by collectors sitting on hundreds of them and releasing them on to the market very slowly.

The world's most valuable stamp, the Tre Skilling Yellow, was sold at auction in Zurich in 1996 for 2.88 million Swiss Francs (about £1.8 m) and again in Geneva in May 2010 for an undisclosed price, all bidders at the auction being sworn to secrecy. If the paper that the stamp is printed on were a commodity sold by weight, it would retail at £55 billion a kilo.

The best-known rare stamp is the 1856 British Guiana 1 cent Magenta, which has been kept in a vault since it last changed hands in 1980. Its owner, John du Pont, heir to the Du Pont chemicals fortune, is currently serving a life sentence for murder.

The most valuable British stamp is a Penny Red printed from plate number 77 in 1864. Plate 77 was corrupt and a few defective stamps went into circulation. There are only six known examples left. One is in the Tapling Collection at the British Library priced at £120,000.

Until Sir Rowland Hill (1795–1879), the social reformer and Secretary of the Post Office, introduced the Penny Black in 1840, it was the receiver not the sender of a letter who paid for the postage. MPs could send letters for free: they did this by stamping it with their 'frank' (a 'true' or 'frank' mark).

Sir Rowland Hill also invented postcodes. He divided London into ten districts each with a compass point and a central office. The original ten areas were EC (Eastern Central), WC (Western Central), NW, N, NE, E, SE, S, SW and W. All were contained within a circle of 12 miles' radius from central London. The present system was introduced in Croydon in 1966. It is made up of the outward code (e.g. OX7 – needed to sort from one town to another) and the inward code (e.g. 4DB – required for sorting within the town).

The first letterboxes were set up in Jersey, thanks to the novelist Anthony Trollope (1815–82). Hill sent Trollope to the Channel Islands in 1852 to see how best to collect mail on the islands, given the unpredictable sailing times of the Royal Mail packet boats. Trollope suggested using a 'letter-receiving pillar' that could be picked up whenever there was a sailing. The first box, erected in November 1852, was olive green. It worked so well that the Post Office rolled them out across the nation. By 1874 so many people had walked straight into the green boxes that red was settled on as a better choice. The Royal Mail still has a trademark on the colour 'pillar box red'.

STEPHEN *Do you know Jimmy Tarbuck? He was doing one of those Royal Command performances, and as he was going off, he looked up into the royal box and said, 'Ooh, that reminds me. I must buy a stamp.'*

When did women first show cleavage?

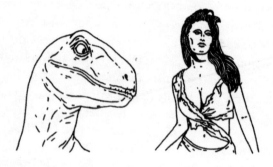

Not until 1946.

Until then cleavage was a word used exclusively by geologists to describe the way a rock or crystal splits.

In the 1940s, the British film studio Gainsborough Pictures produced a series of raunchy bodice-rippers collectively known as the 'Gainsborough Gothics'. *The Wicked Lady* (1945) was an eighteenth-century tale of a husband-murdering, society-beauty-cum-highwaywoman, starring Margaret Lockwood (then Britain's most bankable female star), James Mason and Patricia Roc. It was a huge hit in Britain, but the revealing costumes caused problems in the USA.

The Motion Picture Production Code Administration, popularly known as The Hays Code, was a voluntary system of movie censorship introduced in 1930 by Will Hays

(1879–1954), the US Postmaster General. Its job was to spell out what was and wasn't acceptable to show on the screen. In 1945 it changed its name to The Motion Picture Association of America. The MPAA is still with us today: it's the body responsible for rating films as PG, PG-13, R and so forth.

When *The Wicked Lady* hit the USA, the MPAA demanded changes, but it seems they were overcome by coyness. They hid their embarrassment by using a dry geological term as a euphemism for 'the shadowed depression dividing an actress's bosom into two distinct sections'.

In 1946 *Time* magazine picked up the word when it reported:

> Low-cut Restoration costumes worn by the Misses Lockwood and Roc display too much 'cleavage'. The British, who have always considered bare legs more sexy than half-bare breasts, are resentfully re-shooting several costly scenes.

A new usage was born. Until the end of the Second World War, the partial exposure of a woman's breasts was covered by the French term *décolletage*, first recorded in English in 1894 and derived from *décolleté*, 'low-necked' (1831), from the verb *décolleter*, 'to bare the neck and shoulders'.

It's arguable that *décolletage* is still the prettiest way of putting it. In Middle English the 'cleavage' was bluntly called 'the slot' and, today, the best the International Federation of Associations of Anatomists can manage is the intermammary cleft or intermammary sulcus (*sulcus* is the Latin for 'fold' or 'furrow').

So it seems cleavage is here to stay: and the way it's used is proliferating. A lateral view of breasts is 'side cleavage'. A glimpse beneath is 'neathage' or 'Australian cleavage'. Bottom cleavage – a visible buttock cleft – has been known as 'builder's bum' since 1988. Toe cleavage, the partial exposure of toes by 'low-cut' shoes, is considered both sexy and stylish. According to shoe guru Manolo Blahnik, 'The secret of toe cleavage, a very important part of the sexuality of the shoe, is that you must only show the first two cracks.'

The back of a thong peeking over the top of a pair of jeans (which implies cleavage without revealing it) is called a 'whale-tail'. In 2005 the American Dialect Society voted it the most creative new word of the year.

Which would you rather attend, a Roman orgy or a Greek symposium?

If what you're looking for is a wild night out, choose a symposium every time.

'Orgy' was not the usual word for Greek or Roman social entertainment. An *orgia* was a secret ritual performed in honour of Dionysus, the god of wine, theatre and carnival. The word orgy only emerged in its modern sense of 'a sexually explicit party' in late seventeenth-century England.

Even so, parties in Imperial Rome were often wildly extravagant: the more lavish the soirée, the greater the social and political status of the host. As night fell, slaves would be sent out into the streets to invite hundreds of strangers back to their master's villa. Those asked would be of both sexes, and of any social class – though attractive, fashionably dressed types were preferred. At the venue guests would find lavish quantities of food and drink, along with entertainment from musicians, erotic eastern dancers, and prostitutes of both sexes.

Orgies were a different matter. The Romans had no hang-ups about erotica, but in all the surviving literature, art and even graffiti, there are only one or two references to sex taking place at an *orgia*. Such behaviour was no more recommended or condoned than wife-swapping in church today. Dr Alastair Blanshard of the University of Sydney – a leading orgyologist – believes that the myth about Roman orgies arose in the eighteenth century and survived because it served an ideological purpose. Conservatives took the view that the Roman Empire fell because of its loose morals, while libertines could claim classical (and therefore respectable) precedents for their own fun and games.

On the other hand, the sedate-sounding symposium (from *syn* 'together' plus *posis* 'a drinking') of the ancient Greeks meant 'a drinking party', which frequently descended into debauchery, and even riot. Aristocratic Athenian houses had special 'men's rooms', which existed purely for parties and even had stone floors with built-in sluices to make the post-party clean-up easier.

Greek writers devoted many words to warning about the dangers of symposia, offering advice to hosts on precautions to prevent things getting out of hand, such as watering the wine. The fifth-century BC playwright Euboulos recommended only three cups of wine per man: 'One for health, the second for love and pleasure, and the third for sleep.' At that point, he said, wise men go home – because the fourth cup is for bad behaviour, followed by shouting, rudeness and insults, fights, breaking the furniture, and depression, until we reach the tenth cup – 'for madness and unconsciousness'. A popular symposium sport was the game of *kottabos*, which involved flicking your wine dregs at a target, or at your fellow guests.

During less raucous moments, attendees entertained each other with *encomia*, or eulogies, hence the modern sense of the word as 'a meeting for discussion' which first emerged in the late eighteenth century. On one famous occasion, described in a work by Plato, the encomia were on the subject of love.

CLIVE ANDERSON *In these orgies, did they really do that thing of eating so much, then you sort of brought it up again?*
STEPHEN *Oh, the vomitorium. Of course, vomitorium is not the right word for that, because a vomitorium is actually an exit from a theatre, where literally the people are vomited out.*
RICH HALL *Especially if you've just seen* Mamma Mia.

What effect does testosterone have on men?

Contrary to popular belief, it's a *lack* of testosterone that makes people aggressive; if anything, surplus testosterone seems to make them friendlier.

Both men and women make testosterone, though the levels in women are, of course, significantly lower. It helps grow muscle mass, increases bone density and prevents osteoporosis.

In 2009 Ernst Fehr of the University of Zurich gave 120 women either testosterone pills or placebos, and then involved them in a role-playing situation. The mythic reputation of testosterone is so powerful that those women who *thought* they had been given it acted aggressively and selfishly (even if they'd actually received the placebo), whereas those who really *did* get testosterone behaved more fairly and were better at interacting socially, whether they believed they had received the pill or not.

Testosterone is linked to aggression in animals, so until very recently it was assumed to have a similar effect on humans. This seems not to be the case. It appears that *low* testosterone levels are more likely to cause mood disorders and aggression. Studies into testosterone have only been going on for ten years, so its function is not yet fully understood. Oddly, in the first few weeks of life, baby boys are pumped full of as much testosterone as they'll have in their teens, though this reduces to barely detectable levels by four to six months.

In 2004 Donatella Marazziti and Domenico Canale of the University of Pisa measured testosterone levels in two groups, each composed of twelve men and twelve women. The 'Love Group' consisted of people who had fallen in love in the previous six months, and the 'Control Group' were either single or in stable long-term relationships. The study found that men from the Love Group had lower levels of testosterone than men in the Control Group, while women from the Love Group had higher testosterone levels than their Control Group counterparts. The researchers theorised that, in the falling-in-love stage of a relationship, this apparent balancing act may serve to temporarily eliminate or reduce emotional differences between the sexes.

Testosterone is a hormone. Hormones (from the Greek word for 'impulse' or 'attack') are chemicals released by glands in one part of the body that use the bloodstream to transport messages to, and have an effect on, cells elsewhere.

Progesterone, a hormone associated with pregnant women, is also present in both willow trees and yams, which suggests it has a role that predates the evolution of modern animals.

Oxytocin is a hormone associated with maternal bonding, affectionately referred to by biologists as 'the cuddle chemical'. It can reduce fear, anxiety and inhibitions, and promotes social and sexual bonding as well as parenting. Neuro-economists (who combine psychology, economics and neuro-science to study how decisions are made) have experimented on subjects participating in a game called 'Investor'. They found that a squirt of oxytocin up the nose doubled levels of trust among players.

How many wives can a Mormon have?

One.

Mormons are not polygamous and haven't been for more than a century.

What is now called the Church of Jesus Christ of Latter-day Saints (or LDS) was founded in New York State in 1830 by a twenty-five-year-old farmhand and treasure-hunter named Joseph Smith (1805–44). As a teenager, he had been visited by a resurrected Native American called Moroni and the result of these angelic visions was a supplement to the New Testament, 'translated' and published by Smith in 1830 as *The Book of Mormon*. LDS members revere it as the word of God and a genuine historical document.

Nowhere in the book is polygamy explicitly condoned. But soon after the publication of his new scripture, Smith had a revelation that Christ wanted to him to establish 'a new and eternal covenant' in which a man could take many wives. For personal reasons, he always publicly denied this, confiding in his journal in 1843 that his wife Emma refused to believe it was genuine and that she 'appeared very rebellious'. This didn't stop him 'sealing' himself (in Mormon parlance) to a string of more than thirty 'celestial wives', although there is no conclusive proof that any of these were sexual relationships or that his new wives bore him any children.

Smith paid a high price for these insights. He was threatened with castration by outraged neighbours and was eventually murdered by a mob in 1844 while in jail in Illinois. The persecution of Mormons that followed Smith's death led the LDS to leave Illinois and mount a 2,000-kilometre (1,300-mile) exodus to Utah in 1846–7. It also strengthened the commitment of the church elders to polygamy, or 'the Principle'. In 1852 Smith's successor as president of the church, Brigham Young, made it part of the LDS's public doctrine – and he certainly practised what he preached. By the time he died in 1877 Young had racked up fifty-one wives – with fifty-six children by sixteen of them.

By 1890 the situation had become a political embarrassment. The secular authorities were using the illegality of polygamy under US law to prevent Utah joining the United States and to seize the church's assets, including its temples. On 23 September the president of the church, Wilson Woodruff, produced a timely 510-word account of a night spent struggling with the Lord. It recommended obeying federal law and abandoning the Principle. This was adapted into a manifesto and approved at the LDS conference later that year. The church suspended polygamy and, in 1904, declared it grounds for excommunication.

Today the LDS claims 13 million members worldwide – and not a plural marriage among them. Even at the height of the Principle's popularity, historians believe that no more than 25 per cent of Mormon adults belonged to polygamous households. On the other hand, there are still some 20,000 fundamentalist Mormons who practise polygamy in the USA today, albeit illegally (as portrayed in the 2006 HBO drama series *Big Love*). For the Mormon fundamentalist, 'celestial marriage' isn't an option but an obligation, and the only way to reach the highest level of exaltation in the afterlife.

STEPHEN *The Osmonds. Aren't they lovely? They're members of the Church of Latter-day Saints, I think they call it.*

ALAN *They were rubbish, weren't they?*

STEPHEN *Oh, were they? Oh no!*

ALAN *Apart from little Jimmy Osmond, he was the Long Haired Lover from Liverpool.*

BILL BAILEY *And, of course, there was Big Graham Osmond, the one they kept in the attic. He had one massive hand with a claw. But he wrote all the songs.*

How did Harry Houdini die?

Not from a punch to the stomach.

The death of the Hungarian-born magician and escapologist Erik Weisz in 1926 has become a key part of his legend. The story runs like this.

Houdini was in Montreal, lying on a couch, being sketched after a show, when a young American student called J. Gordon Whitehead was shown into his dressing room. After they chatted, Whitehead asked Houdini whether it was true that punches in the stomach didn't hurt him. According to an eyewitness, 'Houdini remarked rather unenthusiastically that his stomach could resist much, though he did not speak of it in superlative terms.' Whitehead asked if he could hit him. Houdini agreed, at which Whitehead immediately punched him several times in the stomach with all his strength, while Houdini was still reclining on the couch. Evidently in pain, Houdini stopped him, and said he hadn't been able to prepare himself properly.

Later that afternoon Houdini complained of a stomach ache but struggled through two more shows. Two days later in Detroit the pain was so severe he was forced to abandon his performance before the third act (although he didn't collapse on stage, or have to be rescued from the Chinese water-torture tank, as is sometimes claimed). He was rushed to hospital where he was diagnosed with acute appendicitis. Although he survived two operations to remove his appendix, the infection had spread and Houdini died of peritonitis – infection of the intestinal wall – almost a week later. It was Halloween.

The assumption made by both the doctors who treated him – and the life insurance company who paid out – was that the punches to the stomach had ruptured his appendix. This was a reasonable diagnosis at the time, but we now know that this would make it the only recorded case of abdominal trauma ever leading to death in this way. Medical opinion now suggests he was already suffering from appendicitis and that the pain from the punches served to mask the true seriousness of his condition. Put another way, if he hadn't been punched in the stomach he might well have consulted a doctor before his appendix had burst, hugely increasing his chances of survival. In the era before antibiotics, the secondary infection caused by a rupture was almost always fatal.

This isn't the only false legend to have surrounded Houdini's death. Another was this: spiritualists, resentful of Houdini's tireless attempts to unmask their tricks and discredit their profession, poisoned him. This culminated in 2007, when Houdini's great-nephew, George Hardeen, announced he had applied to have the body exhumed to test for the presence of poison.

In fact the application was never made and the whole story was later revealed to be a publicity stunt organised by the authors of a 2006 book *The Secret Life of Houdini*, which had done much to peddle the poisoning theory.

STEPHEN *There's been a recent demand to have Houdini's body exhumed . . .*

CLIVE ANDERSON *You'll never get it out of the coffin.*

ALAN *It won't be in there!*

What does human gas mostly contain?

Despite those schoolboy tricks with matches, all human gas contains very little methane and the majority none at all. It's mostly nitrogen from swallowed air.

On average we each produce about a litre and a half (3 pints) of gas a day, released in ten to fifteen individual 'episodes', many of them while we sleep. Most such discharges contain a mixture of five odourless gases: nitrogen (60 per cent), hydrogen (20 per cent), carbon dioxide (10 per cent), oxygen (5 per cent) and methane (4 per cent). How much of each depends on a number of variables. If we gulp our food down quickly, or our metabolic rate is fast, we may end up with a higher percentage of oxygen in our wind. Fizzy drinks increase the proportion of carbon dioxide, whereas holding in wind allows the more useful gases like hydrogen and oxygen to be reabsorbed through the intestines, leading to a higher proportion of nitrogen.

The most significant variable of all is what we eat. There is a range of complex carbohydrates known as polysaccharides that humans find particularly hard to digest. Three of these sugars – raffinose, stachylose and verbascose – are known to gastroenterologists as 'flatulence factors' because they are present in large amounts in beans, lentils, cabbage, Brussels sprouts, wholegrain seeds and pulses. These make it through to the colon largely untouched by the enzymes in the stomach and small intestine. Once they arrive, all hell breaks loose as the several hundred species of bacteria that live there dine on them voraciously and, in so doing, produce various different gases which we expel as wind. And it's not just beans: the starches in wheat, corn and potato (but not rice) are all on the bacterial menu, as are many of the sugars contained in fruit and the yeasts in bread and beer. These generate the volume of the gas; sulphur-containing foods such as meat, eggs and cauliflower provide its smell.

Most of the gas produced by the bacteria in our gut is hydrogen and carbon dioxide. The one that contributes most of the odour is hydrogen sulphide. This is usually present in very small concentrations (less than 0.5 per cent), but it is so potent that our noses can detect it in concentrations of 0.0047 parts per million. As for the potentially explosive gas methane, most humans, you may be surprised to learn, can't produce it at all.

Methane in the body results from microbes called methanogens (methane-makers), which are not bacteria but members of the *Archaea* kingdom, the oldest life forms on the planet. Only about one-third of humans have methanogens among their gut flora. No one knows exactly why, though it appears to be genetically determined. A child of two methane-producing parents is 95 per cent likely to produce a methane-generating child.

One theory is that some early human populations ate a higher proportion of fibrous vegetable material and came to rely on methanogens to extract energy from the food, rather like cows and sheep (the burps of methane-rich livestock now account for 20 per cent of the planet's annual greenhouse gas emissions). A 2009 study by Arizona State University showed that methane producers are much more efficient at converting the undigested food into fat reserves, making them more likely to become obese. Bluntly put, fat people fart more.

STEPHEN *It seems that we produce about 3 pints of wind a day. Released in ten to fifteen individual episodes.*

ANDY HAMILTON *You can get a box set as well.*

ALAN *Or you can have a feature-length episode.*

New entry!

How long can you keep bottled water?

Much longer than it says on the bottle.

Two years is the usual time period given as a 'best before' date on bottled water. The UK's National Hydration Council, an industry body set up in 2008 to research and promote the benefits of bottled water, explain that this date only appears because EU/UK food regulations require that all foods must display one. If kept in a cool, dry, clean place away from light and strong odours or chemicals, the Council claims, bottled water can last indefinitely.

Given that it's water, would we even be able to taste it if the contents had 'gone off'? Nestlé is the world's bottled water brand leader. Although their website has a 'water taster's glossary', the evidence suggests most of us would struggle. It's true that there are definite differences in the mineral content, taste and effervescence of some genuine 'mineral' waters (e.g. Badoit and San Pellegrino), but 40 per cent of all the water that is bottled and sold is simply purified tap water. In a 2003 edition of their TV show *Bullshit!*, the magicians Penn and Teller demonstrated that diners in a restaurant couldn't tell the difference between bottled water and that supplied by a garden hose at the back of the restaurant.

Despite this, the worldwide growth in sales of bottled water has been phenomenal. The projected volume of sales in 2011 is 174 million litres (38 million gallons): five times more than in 1990. In the United States, which accounts for just under one-third of global consumption, bottled water sales passed sales of fruit juice in 1993, coffee in 2003 and milk in 2005. Now only beer and carbonated soft drinks sell more. For every second of every day, a thousand people buy a plastic bottle of water.

Unfortunately, this also means a huge increase in waste. Of the 30 billion plastic water bottles produced each year, only one in five are recycled. Pumping, purifying, bottling and transporting bottled water uses twice as much water as fits inside the bottle itself. It also burns up 1.5 million barrels of oil, enough to power 100,000 cars for a year. According to the environmental scientist Dr Peter Gleick, this is the equivalent of 'filling up a quarter of every bottle of water we drink with oil'.

If 'best before' and 'sell by' dates are safely ignored for water, they have helped contribute to the rising mountain of food waste. Approximately 40 per cent of all food produced in the US is now wasted, much of it needlessly. In 2006, after extensive testing on 'out-of-date' foods, Oscar Pike, a food scientist at Brigham Young University in Utah, concluded that 'Microbiologically, low-moisture food that is safe when packaged is still safe after storage.'

To prove the point, George Lambert, a veteran of the 1898 Spanish-American war, turned up at a New Mexico state fair in 1969. Wearing his old uniform, he proceeded to eat a seventy-year-old hard-tack biscuit he'd found in the pocket. 'Tastes just like it did then,' he said. 'Wasn't any good then and it isn't now.'

SEAN LOCK *I always think that about Parmesan. I've never understood why it has a sell-by date on it, because it just never goes off, does it? You could put it on a rooftop in Nairobi for a year and nothing.*

DAVID MITCHELL *Like you buy cheese at the supermarket and it says, consume within two days of opening or something.*

STEPHEN *Yeah. Plus it has a label on it saying 'twenty years aged'.*

DAVID *And two days before it's completely inedible, you sell it to me!*

After a disaster, what's the greatest threat to the water supply?

No, we thought that as well – but it's not the dead bodies. It's the survivors.

The World Health Organization (WHO) states unequivocally:

> It is important to stress that the belief that cholera epidemics are caused by dead bodies after disasters, whether natural or man-made, is false.

Cholera is an acute diarrhoeal infection, caused by the bacterium *Vibrio cholerae*. It is transmitted from infected faeces to the mouth, or by food or water that are contaminated. It kills through dehydration and kidney failure. In Europe in the nineteenth century, cholera was so common that it proved a great boon to unscrupulous heirs. People poisoned by means of small quantities of arsenic – known as 'inheritance powder' – were often assumed to have died of cholera, which has similar symptoms.

It can take mere hours to incubate – which is why it spreads so rapidly, overwhelming attempts to contain it – and can kill a healthy adult within a day. Although around 75 per cent of people infected with cholera don't develop symptoms, the germs can be present in their faeces for up to a fortnight, thus helping to spread the disease. People with damaged immune systems – through malnutrition, for instance, or HIV – are the most likely to die.

Most horribly of all, the perfect situation for cholera to spread is a refugee camp, where survivors of disasters are huddled together with inadequate supplies of clean water, and where human waste isn't safely processed. The same applies to a city where the infrastructure has been damaged by, say, an earthquake, a flood, or a 'humane intervention' with so-called 'smart bombs'.

Dead bodies don't come into it: cholera pathogens in a corpse rapidly become harmless. Yet the myth that the disease is caused by 'bodies piling up' is almost universally believed, with even the most respectable news outlets repeating it every time there's an outbreak of cholera following a disaster.

Perhaps the greatest tragedy – or disgrace, depending on your point of view – is that cholera is far from incurable. Effective treatment – a solution of sugar and salts taken by mouth called oral rehydration – is simple and cheap. Given promptly, it saves the lives of more than 99 per cent of sufferers. And yet the WHO estimates that 120,000 people die of cholera every year.

Not that we want to alarm you, but we feel you ought to know: the seventh cholera pandemic in history began in Indonesia in 1961 – and it's still going on, having spread through Asia, Europe and Africa. In 1991 it reached Latin America – which hadn't seen cholera for more than a century. It is, by some margin, the longest of the cholera pandemics so far, probably because modern transport spreads infected people and foodstuffs with such rapid efficiency.

A pandemic is a worldwide epidemic. Pandemics generally end when there aren't enough people left to keep them going – because they've developed immunities, or been vaccinated, or (if you'll pardon the expression) died.

What positive effect did the Great Fire of London have?

It gave Sir Christopher Wren the opportunity to rebuild St Paul's Cathedral. What it didn't do was clear the city of plague.

No one knows what stopped the Great Plague of 1665–66, but despite what generations of schoolchildren have been taught, it definitely wasn't the Great Fire of September 1666.

The plague flared up in early 1665, probably carried on ships bringing cotton from Amsterdam. It was the first major outbreak in thirty years but, by the beginning of the following year, it had already begun to die out. In the last week of February 1666 there were only forty-two plague deaths reported in London, compared to more than 8,000 in each week of September 1665. The king had returned to London on 1 February 1666. Although it killed an estimated 100,000 people (20 per cent of London's population), the plague crisis was over six months before the Great Fire in September.

Also, the areas of London that burned down in the fire – the City, mainly, where 80 per cent of property was destroyed – were not the areas where the plague had been at its worst, which were the suburbs to the north, south and east.

No one really knows why the plague stopped. Perhaps it was spontaneous. That's how epidemics often end: by burning themselves out because they spread so quickly, and have such a high mortality rate, that they have nowhere left to go. It's one of the reasons the Ebola virus hasn't killed more people in Africa: a high (99 per cent) mortality rate means a quicker burn out.

Another possible reason for the disappearance of the plague in London was that the ancient method of barring the houses of known victims was policed much more aggressively. Doors were locked from the outside for twenty to twenty-eight days and guarded by watchmen. It's a fate that doesn't bear thinking about.

Even more difficult to comprehend is the story of the small hamlet of Eyam in Derbyshire. In September 1665 a bundle of infected cloth arrived from London for the local tailor. He was dead within a week. As the plague began to rage, the villagers (led by the Anglican vicar and the Puritan minister) voluntarily cut themselves off from the rest of the world so that it wouldn't spread elsewhere. When the first visitors were finally allowed to enter a year later, they found that three-quarters of the inhabitants were dead.

The disease had struck viciously, but apparently at random. Elizabeth Howe never became ill, despite the fact that she had buried her husband and their six children. Another survivor, against all probability, was the man who helped her do it – Marshall Howe, the unofficial local gravedigger.

What did the Black Death turn people against?

It wasn't witches and it certainly wasn't rats. Rats weren't correctly identified as the cause of bubonic plague until 1898. The immediate effect of the Black Death was to turn people against water.

Despite the Middle Ages' reputation as an era of un-interrupted filth, most medieval European cities and towns had bathhouses. As well as hot water and steam, a good bathhouse offered food, wine and 'other' services. They became the perfect place for romantic assignations and some were little better than high-class brothels (rather like modern 'massage parlours'). Even so, for almost 400 years, bathing and cleaning the whole body, either in public or private, was considered both normal and desirable.

The Black Death changed all this. Between 1347 and 1350, 25 million people – one-third of Europe's population – were wiped out and no one could agree how and why the disease had spread. Then, in 1348, a group of medical scholars at the

University of Paris published their learned opinion about the plague's cause: noxious air entering the body through the nose and mouth or the pores of the skin. Suddenly soaking in a bath was tantamount to suicide. Water became something to be avoided at all costs, the bathhouses were closed, and for the next 300 years almost no one in Europe washed at all.

The new theory meant the more blocked-up the pores the better, and the same bodily emissions that bathing had once removed now offered protection against the seeping, noxious vapours of disease. Oils, powders and scents were used to cover the smell of body odour, and hair was brushed and powdered but washed only in extreme circumstances. People of all ranks and professions swarmed with lice and fleas, and monarchs were even dirtier than their subjects. James I claimed to have only ever washed his fingers. Louis XIII (1601–43) boasted, 'I smell of armpits.'

Nor did the madness end there. What magical cleansing substance do you suppose replaced water? Alcoholic sprays? Unguent oils? No: during the seventeenth and eighteenth centuries people 'cleaned' themselves with *linen*. Clean linen magically absorbed all dirt and sweat from the body of the wearer, sucking it from the skin just as plants sucked nutrients from the ground. Instead of bathing, Louis XIV (1638–1715), the Sun King, changed his shirt three times a day. A gentleman's standing was judged by the amount of clean linen he owned.

During the late eighteenth century, water gradually made a return to respectability through the medicinal properties of public spas. In England plunging into cold water became fashionable as a cure for almost anything. John Wesley (1703–91), the founder of Methodism, who coined the phrase 'cleanliness is next to godliness', claimed in his bestselling *Primitive Physick* (1785) that cold bathing had been effective in treating blindness, melancholy and cancer.

(Although we shouldn't forget Wesley also recommends honey and onion paste to cure baldness, a warm treacle massage to relieve gout and sticking wine-soaked bread in one's nostrils to control overeating.)

STEPHEN *During the Great Plague of London, doctors recommended patients store their farts in a jar and then when they were feeling unwell, smell them, and apparently this would help.*

JO BRAND *But, as I always say, better out than in. Bit like Simon Cowell in a lifeboat.*

What was the name of the Earth's original continent?

Many of us are familiar with the idea that the world's continents once fitted snugly together into one huge single 'supercontinent' called Pangaea. Fewer people are aware that Pangaea (Greek for 'whole earth') had two subdivisions: Laurasia in the north and Gondwanaland in the south.

What most of us don't know is that Pangaea was only the seventh and last of a series of supercontinents that coagulated and split apart at regular intervals after the Earth formed 4.5 billion years ago. Pangaea existed between 550 and 200 million years ago – which is relatively recent in geological time. In fact, if the entire history of the world were expressed as a week starting on a Monday, Pangaea would only have appeared early on Sunday morning.

The very first supercontinent was called Vaalbara and it started forming over 3.6 billion years ago. Its name unites

Kaapvaal and Pilbara, two pieces of land (one in southern Africa and the other in north-western Australia) that were once adjacent to one another. Vaalbara was succeeded by Ur, then Kenorland, Columbia, Rodinia, Pannotia and finally Pangaea. Each cycle of joining and separation took about 300 to 500 million years.

Such vast movements are driven by the Earth's internal structure. The planet's radioactive interior is extremely hot: at 3,997 °C (7,227 °F), it's hotter than the surface of the Sun. As a result, about a third of the Earth's rock has melted into a viscous liquid called *magma* (from the Greek for 'ointment'). This sits between Earth's deep core, which, though equally hot, is prevented from liquefying by intense pressure, and its cool, rocky skin known as the lithosphere (from *lithos*, Greek for 'stone'). The outermost edge of the lithosphere is the thin rind we call the Earth's crust. This looks and feels sound to us, but it's more like the crackling on a joint of roast pork – the lightest, puffiest bit of the whole thing.

The lithosphere isn't a seamless girdle of rock: it is made up of seven major and thirteen minor 'plates' that float like flat slabs of cracked toffee on the thick rock syrup of the magma. Convection currents in the magma (as in a very slowly simmering pan) propel the plates beneath our feet at a rate of about 6 centimetres (2.5 inches) a year – the same speed at which human fingernails grow. At present these shifts mean the Atlantic Ocean is growing each year, at the expense of the Pacific, which is shrinking. Readjustments and collisions of these plates (called 'tectonic' from the Greek *tetkton*, builder) are what cause earthquakes, throw up mountain ranges and gouge out ocean trenches. The next supercontinent is not due to form for 250 million years, but it already has a name – Pangaea Ultima.

Despite its reassuringly sturdy appearance, approximately 50 per cent of the mass of most rock is oxygen. Seventy-five per cent of the Earth's crust is composed of oxygen and silicon, usually in the form of silica, silicon oxide. Aluminium, iron, calcium, sodium, magnesium and potassium make up the next 23.4 per cent. Everything else – including all the gold and silver – accounts for just 1.6 per cent. Though oxygen is a gas in its pure state, it is the most abundant element on the planet and accounts for half its total mass.

What time is it at the South Pole?

Unofficially at least, it's always the same time as it is in New Zealand.

It's impossible to tell the time using the sun at the South Pole, because whichever way you face is north and all the Earth's time zones converge. Theoretically, it's always noon – but then again it's also always midnight. So, to avoid confusion, the time zone across Antarctica is defined as UTC (which stands for Universal Time, Co-ordinated, better known as Greenwich Mean Time or GMT). This is the default time used by clocks on the Internet, in aviation and by weather forecasters. It allows all the international Antarctic research stations to communicate with each other, which is important in an emergency.

However, while UTC is the official time across the continent, the 200 scientists and researchers working at the pole in the Amundsen-Scott South Pole Station actually use New Zealand time (UTC +12 or +13 in the summer) because all their supplies come via the large McMurdo Base, which is in New Zealand territory. Practically speaking, those intrepid souls based at the pole go to bed and get up at the same time as office workers in Auckland.

The South Pole is cold and remote as it gets. Other than the transient human population, nothing lives there – although exasperated seabirds called skuas occasionally appear, blown off course by the fierce wind. The pole is 1,230 kilometres (763 miles) from the sea, and perched on the summit of an ice shelf that is 2.84 kilometres (1.76 miles) deep. Its annual average temperature is −49 °C (−56 °F), but it can reach −82.8 °C (−117.0 °F).

A US Navy team established the original (wooden) South Pole station in 1956. They were the first people to set foot there since Robert Falcon Scott's ill-fated mission in 1912. A new, two-storey, 7,400-square metre (80,000 square feet) version opened in 2008 and is constructed on jacks, so that it can be raised to compensate for the 1.2 metres (4 feet) of snow that builds up around it each year.

The sun at the South Pole is continually up for half of the year, and continually down for the rest of it. Summer lasts for one very long day and winter for one very long night. During the six-month-long winter, when the sun never rises at all, the population of the base reduces to fifty. Distractions from the darkness include Antarctica's only newspaper – the ironically titled *Antarctic Sun* – as well as yoga, salsa classes and bowling. They also grow their own vegetables (including eggplants and jalapeño peppers) using a hydroponic system that substitutes water and chemical nutrients for soil.

Regular visitors to Antarctica have evolved their own slang. To 'have a *monk-on*' is to fall into an introspective mood; *big eye* is insomnia caused by the changes in the length of daylight; *greenout* is the experience of seeing vegetation again after a long period on the ice, and an *Antarctic 10* is someone of the opposite sex who would probably score '5' on the attractiveness scale anywhere else.

STEPHEN *The North Pole becomes the South Pole and vice-versa every million or so years.*

ALAN *So, any minute now, everyone's fridge magnets are just going to fall on the floor?*

STEPHEN *No, that's not how fridge magnets work. What will happen is compasses will point to the south, rather than the north.*

ALAN *North, not south? I don't live in south London, and I don't care what you say!*

What was the original name given to Australia by European explorers?

They called it New Zealand.

The first European to reach Australia was Willem Janszoon from the Netherlands in 1606. He landed in what is now Cape York, Queensland, thinking it was part of New Guinea. He proposed the name 'Nieu Zelandt' (New Sea-Land) after the island province in western Holland. It didn't stick, and by the time the Dutch had finished charting the western and northern coastlines they'd started to call it *Hollandia Nova* ('New Holland').

In August 1642, the governor general of the Dutch East Indies, Anthony Van Diemen, dispatched another unrelated Janszoon ('Jan's son') to explore further. In November of that year, Abel Janszoon Tasman found what he thought was an undiscovered coast of the great southern continent or *Terra Australis*, as described by Marco Polo. He named it Anthony Van Diemen's Land after his boss but two centuries later, in

1856, the British gave credit where it was really due and renamed it Tasmania.

From there, Tasman sailed off and discovered the South Island of today's New Zealand, which he called Staten Land on the grounds that he thought it was attached to Staten Island off the coast of Argentina – which, of course, it isn't.

After those early Dutch expeditions, there were no European landings in northern Australia until Matthew Flinders's circumnavigation of the continent in the early nineteenth century.

The Aborigines had been in Australia for 50,000 years before the Dutch arrived, and the Dutch weren't even the first outsiders to get there. Fishermen from Makassar in Indonesia had traded edible sea cucumbers with the Yolgnu, an Aboriginal people from the Northern Territories, for at least a century before the Dutch landed.

This was how the Yolgnu came to hear of Europeans – described to them as the *Balanda* (or 'Hollander') people. From the Makassans the Yolgnu also learned how to sail small boats known as *prau* and how to smoke tobacco. They obviously liked it because there is a Yolgnu song cycle that lays down sensible guidelines for how it should be used.

The Portuguese had brought tobacco to Indonesia in the early sixteenth century and it was being grown in Java as early as 1601. It's odd to think that the Australian Aborigines were smoking the leaves of a plant imported from the New World by Europeans before they'd met any of them face to face.

The Makassans continued to visit until 1906, when the Australian government decided they didn't like this exclusive tax-free trading arrangement with an Aboriginal tribe. Without consulting the Yolgnu, they refused the Makassans a permit for harvesting sea cucumber and five centuries of peaceful cultural exchange came to an abrupt halt.

STEPHEN *The Dutch discovered almost everything first.*

ALAN *And then they go home.*

STEPHEN *They're just thought of as being homosexuals who smoke joints. Actually there's a lot more to them than that. A lot more.*

New entry!

Name the world's fastest man

It's not Usain Bolt. The title belongs to a Stone Age Australian called T8.

In 2003 archaeologists from Bond University in Queensland discovered some fossilised human footprints on Australia's Gold Coast. They date back 20,000 years, and careful analysis of their configuration has shown that one of the males – known as T8 – must have been running at 37 kilometres per hour (23 kilometres per hour).

Although Usain Bolt has reached 42 kilometres per hour (27 kilometres per hour), for a second or so (usually at the 70-metre mark), he was on a running track with spiked shoes. T8 was in mud, barefoot, and was accelerating. We don't know how much faster he got, but we can be pretty sure it was faster than Bolt. And he may not even have been the fastest of the 150,000 humans living in Australia at the time.

In his book *Manthropology*, anthropologist Peter McAllister argues that, with modern training, Paleolithic aborigines would have been able to reach 45 kilometres per hour (28 miles per hour). The fossil record suggests that hunter-gatherers were much fitter and more physically robust than modern man, whose comparatively sedentary lifestyle has led to a gradual loss of athleticism.

Not that T8 diminishes the extraordinary nature of Bolt's achievement.

If the 100-metre results since records began are plotted on a graph, they form a neat curve, which has led to the statistical prediction that humans will reach the limit for running the 100 metres (at about 9.45 seconds) in 150 years' time. For many years, the curve has accurately predicted how record times would improve. But Bolt's two runs of 9.69 and 9.58 in 2009 – which shaved 0.14 seconds off his fellow Jamaican Asafa Powell's record set in 2008 – exceeded expectations. The model didn't indicate a 9.69-second run until 2030.

The first modern man to run the 100 metres in under ten seconds was American sprinter Jim Hines at the 1968 Mexico Olympics. The record has been broken twelve times since then. The nine-second barrier for the 100 metres seems unlikely ever to be broken: there is evidence that the physical stress required to reach such a speed from a standing start would crack a sprinter's bones and pull tendons from their connection points.

But who knows? After all, Bolt – and maybe T8 before him – has already run the distance in that time: in a relay where he had a running start.

STEPHEN *Name the fastest human runner of all time.*
JIMMY CARR *I'm going to go Usain Bolt.*
KLAXON
JACK DEE *He's not as fast as Jimmy Carr when it's his round.*

What can we expect to experience at the point of death?

Yes, it seems our life really does flash before our eyes.

Research published by Indiana University in 2006 suggests that this apparently useless psychological phenomenon might be the result of an important survival mechanism.

When confronted by danger, people like firemen and doctors often rely on automatic (rather than considered) decision-making. They may later rationalise their actions as the 'obvious' things to have done, but in the instant there is evidence that their brain has rifled through its entire filing system in search of a matching experience. Our memories record much more detail than we consciously realise, so that when a fireman tells everyone to leave a building seconds before it collapses, this isn't because he is psychic – it's because his brain has subconsciously picked up subtle clues and matched them with what he has professionally come across before.

Obviously, this confers a strong evolutionary advantage: such snap decis ons can save our own lives and those of others. But what happens when we are confronted with something we have never experienced, like drowning or falling from a plane without a parachute? According to the current theory, in such unique circumstances images are rapidly pulled from the memory, compared with the reality as it happens, and rejected as unsuitable. When none of the options matches the current danger, in desperation the brain widens its search and eventually opens the floodgates to let all memories through at once. Then, a whole life – quite literally – 'flashes before the eyes'.

This is what happened to Rear-Admiral Sir Francis Beaufort, the inventor of the Beaufort Wind Force Scale, in 1795. At the age of twenty-one he narrowly avoided drowning in Portsmouth Harbour, later recording his impressions in this classic account: 'The effect on my most affectionate father, the moment in which it would be disclosed to the family, and a thousand other circumstances minutely associated with home, were the first reflections. Then they took a wider range, our last cruise, a former voyage and shipwreck, my school and boyish pursuits and adventures. Thus travelling backwards, every past incident of my life seemed to glance across my recollection in retrograde succession: not however in mere outline, as here stated, but the picture filled up with every minute and collateral feature. In short, the whole period of my existence seemed to be placed before me in a kind of panoramic review . . .'

It's interesting to note that Persian, Portuguese, Italian, Russian, German, Norwegian, Romanian, Spanish, Swedish, Arabian, Dutch and French all have phrases which equate to the English. The French is *J'ai vu toute ma vie défiler devant mes yeux*; the German is *Mein ganzes Leben passierte Revue*; and the Swedish is *Livet passerade revy framför mina ögon*.

Skol! Live long and prosper.

Can anything live forever?

Yes.

Introducing the Immortal jellyfish . . .

The adult form of the species *Turritopsis nutricula* looks like any other small jellyfish. It has a transparent bell-like body, about 5 millimetres (⅕ inch) wide, fringed with eighty or so stinging tentacles. Inside is a bright red stomach, which forms the shape of a cross when seen from above.

Like most of the *Cnidaria* family (from *knide*, Greek for

'stinging nettle'), the tiny *Turritopsis* is predatory, using its tentacles to first stun plankton and then waft them up through its mouth-cum-anus. The females squeeze their eggs out through the same passage, after which the males spray them with sperm. The fertilised eggs fall to the ocean floor where each one attaches itself to a rock and starts growing into what looks like a tiny sea anemone: a stalk with tentacles called a *polyp* (from the Greek *poly* 'many' and *pous* 'foot').

Eventually these polyps form buds that break off into minute adult jellyfish – and the whole process starts all over again.

Reproduction by budding occurs in thousands of species – including sponges, hydras and starfish – and has gone on with few modifications for half a billion years. What makes *Turritopsis nutricula* so special is that it has evolved a skill unmatched, not just by other jellyfish, but by any other living organism.

Once the adult *Turritopsis* have reproduced, they don't die but transform themselves back into their juvenile polyp state. Their tentacles retract, their bodies shrink, and they sink to the ocean floor to restart the cycle. Their adult cells – even their eggs and sperm – melt into simpler forms of themselves, and the whole organism becomes 'young' again.

Newts and salamanders can grow new limbs using this cell reversal process, but no other creature enjoys an entire second childhood. Among laboratory samples, all the adult *Turritopsis* observed, both male and female, regularly undergo this change. And not just once: they can do it over and over again.

So although many *Turritopsis* succumb to predators or to disease, if left to their own devices, they never die. And, because individual specimens haven't been studied for long enough, we have no idea how old some of them may already be. What we do know is that, in recent years, they have spread out from their original home in the Caribbean to all the

THE USES OF INTERESTINGNESS

There are books in which the footnotes, or the comments scrawled by some reader's hand in the margin, are more interesting than the text. The world is one of those books.
GEORGE SANTAYANA (1863–1952)

We think all books, even the ones that are handsomely bound and come with an index, are still works in progress. If the pursuit of interestingness has taught us anything it is that there is no final word on any subject. For this reason we encourage you to scrawl furiously in the margins of this book or, better still, visit our website and pick up the conversation with us there. The address is www.qi.com/generalignorance. We'll happily share our sources and correct any errors we have made (and there are bound to be some) in future editions.

QI books are the product of long months of research by many people. The one you hold in your hands would not have happened without the first-class input of James Harkin, Mat Coward and Andy Murray, who researched and wrote the early drafts of many of the questions. They, in turn, relied on the work of the extended Elven family: Piers Fletcher and Justin Pollard (QI's Producer and Associate Producer respectively), Molly Oldfield, Arron Ferster, Will Bowen, Dan Kieran and the members of the QI Talkboard.

In the fifth century BC, Euripides, the great Athenian playwright, wrote that 'the language of truth is simple'. He didn't say it was easy. What success we have had in making complicated things seem simpler is due to the clear-sighted editing of Sarah Lloyd.

As for book-making, no one does it better than the team at Faber. Special thanks must go, once more, to Stephen Page, Julian Loose, Dave Watkins, Eleanor Crow, Hannah Griffiths and Paula Turner.

In a low moment the Victorian aesthete, John Ruskin, once complained: 'How long most people would look at the best book before they would give the price of a large turbot for it?' It's a good question. As we write, the wholesale price of turbot is about £9 per kilogram. We will make no further claims, except to say interestingness lasts longer and contains no bones.

The Two Johns,
Oxford

INDEX

ff

Faber and Faber is one of the great independent publishing houses. We were established in 1929 by Geoffrey Faber with T. S. Eliot as one of our first editors. We are proud to publish award-winning fiction and non-fiction, as well as an unrivalled list of poets and playwrights. Among our list of writers we have five Booker Prize winners and twelve Nobel Laureates, and we continue to seek out the most exciting and innovative writers at work today.

Find out more about our authors and books
faber.co.uk

Read our blog for insight and opinion on books and the arts
thethoughtfox.co.uk

Follow news and conversation
twitter.com/faberbooks

Watch readings and interviews
youtube.com/faberandfaber

Connect with other readers
facebook.com/faberandfaber

Explore our archive
flickr.com/faberandfaber